Engaging Students as Partners in Learning and Teaching

Engaging Students as Partners in Learning and Teaching

A Guide for Faculty

Alison Cook-Sather,
Catherine Bovill, and Peter Felten

Maryellen Weimer, Consulting Editor

JB JOSSEY-BASS™

A Wiley Brand

The Jossey-Bass Higher and
Adult Education Series

Contents

Preface

Faculty think a lot about teaching. We regularly create new courses or revise existing ones. We talk with colleagues about our classes and our students, perhaps even inviting other faculty to observe and give us feedback on our teaching. We reflect on our course ratings. We read articles and books about teaching. We participate in workshops and consult with our campus learning and teaching centers. However, in all of this, how often and how carefully do we listen to students and respond to their ideas? How often do we collaborate and work alongside students to enhance learning?

These simple questions are the foundation of this book. Faculty talk with students frequently, of course, but what we advocate here is something distinct and different. Many of the good practices faculty use to gather responses from students, such as asking questions and gathering mid-semester feedback, are helpful, but they typically do not lead to authentic partnership between students and faculty. In most of these cases, faculty frame the questions, students provide answers, and then faculty alone decide whether, and how, to respond to that information. This process often resembles a customer-service relationship. How satisfied were you with the teaching in this course? What did you like best, and least, about the class? Partnership, on the other hand, is based upon the principles of respect, reciprocity, and shared responsibility. This changes the types of questions we ask in student-faculty partnerships to be more like this: How can we, together, deepen student learning in this course?

Our commitment to student-faculty partnerships is rooted in three foundational beliefs:

- Students have insights into teaching and learning that can make our and their practice more engaging, effective, and rigorous.

- Faculty can draw on student insights not only through collecting student responses but also through collaborating with students to study and design teaching and learning together.

- Partnerships between students and faculty change the understandings and capacities of both sets of partners— making us all better teachers and learners.

In this book we explore how and why faculty and students can engage as partners in learning and teaching in higher education. This collaborative process may not come naturally to students or faculty. Students often come to higher education from schools that emphasize high-stakes testing, not shared inquiry. Faculty have spent years developing disciplinary expertise, sometimes in rigidly hierarchical graduate programs, creating intellectual and cultural distance between our students and ourselves. Despite these and many other barriers, which we will explore more fully later, many of us have cultivated pedagogical habits that treat students as active contributors to learning and in some cases practices that invite students to be active contributors to teaching. As we will show, student-faculty partnerships—through which participants engage reciprocally, although not necessarily in the same ways— have transformational potential for individuals, courses, curricula, and institutions.

This book was born of the collaborative spirit it advocates. As coauthors, we come from three different higher education contexts: a small liberal arts college in the northeastern United States, a large 'research intensive' university in Scotland, and a medium-sized liberal arts university in the southeastern United States. We each take a different approach to working in partnership with students and to facilitating partnerships between faculty and students, and we each have walked a different path to the institutional and research programs we have developed. Yet we share a commitment to deep and extended collaboration among faculty and students as a primary mode of exploring, affirming, and transforming teaching and learning in higher education. In this book we share what we have learned about developing and supporting student-faculty partnerships, on our own campuses and in our work together.

Like the individuals in any partnership, we came to this common work with different histories and goals. We will introduce ourselves briefly here so that what unites and what distinguishes the three of us will be clearer.

Alison's Story

One of the most vivid memories I have of researching graduate schools is of plopping down in one professor's office and stating, without context or explanation, "I want to study student voice!" As a former secondary English teacher, I had worked closely with students to understand their perspectives on their learning, and I wanted to carry that commitment into graduate school. Although I didn't end up working with that professor, I did end up keeping the question of student voice at the forefront of my work.

After completing my doctoral work, I took on the job of directing and teaching in the Bryn Mawr/Haverford Education Program in 1994. Bryn Mawr and Haverford are two selective liberal arts colleges that share a close collaborative relationship, both emphasizing deep disciplinary study. The Education Program that the colleges also share offers secondary teaching certification, as well as a minor in educational studies to undergraduates and recent graduates who wish to integrate work in education with their major courses of study. During my first year working with secondary certification candidates, I remember talking with a close friend and high school teacher, Ondrea Reisinger, about a problem in secondary teacher preparation: the absence of student voices. She and I designed a project I maintained for 15 years (and that is sustained to this day) that positioned her (and subsequently other teachers') secondary students as teacher educators.

For the full semester prior to the student teaching experience, the high school students work in partnership with the college undergraduates seeking certification to teach at the secondary level. They maintain a weekly email exchange and meet several times. Over the course of the semester, the secondary students become true collaborators in preparing the college students to teach; they and their college partners learn about one another's experiences and perspectives, question and revise their assumptions about one another, and learn to communicate across and grow from their differences (see Cook-Sather 2002a for a description of the secondary teacher preparation program and Cook-Sather 2010 for a comparison between that and the college program I now direct).

The program I currently run as part of Bryn Mawr College's Teaching and Learning Institute, called Students as Learners and Teachers (SaLT), builds on and extends this model at the college level. Piloted in 2006 with support from The Andrew W. Mellon Foundation, this program pairs undergraduate students with faculty members who wish to analyze and, perhaps, revise their pedagogical approaches over the course of a semester. The undergraduate students who assume the role of pedagogical consultant to faculty members are not enrolled in the courses within which the partnerships unfold, and often they are unfamiliar with the subject matter being taught. The focus of their partnerships is teaching rather than content; the student consultants explore with faculty members classroom dynamics, pedagogical approaches, and the learning experiences of students enrolled in the course. (This program is discussed further in Chapter 1 and in detail in Chapter 4.) My role is to provide the forums for the partners, facilitate same-constituency (student consultant-student consultant, faculty-faculty) dialogue, and support cross-constituency (faculty-student) dialogue (see Cook-Sather 2008, 2009b, 2010, 2011b, 2011c, 2012, 2013b).

Both these projects put into practice my strong conviction that students have essential perspectives that, when brought into dialogue with teachers' perspectives, can raise awareness, deepen engagement, improve teaching and learning for all involved, and foster a culture on campus that embraces more open communication about, and shared responsibility for, education. The generous support the SaLT program has received from The Andrew W. Mellon Foundation and the Provosts of Bryn Mawr and Haverford colleges affirms these convictions. The ways in which faculty with whom I have worked for the past seven years have taken up partnership with students are truly inspiring: they partner with students to plan new courses (Jiang and Wang, 2012; Shore, 2012), assess and revise existing courses (Battat, 2012; Conner, 2012; Nath, 2012; Walker, 2012), and develop, teach, and assess innovative new programs (Cohen, Donnay, & Hein, 2012; Francl, 2012; Lesnick, 2012).

Cathy's Story

I grew up with a strong sense of the importance of social justice, the value of cultural diversity, and the key role of critical education in developing individual and community potential. This was certainly in some part due to the influence of my mother and grandmother, who were both activists in the women's peace movement. After graduation, my work in health promotion, community, and international development introduced me to the literature, practices, and experiences of participatory approaches in a range of development, educational, and research settings. These influences have informed my teaching practice over the last 20 years, particularly my approach to teaching in higher education. In my role as a faculty developer, previously at Queen Margaret University in Edinburgh, and since 2007 at the University of Glasgow, I have used a range of approaches that aim to enhance the participatory possibilities of higher education teaching and learning practices. I have invited faculty participants to design and carry out their own assessment of the courses that they are studying and to collaboratively write up these experiences for publication and presentation; reconsider the role of both faculty and students in the assessment process; co-create grading criteria; and collaborate in making decisions about curricular design, content, and processes (Bovill et al., 2010; Bovill, 2011). I have also worked alongside, advised, and supported colleagues at the University of Glasgow and at many other universities to pursue their goal of engaging students as partners in teaching and learning.

These experiences led me to seek out the work of others in co-creating learning and teaching processes and to consider some of the difficult questions raised by engaging students as partners, such as what kind of engagement we are aiming for and how we ensure that we meet the needs of our increasingly diverse groups of students. Since 2005, I have undertaken research into the motivations, methodologies, outcomes, and lessons from a range of examples of students and faculty working as partners in curricula design processes (Bovill et al., 2011; Bovill, 2013a). This work has been thrilling. Faculty and students who have collaborated in learning and teaching partnerships are almost entirely enthusiastic and positive about their learning experiences, and it has made the research fascinating, stimulating, and enjoyable. I believe that engaging students as partners in teaching and learning leads to a range of compelling outcomes with particularly interesting impacts upon enhancement of metacognitive understanding of learning and teaching processes for both faculty and students. However, I also believe that engaging students meaningfully in making decisions about their learning poses a challenge to existing assumptions, practices, and structures within universities about how the aims, content, and processes of learning and teaching are conceptualized and decided. We explore this challenge to existing ways of thinking and practicing in Chapter 1.

Peter's Story

I began thinking about student voice the first time I taught a graduate course, shortly after finishing my PhD in 1995. I wanted my students to dig deeply into their discipline and their own learning, so I asked them to co-construct with me some portions of the course, including the rubric to assess their final research papers. I more-or-less made this up as I went along, inspired by theoretical writings from people like Freire (1970) and Brookfield (1995) but without a blueprint. The process worked better than I had expected. Students engaged seriously in the process, and the final rubric turned out to be clearer and more rigorous than I would have been able to create on my own.

Having done this once with graduate students, I began taking cautious steps in a similar direction with my undergraduates. Over the next several years I experimented by regularly engaging students in the development of rubrics and study guides, all the while reading whatever I could find on the topic. Colleagues at Vanderbilt University's Center for Teaching, particularly Allison Pingree, further shaped my thinking by emphasizing the relational nature of teaching, drawing on Carol Gilligan (1993) and Parker Palmer (1997), among others. I had been trained as an historian to think about what I wanted to teach, when I thought about teaching at all; now I was beginning to focus less on my teaching and more on my students' learning, what Barr and Tagg (1995) describe as a shift from an instructional to a learning paradigm.

My engagement with this work took off in the fall of 2005 when two colleagues at Elon University, Deborah Long and Richard Mihans, consulted with me about a "broken" course in their department. As the new-to-campus director of a new teaching and learning center at a liberal arts university, I raised several possibilities with them, ranging from cautious to innovative. They jumped at the boldest of my options, the idea of working in partnership with students to redesign the course. Together we decided to adapt the center's effective and popular course-design process to integrate students. This work went considerably further toward full partnership than I had gone before, creating a ten-person team (seven undergraduates, my two faculty colleagues, and me) that met a dozen times over two months to reinvent the course. We deliberately included more students than faculty as one way to shape the power dynamics in the group (in 2013 an article by Carey highlighted the perils of planning partnerships where students are in the minority and therefore extra vulnerable). This process led to a much-improved course, meeting our primary goal (Mihans et al., 2008). It also solidified my commitment to engaging students in teaching and learning. Since that winter in 2006, Elon's teaching center has been supporting faculty and student partnerships to design new courses or to reimagine existing courses, and I marvel at the impressive work my faculty and student colleagues have done together (for example, Delpish et al., 2010; Moore et al., 2010; Pope-Ruark, 2012).

Our Intended Audience and Approach

Over the years we have talked with many faculty who have developed diverse ways of establishing partnerships with students. Our aim with this book is to invite you to join us in this work, not by copying off a script or reproducing what we or others have done, but rather by adapting and extending the principles and models we offer here. Partnerships are always contextual. A simple set of prescriptions or a one-size-fits-all model is unlikely to be helpful;

however, working in partnership with students need not be overly complex, nor do you need a sophisticated theoretical framework to do this work. Indeed, we believe that many faculty and students are already poised to take a step toward one another.

We have written this book for faculty colleagues who wish to take this step, or to continue with subsequent steps in partnership with students. Whether you are an isolated faculty member just beginning to think about partnership, one of several colleagues on your campus who want to develop more extensive student-faculty collaborations, or an experienced practitioner who is leading other teachers in this work, our practical advice and theoretical perspectives aim to help you feel prepared and confident as you start or deepen your partnerships with students. The evidence we present of positive outcomes for both students and faculty will, we hope, give you a sense of what is possible. The examples of student-faculty partnership included in this book are drawn from programs we run or that we have studied as part of our research and also from examples colleagues have shared, both formally in print and more informally in conversation. Because we do not intend or claim to offer an exhaustive set of examples, we have chosen those that we feel effectively introduce a range of possibilities for partnership.

In many of the following chapters we include the voices of faculty and student partners. We have several reasons for including these voices. First, we believe that stories and insights offered by those who have direct experiences of partnership are often more powerful than someone else's summary or analysis. Second, in the spirit of partnership within which this book is written, we are committed to sharing some of its pages with the voices of those who have undertaken partnership work. Finally, we hope that hearing directly from participants in student-faculty partnerships will enable you to discern resonances or contrasts with your own efforts or aspirations. We cite the names of many of the students and faculty we quote throughout the book; however, some of these quotations were gathered while conducting research, and therefore we must preserve the anonymity of participants in those particular inquiries.

Some of what participants say reiterates the arguments we are making, but from a different angle. We also occasionally repeat ourselves across the chapters. We are quite intentional in this. We have learned from our own experiences and from many conversations with colleagues that true partnership requires significant shifts for many of us, and therefore, revisiting some key concepts and challenges at different points across the book is intended to be helpful. Partnership is something of what Meyer and Land (2005) have called a threshold concept—both for faculty and for students (Cook-Sather, 2013a; King and Felten, 2012; Werder et al., 2012). As such, working through the complexities of partnership can be troublesome and often takes patience, requiring careful thinking, planning, experimentation, and reflection. As you will see in the examples we provide, partnership is iterative—it is work that requires revisiting and revising throughout the process.

Structure of the Book

We recognize that some people like to start with theory and then see practical examples, while others prefer to see examples first and then move to a consideration of the underlying theory. Because the partnership approach we advocate in this book requires such a significant rethinking of current notions and practices, we have chosen to present some practical examples early in the book to enable you to envisage what student-faculty partnerships might look like in practice. We share the principles that guide us and our definition of partnership up front, but we move quickly to the examples before stepping back from these to discuss benefits, cautions, and practical approaches that can help you develop your own version of student-faculty partnerships. So if you read the chapters in order, this is what you will find:

- Our guiding principles and definition of partnership

- Responses to preliminary questions you may have about student-faculty partnerships

- Examples of individual, program-level, and institutional-level student-faculty partnerships

- Research into the outcomes of partnerships

- Cautions to prepare you for challenges you may face in adopting a partnership approach

- Practical strategies for developing partnerships

- Discussion of further questions you may have

- An outline of approaches to assessing the processes and outcomes of student-faculty partnerships

- Some reflections on next steps in and toward a partnership movement

You may choose to read the chapters in the order they are presented, or you may jump around, creating your own order or focusing first on where you have greatest interest or the most questions. In many chapters we refer you to other places in the book that you might find helpful.

In Chapter 1 we open with a discussion of the three principles that we believe are the essential foundation of any student-faculty partnership, regardless of the particulars of individual practice: respect, reciprocity, and responsibility. Building on these principles, we detail what we mean by student-faculty partnerships and how they are different from the feedback exchanges faculty typically have with students. We identify norms in higher education that need to be revised in order for student-faculty partnerships to develop and flourish, we touch on precedents for student-faculty partnership, and we present a glimpse into the kinds of engagement and active learning that are possible through more collaborative forms of relationship. Our intention is not to present student-faculty partnerships as a panacea; indeed, concerns about power and culture, for example, underscore the need for careful and intentional steps in the process. However, the potential for significant learning, development, and even transformation that arises from these practices should prompt everyone in higher education to consider the possibilities of student-faculty collaboration.

In Chapter 2 we address some preliminary questions you might have about developing student-faculty partnerships. These are the kinds of questions we have been asked repeatedly by many faculty colleagues, questions such as: How can students possibly help me explore or design learning and teaching, given that they are not experts in either subject matter or pedagogy? I have enough to do already without having to set up all these meetings with students; wouldn't it be quicker to do this on my own? And, why change my practice if I'm currently an effective teacher and my students are learning a lot? If you also have such questions, we hope our responses reassure you that you are not alone in raising them and prepare you for the subsequent two chapters, which offer you examples of student-faculty partnerships across a variety of contexts.

In Chapter 3 we outline numerous examples of partnerships that individual faculty have developed with students in a wide range of settings, whether or not they have support from colleagues or their institutions. We take as a starting point faculty-driven and faculty-developed approaches and present many varieties of student-faculty partnership involving different types of students, a focus on different elements of learning and teaching, and different levels of partnership. The examples we provide cannot and do not extend to every possible approach to this work. Instead, this chapter aims to give you some ideas of what might be possible for individual faculty who wish to engage students in meaningful partnerships. We have arranged our examples under three headings: (1) designing a course or elements of a course; (2) responding to students' experiences during a course; and (3) assessing student work. These are not, however, intended to be fixed categories; some examples from each could easily fit into one or more of the others.

In Chapter 4 we present different program-level student-faculty partnerships. We outline examples of programs that support (1) designing or redesigning a course before or after it is taught; (2) analyzing classroom practice within the context of a course while it is being taught; and (3) developing research partnerships that catalyze institutional change. Under each heading we offer several short examples and one extended example of student-faculty partnerships. We feature, as case studies, programs with different purposes and in various contexts.

In Chapter 5 we synthesize the research on outcomes of student-faculty partnerships. We explore mutual benefits for students and faculty, including enhancing engagement, motivation, and learning; developing metacognitive awareness (awareness of one's own thinking and action) and a stronger sense of identity; and improving teaching and the overall classroom experience. We also discuss the ways in which student-faculty partnerships can benefit programs and institutions by creating a more collaborative culture in higher education contexts.

In Chapter 6 we focus on some of the challenges inherent in this work and some cautions should you choose to adopt a partnership approach. These include the necessity of working to find a balance of participation, power, and perspective; the imperative to consider perspectives from underrepresented students and faculty; the necessity of being careful and intentional regarding the language we use to describe this work; the wisdom of starting small rather than taking on too much too quickly; the danger of adopting processes and programs uncritically and embracing a one-size-fits-all model; and the risk of assuming that all students and faculty will be receptive to the idea of partnership. Like Chapter 2, this chapter aims to address explicitly potential problems and pitfalls with the goal of helping you avoid common difficulties where possible and thoughtfully manage them where they are an inevitable dimension of this work.

In Chapter 7 we offer a set of practical strategies intended to guide you as you create or further develop student-faculty partnerships across different contexts. We offer three sections of concrete strategies: (1) getting started with student-faculty partnerships; (2) sustaining and deepening student-faculty partnership practices; and (3) negotiating roles and power within partnerships. This chapter should help you understand the big picture, the overarching ideas that unite the many forms of partnership, while also providing some broad yet concrete recommendations for practice. We outline approaches that can be used to develop a continuum of possible partnerships and that can be adapted to suit particular teaching and learning contexts.

In Chapter 8 we pose and address a further set of questions that may arise after you have deeply explored the notion of student-faculty partnership or have tried out some partnership activities. We offer responses in this chapter to questions about how to pursue partnerships in an institution that might not have a culture conducive to doing so, how to think about the role of change in student-faculty partnerships, and how to return to "regular" teaching and learning after having been in partnership. We also address other questions, including: How can I be in partnership with students if I am grading them? How do I engage disengaged students? Do I have to do everything my student partner recommends?

In Chapter 9 we present diverse approaches to assessing the outcomes of student-faculty partnerships. Consistent with the repositioning of students as partners throughout the book, we critique the role that students currently play in assessment as well as explore the potential roles they could play in assessing teaching and learning in higher education contexts. We then offer guiding principles for, and examples of good practice in, capturing and assessing the outcomes of student-faculty partnerships in different contexts.

In Chapter 10 we provide a short summary of the main insights and arguments we have offered throughout the book. We also propose several areas for further consideration, including expanding student-faculty partnership work into new contexts both to support and to create new faculty roles; connecting with more diverse students; and preparing the next generation of faculty for a new kind of higher education. Finally, we posit that student-faculty partnerships might be understood—and embraced—as a movement.

A Note on Terminology

Educational terminology varies in different parts of the world, sometimes producing confusion or outright misunderstanding. We have adopted the common North American definition of words throughout this book but have noted below some of the terms that may perplex people in other parts of the world where meanings may differ.

> **Assessment**: Stepping back from and analyzing progress in any educational endeavor—learning, teaching, research, pedagogical partnership—either in a formative way (during the process with the goal of using what is gathered to revise approaches) or in a summative way (with the goal of measuring and making judgments about what has been learned, taught, or accomplished after the process is completed). In some contexts "assessment" and "evaluation" are used interchangeably; in others, the way we define "assessment" here is more frequently called "evaluation."
>
> **College**: A two- or four-year institution of higher education.
>
> **Faculty**: Those responsible for teaching in higher education. In the United Kingdom, faculty are often called "academic staff."
>
> **Faculty development**: The common U.S. term for academic or educational development.

Major: The main course of study undergraduate students pursue.

Minor: A smaller constellation of courses students often complete in addition to a major.

Service learning: An approach to teaching and learning that integrates meaningful community service with teaching and that supports regular, ongoing reflection to enrich the learning experience, teach civic responsibility, and strengthen communities.

Students of color: Students who claim or are assigned racial or cultural characteristics that distinguish them from "white" students or those from European backgrounds (e.g., African American). This term replaces "minority" and "nonwhite," and is intended to be inclusive of all those who have experienced racism.

Acknowledgments

We wish to express our thanks to two individuals at Jossey-Bass: David Brightman, for his enthusiasm about the project and his flexibility through the composing and revising processes, and Maryellen Weimer, who offered several rounds of very thoughtful feedback on the evolving manuscript. We also want to thank faculty and student participants in the projects we describe for taking up student-faculty partnership work, and our critical-friend readers, both faculty and student colleagues, who offered feedback on drafts, including Sophia Abbot, Mick Healey, Pat Hutchings, Deandra Little, Daphne Loads, Desiree Porter, Kay Sambell, Elliott Shore, Luke Shore, Amanda Sykes, and Steve Volk. Finally, we wish to thank our families for their ongoing patience and unwavering support as we worked over months and across continents to pull this book together.

About the Authors

Alison Cook-Sather is the Mary Katharine Woodworth Professor of Education and Coordinator of the Teaching and Learning Institute at Bryn Mawr College. Supported by grants from the Ford Foundation, The Arthur Vining Davis Foundations, and the Andrew W. Mellon Foundation, Dr. Cook-Sather has developed internationally recognized programs that position students as pedagogical consultants to prospective secondary teachers and to practicing college faculty members. She has given more than 65 keynote addresses, other invited presentations, and papers at refereed conferences in Brazil, Canada, Spain, the United Kingdom, and throughout the United States, and she has published over 40 articles, 14 book chapters, and 5 books on how students can become partners with teachers and scholars to make education a mutually engaging and empowering process. Her books include *Learning from the Student's Perspective: A Sourcebook for Effective Teaching* (Paradigm Publishers, 2009), *International Handbook of Student Experience in Elementary and Secondary School* (co-edited with Dennis Thiessen, Springer Publishers, 2007), *Education Is Translation: A Metaphor for Change in Learning and Teaching* (University of Pennsylvania Press, 2006), and *In Our Own Words: Students' Perspectives on School* (co-edited with Jeffrey Shultz, Rowman & Littlefield Publishers, Inc., 2001). In 2010, Dr. Cook-Sather was named the Jean Rudduck Visiting Scholar at the University of Cambridge in England.

Catherine Bovill is a senior lecturer in the Academic Development Unit at the University of Glasgow in Scotland. She is currently coordinator of the Postgraduate Certificate in Academic Practice offered to all new academic members of staff in the University. Dr. Bovill holds a range of positions externally, including being an associate editor for the *International Journal for Academic Development* and an external examiner at St Andrews University, Scotland. Her research focuses on students and faculty co-creating curricula; conceptualizations of curricula; faculty development; peer observation of teaching; and the internationalization of higher education. Dr. Bovill has been invited to present her research on students and faculty co-creating curricula at a range of settings in the United Kingdom, Europe, the United States, and Australia. Her current and recent projects include a British Council funded project supporting faculty in Iraq to implement tudent-centered learning curricula across a university (Jordan et al., 2013); a survey of pedagogic research in Scotland (Bovill et al., 2012; Bovill et al., 2013); and acting as a co-facilitator and expert advisor to institutional teams from across the United Kingdom, participating in the Higher Education Academy (HEA) *Students as Partners Change Academy Programme*. In 2013, Dr. Bovill and Professor Vivienne Baumfield, from the School of Education at the University of Glasgow, received funding from the HEA to support a Mike Baker Doctoral Student—Cherie Woolmer—to undertake a Ph.D. entitled *Evaluating the Impact of Student-Staff Co-created Curricula in Higher Education*. Dr. Bovill currently supervises six Ph.D. students, and she was voted "Best Research Supervisor" in the 2011–2012 University of Glasgow Student Representative Council student-led teaching awards.

Peter Felten is assistant provost, executive director of the Center for Engaged Learning and the Center for the Advancement of Teaching and Learning, and associate professor of history at Elon University in North Carolina. He has published widely on engaged learning, educational development, and the scholarship of teaching and learning, including most recently the co-authored books *Transformative Conversations: A Guide to Mentoring Communities Among Colleagues in Higher Education* (Jossey-Bass, 2013) and *Transforming Students: Fulfilling the Promise of Higher Education* (Johns Hopkins University Press, 2014). He has served as president of the POD Network, the professional association for educational developers in the United States, and in 2013 he co-chaired the annual conference of the International Society for the Scholarship of Teaching and Learning. He is on editorial boards including the *International Journal for Academic Development* and *Teaching and Learning Inquiry,* and he has presented more than 75 invited workshops and plenary addresses at universities and conferences in five countries.

Engaging Students as Partners in Learning and Teaching

What Are Student-Faculty Partnerships?
Our Guiding Principles and Definition

Partnerships are based on respect, reciprocity, and shared responsibility between students and faculty. These qualities of relationship emerge when we are able to bring students' insights into discussions about learning and teaching practice in meaningful ways—ways that make teaching and learning more engaging and effective for students and for ourselves. In our own teaching and in the partnership work we have studied, we have found that respect, reciprocity, and shared responsibility are fostered when we draw on students' insights not only through collecting their responses to our courses but also through working with them to study and design teaching and learning together. So what do we mean by working with students in this way?

We begin this chapter with a discussion of the three principles that guide our vision of student-faculty partnerships, and we move from that discussion into our definition of student-faculty partnership. We then offer a brief story that illustrates what is possible when students and faculty engage in partnership. We conclude this chapter by reflecting on the ways in which our notion of partnership may seem radical—even countercultural—within many higher education institutions; however, this work is not without precedent. With this foundation established, we hope you can move through the subsequent chapters of the book with a clear vision of student-faculty partnership.

Guiding Principles for Student-Faculty Partnerships

All practice is guided explicitly or implicitly by underlying principles: they are the spoken or unspoken commitments according to which we act. We have come to believe that student-faculty partnerships rooted in the principles of respect, reciprocity, and responsibility are most powerful and efficacious. Each of these principles is foundational to genuine relationships of any kind, and each is particularly important in working within and, in some cases, against the traditional roles students and faculty are expected to assume in higher education. All three of them require and inspire trust, attention, and responsiveness. They embody what Delpit (1988) has described as listening not only with "open eyes and ears but also open hearts and minds" (p. 298), and they lead to informed action and interaction.

You are likely to have your own associations with each of these terms, so we spend a little time next explaining what we understand by respect, reciprocity, and responsibility, particularly within the context of student-faculty partnerships.

Respect

Respect is an attitude. It entails taking seriously and valuing what someone else or multiple others bring to an encounter. It demands openness and receptivity, it calls for willingness to consider experiences or perspectives that are different from our own, and it often requires a withholding of judgment. In our research, student partners frequently comment on the centrality of respect to their collaborative work with faculty; for instance, one student advises faculty to "be as open as you possibly can. The key to these types of exchanges is respect, honesty, and an ability to expose yourself to new and different perspectives."

Partnership is built on and through communication. Therefore, this first principle is foundational to pedagogical partnerships because, as one student asserted, "You can't have good communication without respect. If I don't respect you, we can't communicate" (Sanon et al., 2001, p. 119). Since dialogue is important in any partnership, you need to establish respect between yourself and those with whom you work, through the expression and reception of open eyes, ears, hearts, and minds. While we advocate that everyone entering a partnership bring an attitude of respect, we have found that it takes time to build trust in practice. The structures and norms of higher education do not necessarily foster the kind of respect that makes student-faculty collaboration into genuine partnership work, so we urge you to take the time to nurture trust and respect.

Some manifestations of respect that you will see in the chapters of this book include the explicit and regular acknowledgment of the different perspectives students and faculty bring to this work. There are examples that make it clear that while student and faculty experiences, perspectives, and even goals are sometimes different, each is taken into consideration and valued. Respect also informs the structures that support the active and engaged participation of both students and faculty members: the examples of partnership in this book illustrate the range of ways that partners and programs create forums and projects that enable students and faculty to contribute in meaningful but different ways to exploring and developing pedagogical practice.

Reciprocity

There is a close connection between respect and reciprocity, the second of our principles. Lawrence-Lightfoot (2000) asserts, "Respect: To get it, you must give it" (p. 22). Likewise, Rudduck and McIntyre (2007) argue that teacher-student relationships "have to be respectful, and the respect must be in both directions" (p. 53). However, while respect is an attitude, reciprocity is a way of interacting. It is a process of balanced give-and-take; there is equity in what is exchanged and how it is exchanged. Therefore, what this principle embodies is the mutual exchange that is key to student-faculty partnerships. As we state in multiple places in this book, we are not suggesting that students and faculty get and give exactly the same things in pedagogical partnerships. Indeed, partnerships invite faculty and students to share differing experiences and perspectives; those differences are part of what can make partnerships so rich and diverse.

The most basic manifestation of reciprocity in partnerships occurs when students offer their experiences of, and perspectives on, what it is like to be a learner in a course while faculty offer their experiences of, and perspectives on, teaching that course. As the examples and statements we include throughout the book illustrate, when these distinct yet valid sets of experiences and perspectives are shared, partners have the potential to deepen understanding and improve teaching and learning. Reciprocity also involves students taking on some responsibility for teaching and faculty re-envisaging themselves not only as teachers, but also as learners alongside their students.

A general example might help illustrate this principle. In a discussion among a group of students and a faculty member about revising a course syllabus, one student might explain how she experienced a particular assignment, noting how the framing question piqued her curiosity but that the grading rubric seemed to limit her creativity in responding to the assignment. Another student might have a different take on this, highlighting different aspects of the assignment and how they worked for him. A third student might agree with some points the first student made and some points the second student made, but have yet a third angle to share. The faculty member could explain what she had in mind with the assignment, the pedagogical rationale for it, and why she designed it as she did. In this exchange, each would gain insight into the others' perspectives, and the result might be that the faculty member affirms some aspects of the assignment and revises other aspects. The students develop a better sense of what is involved in crafting course assignments—an understanding that increases their capacities as students, with potential for future benefit. At the same time, the faculty member learns from students' perspectives that there are alternative approaches to inviting students to demonstrate their learning in this course, and which approaches students seem to value more and why.

Responsibility

Our third principle is both a prerequisite for, and an outcome of, student-faculty partnerships. One faculty member captured the connections between reciprocity and responsibility this way: "Participating in this project gave me a sense of students being able and wanting to take certain pedagogical responsibility, and the counter of that is me taking a learning responsibility." In this recognition we see the give and take of reciprocity and we also see how partnership work changes student and faculty orientation toward responsibility. Students now have some responsibility for pedagogy and faculty share some responsibility for learning.

Reliability and trustworthiness, on both the student side and the faculty side, are essential if partnerships are to develop productively. At the same time, we find that participating in student-faculty partnerships prompts both students and faculty to be more responsible and responsive. In our research we have heard over and over the student refrain that collaborative work with faculty makes them realize that "it is up to the entire community to make learning spaces function, so that means students have just as much responsibility as professors." As we will discuss in detail in Chapter 5, faculty who work in partnership with students typically have a similar reaction, often redefining their understanding of their responsibilities to the students they are teaching.

When both students and faculty take more responsibility for the educational project, teaching and learning become "community property" (Shulman, 2004a), with students recognized as active members of that community and collaborative partners equally invested in the common effort to engage in, and support, learning.

So What Exactly Do We Mean by Partnership?

Partnership is a slippery term to define (Harrison et al., 2003), and student-faculty partnership might be particularly so because of the vast diversity within higher education. However, Bird and Koirala (2002) identify four key qualities of meaningful partnerships that are closely related to the principles we offered in the previous section and that also inform our definition: (1) trust and respect, (2) shared power, (3) shared risks, and (4) shared learning. These qualities are not always present in college and university classrooms, but we believe that they can be cultivated and nurtured in ways that both constitute partnership and allow student-faculty collaboration to develop.

Partnerships rarely emerge suddenly in full bloom; instead, they grow and ripen over time as we engage with students. We invite students to think about the teaching and learning process. We solicit student feedback and then use that information to change our teaching. We create spaces in class for students to step into the role of the teacher by leading discussions or presenting their research. We challenge students to work together to solve complex problems or to make sense of difficult texts, while we listen carefully and watch, providing guidance or asking questions to help students avoid dead-ends and to focus on central issues. These practices, and many more, imply a degree of student engagement and activity focused on learning and teaching. However, they may or may not involve students collaborating with faculty as partners, or achieve the respect, reciprocity, and responsibility as we define them above, or reflect the qualities of meaningful partnership that Bird and Koirala (2002) identify.

We define student-faculty partnership as a collaborative, reciprocal process through which all participants have the opportunity to contribute equally, although not necessarily in the same ways, to curricular or pedagogical conceptualization, decision making, implementation, investigation, or analysis. This definition stands in contrast to the student-as-consumer model that has become increasingly prevalent in higher education. It also departs from the traditional "sage-on-the-stage" model of teaching. Partnership, as we define it, positions both students and faculty as learners as well as teachers; it brings different but comparably valuable forms of expertise to bear on the educational process. In this way, partnership redefines the roles of student and faculty not only in relation to one another but also in relation to the institutions within which we work. Partnership redefines processes and therefore our approach to analysis, pedagogical practice, and research in ways that emphasize affirmation as well as create opportunities for change.

We want to be clear, though, that when we talk of partnership (particularly when we use terms like "shared power"), we do not mean that faculty and students are the same. Hildyard and colleagues point out that "many participatory projects rest on the dubious assumption that simply identifying different 'stakeholders' and getting them around the table will result in a consensus being reached that is 'fair' to all." They argue that "such an assumption only holds, however, if all the actors involved are deemed to have equal bargaining power (which they do not)" (Hildyard et al., 2001, p. 69). In student-faculty collaborations, we need to acknowledge that our roles, expertise, responsibilities, and status are different. And they should be. Partnership does not require a false equivalency, but it does mean that the perspectives and contributions made by partners are equally valued and respected and that all participants have an equivalent opportunity to contribute. We spend many years developing and honing our scholarly expertise. Likewise, students spend many years experiencing and, in some cases, analyzing learning that might or might not be optimal and engaging. Partnership brings these forms of experience and expertise into dialogue in ways that inform and support more intentional action. One faculty member who participated in a partnership program explained her understanding of this approach in these terms:

> I think when most faculty hear of a program in which students are involved as commentators and collaborators, they assume that the program is giving the students unfettered authority or equality in the teaching process. But I realize now that taking student contributions seriously DOES NOT mean blindly or directly following their opinions and suggestions, but rather taking them seriously, carefully reflecting on and analyzing them, and then addressing the core concerns behind them in a way that is consistent with my overall goals and values.

So while we recognize that the partnership model we advocate represents a significant shift in attitude and approach, and in some contexts, perhaps a dramatic shift, we also want to emphasize that studying and designing teaching and learning in partnership with students does not mean that we simply turn the responsibility for conceptualizing curricular and pedagogical approaches over to students, nor does it suggest we should always do everything they recommend to us. Rather, it means that we engage in a more complex set of relationships involving genuine dialogue with students. Otherwise, we are in danger of what Cleaver describes as "swinging from one untenable position (we know best) to an equally untenable and damaging one (they know best)" (Cleaver, 2001, p. 47).

According to our guiding principles and definition, partnership involves negotiation through which we listen to students but also articulate our own expertise, perspectives, and commitments. It includes making collaborative and transparent decisions about changing our practices in some instances and not in others and developing mutual respect for the individual and shared rationales behind these choices. Indeed, it means changing our practices when appropriate, but also reaffirming, with the benefit of students' differently informed perspectives, what is already working well. Sometimes it means following where students lead, perhaps to places we may not have imagined or been to before. In all of these cases, respect and reciprocity are integral to the learning process: we share our perspectives and commitments and listen openly to students' insights, they share theirs and listen to ours, and in the exchange, we all become wiser.

How Radical Is the Notion of Student-Faculty Partnership?

The qualities of student-faculty relationships that we are describing might sound quite unfamiliar or even fanciful to some readers. Each of us has been told: "That might work with your students, but I cannot see it happening with mine." While we do not promise that partnership will be easy or comfortable (at least not at first), we are convinced it is possible—and desirable—across contexts in higher education. Initiating partnerships, however, requires stepping out of traditional roles, something that always is a challenge both to imagine and to do. In many instances, faculty take sole responsibility for creating and teaching courses. This orientation is often experienced by faculty in a largely positive way, enacting our professional obligations and honoring academic freedom. However, this approach also means that students are completely outside the course planning and teaching process.

In essence, students are primarily responsible for proceeding through the pre-planned weeks of the curriculum, regardless of whether they know why they are doing what they are doing. While some students may be quite active and engaged in this environment, others float along, adrift in their education, because that is often what they think we expect of them (Arum and Roska, 2010; Mann, 2008). Students may choose not to complete the reading or speak up in class. They may do the minimum they can get away with, and then complain about the (sometimes generous) grade they receive. Too often faculty and schools unintentionally convey these low expectations to students, and students who feel voiceless, passive, and disempowered then act that way (Green and Popovich, 2012). Indeed, many of our pedagogical assumptions and practices may be contributing to a sense of disengagement. Sambell and colleagues conclude that in many higher education classrooms "our approaches seem to suggest that students are 'problems' or lacking in some way," requiring us to structure and dictate their every action in a highly detailed syllabus (Sambell et al., 2012, p. 149). This is a cycle that alienates both students and faculty from each other, as well as from the shared task that brings us together in the first place.

The experiences we bring to higher education also create distance between faculty and students. In some ways, that distance is hard earned. Faculty have spent years pursuing graduate studies, and sometimes decades after that honing our craft, to become disciplinary experts. Students are not our peers in knowledge, skills, or learning, so it is no surprise that we see them as the recipients, the beneficiaries, of our scholarly achievements. This leads to a situation in which students are considered the people we teach *to*, not the people we are in class *with*. At the same time, students often come to university after years of being taught to be relatively passive learners. In many cases, they have been rewarded for following a prescribed curriculum that prepares them to successfully pass a standardized test that then gives them access to the next high-stakes exam. In many contexts, schooling is a slog, not an opportunity to explore, to learn, and to grow.

We envision partnership as creating the conditions for curiosity and common inquiry, breaking down the barriers that often distance students from faculty. While that might seem radical to some, student-faculty partnerships are not a new phenomenon in education. A century ago John Dewey championed schools where students would have a stronger voice in their own learning experiences (Dewey, 1916). Since then, many theorists and reformers have advocated similar or even more radical ideas (Bovill, 2013b), and students have sometimes asserted their desire to contribute to curricular and institutional decision making. Indeed, some of today's faculty and academic staff were, not so long ago, among those students who cried out for a more engaged and engaging university.

Although student-faculty partnerships are not entirely new or novel, they are outside the norm at many colleges and universities. We believe that this situation needs to change. Even in a climate when both time and money are all too rare, we believe that flexible, sustainable, and often simple practices of partnership can transform students, faculty, and institutions, helping all of us to achieve our aspirations for higher education. While breaking old habits and shifting established culture can be difficult for students and faculty, our current practices are socially constructed, not inevitable. They have developed over time, and they will continue to change as students, faculty, and education evolve. Indeed, the growth of free, online education is just one example to suggest that under the right circumstances many students will voluntarily study challenging material for no extrinsic reward. Research consistently demonstrates that students will work hard and engage deeply when they experience learning as personally meaningful (Schlechty, 2011; Nygaard et al., 2013). To tap into that motivation and engagement, we need to move away from the isolation fostered by our traditional roles as students and faculty. Instead, we can strive to act as partners, equally invested in the common goal of learning. Embracing change like this requires openness to what Shulman (2004b) has called "visions of the possible" that can inspire our thinking and practice, even when such visions might be offering just a glimpse of a distant horizon.

One Vision of the Possible

To give you a quick sense of what participant experiences within some of these programs can look like and what partnerships can lead to, we will offer a brief story that we see as an illustration of the transformative potential of an institutionally supported student-faculty partnership. This story unfolds within the context of Bryn Mawr College's Students as Learners and Teachers (SaLT) program, which we introduced in the Preface. In this program, participating faculty and students meet throughout the semester to discuss what they are learning through their partnerships, how their understandings of teaching and learning are being clarified or challenged, and the ways in which they might be reaffirming or revising pedagogical approaches in the classrooms under study. In this and other forums the program provides, teachers not only learn about themselves as teachers, students learn about themselves as learners.

In one meeting of SaLT participants, a student reflected on her experience and shared with the group how her first semester as a consultant changed her orientation toward teaching and learning:

> When I was writing the last paper I had [in a particular class], I found myself looking at the prompt and thinking more. The professor wasn't necessarily explicit about making connections, but I found myself being able to look at what the assignment was and being more able to decipher what the professor was emphasizing and what they were looking for. I think I ended up writing a better paper as a result. And it was sort of interesting to realize that I don't think I would have thought of this last semester; I would have just answered the question. Whereas this was more like, what is the intent behind the questions, and why are these questions set up as they are?

This student attributed her critical, active approach toward learning to her consulting partnership with a faculty member. After hearing this student speak, a faculty member mused, "The kind of reflective understanding that the student consultant gets through her work with a faculty member isn't inert; it makes her a much better learner."

While that story is about a particular student in a specific context, it suggests possibilities for diverse students at many different types of institutions. This student's story highlights how she became a better student—more reflective and better prepared for her own academic work—through her conversations with her faculty partner, and how this then altered how she approached work for other classes. She became a more actively engaged learner through partnership, and she carried that active engagement beyond her partnership.

All of us can recall students like this. These students are so engaged with their studies that they truly make the work their own. They might be common or rare on your campus, but they are everywhere. They don't just answer our questions, they ask their own (often better) questions—and then they relentlessly pursue answers. Many other students we quote throughout the book illustrate how this passion and engagement can be kindled. Such engagement is the fundamental goal of student-faculty partnerships and, as the story above illustrates, is also fostered by them. We believe this collaborative work leads to a radical shift in teaching; rather than faculty and students facing each other across a room in a combative manner, we are sitting on the same side of the desk, working together to pursue the common goal of learning and development.

Throughout the chapters in this book, we include stories like this, as well as shorter reflections from participants in student-faculty partnerships, to give you a sense of how faculty and students experience this kind of respect, reciprocity, and shared responsibility. As we state in our Preface, our inclusion of so many faculty and student voices reflects our commitment to participatory dialogue and shared meaning making. The quotes are also consistent with our core belief that we create meaning through sharing stories, as well as engaging in systematic and intentional study (Shadiow, 2013).

Conclusion

In this chapter, we have articulated our core beliefs about the transformative potential of student-faculty partnerships. We emphasize that in partnership students and faculty make distinct contributions that are equally valued in the pursuit of common goals. What each brings to the partnership—the experiences, expertise, and perspectives—is respected and valued and drawn upon as students and faculty together explore, affirm, and, where appropriate, revise curricular and pedagogical approaches. In this discussion we have attempted to balance what we mean by partnership and what we do not mean, what we advocate and what we do not, and both the contextual constraints we all face and the historical precursors of such an approach.

Our discussion thus far may have raised questions for you, or perhaps you have come to this text with a number of questions. In the next chapter, we address many of the questions we are regularly asked, and we hope our responses prepare you to read about some concrete examples of student-faculty partnerships, which we present in Chapters 3 and 4.

2

Preliminary Questions about Student-Faculty Partnerships

Whether you have already been involved in student-faculty partnerships or are just beginning to think about ways in which you might try to establish them, you are likely to have questions about some of the complexities involved in setting up, implementing, and sustaining partnerships. Most faculty have pragmatic concerns about how partnerships might be possible within different disciplinary, institutional, and national settings where very real challenges exist.

We urge you to take your questions and concerns seriously, and we advise against leaping into partnership without first carefully thinking through your goals, strategies, and context. To help you get started, we offer some preliminary responses to questions that we are often asked about student-faculty partnerships. We raise and address additional questions in Chapter 8.

Students are not experts in either subject matter or pedagogy. How can they possibly help me explore or design learning and teaching?

Indeed, most students are neither disciplinary nor pedagogical experts. Rather, their experience and expertise typically is in being a student—something that many faculty have not been for many years. They understand where they and their peers are coming from and, often, where they think they are going. As Sorenson (2001) wrote in describing one of the first formal student-faculty partnership programs in the United States, "as experienced students, they are experts about sitting in classes, understanding new concepts, and creating their own learning" (p. 179). They can contribute to explorations of curricular and pedagogical questions by bringing their backgrounds and perspectives into our thinking and planning as faculty members. This not only expands our understanding of existing student learning and teaching experiences but also can be the beginning of shared dialogue and deeper understanding about learning and teaching content and processes as we exchange perspectives.

Therefore, as we suggest in a number of ways throughout this book, we advocate cultivating or deepening respect for students as partners based on their positions, experiences, and insights as learners. We propose that you think of students as legitimate informants (Feuerverger and Richards, 2007) on the student experience—those with perspectives we cannot have as teachers. We recommend that you conceptualize students as differently positioned witnesses to what happens in and outside of your classroom or online teaching space. You may find that in many cases, students have invaluable insights into curricular structures, assessment methods, learning goals, and even disciplinary content—although they are unlikely to use those terms.

We recognize that many faculty may be uncomfortable with the necessary change in power relations that a more collaborative and democratic pedagogical planning process requires. We discuss issues of power extensively in Chapter 7. We encourage you to be honest with yourself and with your partners about the potential discomfort you (and they) might experience as you begin this work. Fielding (1999) aptly calls partnership a form of "radical collegiality" between learners and teachers. While unfamiliar or even scary, such an orientation also can be exciting and empowering.

I have enough to do already without having to set up all these meetings with students; wouldn't it be quicker to do this on my own?

It depends on how you think about time. People typically find time for the things they consider most important. Working with students as partners in the design or revision of a course probably takes more time than doing these alone. However, time investments up front can pay off later as students take a more active role in the learning process (Wolf-Wendel et al., 2009), and working in partnership with students rather than working against them actually saves time as students assume more responsibility for the learning, as well as sometimes the teaching, that happens in a class. The time you spend creating and building partnership that enhances student engagement and accountability is time you save later on: repeating or clarifying when students don't understand; reviewing with students during office hours; responding to drafts of student work; and coping with the frustrations of teaching disengaged students. As the Bryn Mawr student in Chapter 1 explained, partnership helps students to become more invested in and responsible for learning.

My students don't want to design their own learning; they have paid for their education and see teaching and curriculum design as my job. How can I convey the desirability of partnership?

Because partnership challenges the consumer model of learning and the transmission model of teaching, both of which most students have come to expect through many years of schooling, students can feel confused and even frustrated when we propose a different approach. As Bain and Zimmerman (2009) have pointed out, there are students who choose to adopt a surface or strategic approach to learning, skimming across course content or learning only what is necessary for a good grade. Sometimes they make these choices because of the way we design courses and programs. Most students, however, once they have the chance to realize that their expectations of learning result from habit and not desire, recognize that having a hand in designing their own learning is far more engaging, interesting, and meaningful as a form of education. In Chapter 5, we share with you the experiences of student partners who report the process to be invigorating and empowering; we have heard from many students that this makes their higher education experience far more rewarding.

However, it takes time and flexibility to achieve a revision of what higher education can be, so start small by asking for student input on parts of your course—a single assignment or activity— and give them a chance to see what happens and how it feels when they have that voice. What most faculty find is that if students are invited to work in partnership, even just for a bounded and fo- cused part of the course, their engagement deepens and they begin to shift their thinking. This will vary with students and contexts, of course, but moving toward partnership with students, by tak- ing slow, cautious steps to ensure that students trust the changes, is one of the best ways to inspire students' openness to designing their own learning.

In order to enable this shift to happen more often and in more contexts, we have some work to do to change our own and our students' ways of thinking about learning and teaching from pre- dominant consumer models. As the United Kingdom's National Union of Students points out: "If we seek to engage students mere- ly in order to find out what they want and give it to them, we re- produce this dangerous narrative of consumerism and lose sight of the responsibility of educators to challenge and stretch students" (NUS, 2012, p. 5). A transmission model of education is unlikely to help students become independent and critical thinkers, effec- tive team players, clear communicators, skilled at self-assessment, and socially aware. In contrast, partnerships and other opportunities for students to take more responsibility for learning and teaching can lead to a range of compelling knowledge, skills, and value- based outcomes (which we outline in Chapter 5). However, we should not assume that students already recognize the possibilities of partnership. Explicit invitations and explanations complement practices that build trust and give students experience acting as partners.

Will students want to do this if they don't get credit for it?

In some forms of partnership, faculty work with a whole current cohort of their students (such as an entire class section) rather than engaging a selected group of interns or consultants. When an entire cohort is involved, and when the partnership work forms an integral part of an ongoing course, students typically are not compensated in any way for their contributions other than with the usual credit for undertaking that particular course.

When faculty work outside of an ongoing course or with a small number of student partners, students are more likely to be compensated in some way. Different institutions have different norms and practices regarding student compensation. In some cases, receiving course credit or pay will be essential to students because they need the income or a certain number of credits per semester, or some combination of these. In other instances, students do not receive tangible benefits but participation is acknowledged by, for example, conferring a formal title on their work (e.g., Student Consultant, Research Partner) that students can include on their résumés and that shows that we value their participation.

What do I do if the culture of my department or institution is not conducive to student-faculty partnerships?

Consider starting small, perhaps by working with a handful of students or talking with a few like-minded colleagues, beginning with people you suspect will be open to the idea of partnership. Set attainable goals such as redesigning a single assignment with students in a course rather than trying to enlist an entire department to redesign the curriculum in partnership with students. Consider piloting some partnerships and let faculty and students learn for themselves what the possibilities are. And also look for opportunities to advocate for partnership in appropriate venues on campus, whether in formal committee meetings or through informal conversations with faculty and administrators. The language of student-faculty partnership typically aligns with institutional mission and values, allowing you to frame your work as returning to the fundamental goals of your department or university.

Once you can demonstrate the efficacy of partnership work, word will spread among colleagues and the culture may start to shift. In our work, we have found that some colleagues who are initially dismissive or suspicious of student-faculty partnerships change their minds when they have the opportunity to try out a partnership in a low-stakes and well-supported situation. Colleagues may become more open when working in collaboration with one other faculty member and a couple of students, while joining an ongoing program of partnership may help other colleagues feel that they are part of a larger movement, not stepping out alone into unfamiliar terrain.

Finally, be alert for sources to support and fund your partnership work. Often institutions have internal innovation grants, and some external funders are in search of unique and distinctive learning and teaching projects. If you have funds, participants as well as other colleagues may consider your project more legitimate. When you succeed, the project can become an accomplishment that the institution or the external funder can celebrate and promote.

How do I deal with my university's policies that do not support this kind of work? For instance, I am required to have my syllabus and learning outcomes clearly established before my course begins.

Cooke and Kothari (2001) argue that "participatory ideals are often operationally constrained by institutional contexts that require formal and informal bureaucratic goals to be met" (p. 8). Indeed, many universities require faculty to create explicit learning outcomes for courses and programs. Frequently, this enables students and faculty to be clear and transparent about the purposes and processes of learning and teaching in a course—and that's a good thing. This kind of requirement can restrict (but not eliminate) possibilities for student-faculty partnership in teaching and learning because even if the ends of a course are fixed, the means often are not. For example, you might collaborate with students to decide how best to achieve the established learning outcomes. Encouraging students to become partners in this way puts students and faculty on the same team: striving together to reach goals. Knowing the aims and outcomes of a course and contributing to ways of meeting those can facilitate students' development of greater metacognitive awareness. As we discuss in Chapter 5, such metacognitive awareness—understanding why we learn the way we do and making choices to learn most effectively—can, in turn, contribute to students' capacity to meet course goals. The key here is to take the three qualities of relationship we emphasize—respect, reciprocity, and shared responsibility—and to turn them into a mode of working within whatever requirements and constraints you face.

It's OK for you in your course, but in my discipline we have a professional accrediting body. I have to be sure that my students can demonstrate they are competent to meet the professional body's requirements at the end of my course. How can I create a meaningful partnership without risking competency and accreditation?

Faculty from disciplines with professional body requirements may consider that the guidelines set out by these bodies seriously limit the possibilities of cocreation. However, it is important to check what exactly your professional body stipulates, rather than what is commonly believed to be stipulated. Sometimes, for example, professional body requirements focus on graduate competencies and not on when within a degree program a competency is to be developed. Typically, some flexibility exists within courses and programs for faculty and students to design learning and teaching in ways that they consider most effective for developing professional knowledge, skills, values, and competencies. That flexibility may allow some room for partnerships to develop. Indeed, partnership may help students develop key skills in learning how to learn, as well as self-assessment, teamwork, and other values essential in professional settings and for meeting the mandated competencies.

When is the best time during one's career to devote time and energy to partnership? For example, I'm a new faculty member and have only just worked out my lectures for the first time last year. Do you think partnership with students is more suitable for experienced faculty members?

There is no single best career stage for partnership, and we think this work is appropriate for faculty of all ages and stages. However, because faculty roles and responsibilities vary widely across disciplines and types of institutions, we encourage you to think carefully about how partnership connects to institutional values, how it fits into your career development, and how it might be both supported and rewarded on your campus.

If you are at an institution that encourages collaborative work with students, perhaps through a teaching center or an undergraduate research office, you could try out pedagogical partnership with plenty of support in a context that values time spent on teaching. For instance, all new faculty members at Bryn Mawr and Haverford Colleges are invited to participate in a weekly seminar with other faculty and a semester-long partnership with a student consultant as part of the SaLT program during their first semester at the colleges. Many new faculty find this tremendously helpful in coming to understand the institutional culture and in making the shift from their own graduate work to undergraduate teaching. At the same time, experienced Bryn Mawr and Haverford faculty also choose to participate in this program because it helps them rethink and reinvigorate their teaching.

If your institution does not have programs and resources dedicated to partnership, and many do not, then you may want to reflect on what you will need to create sustainable partnerships. Are there colleagues who could help you or students who seem ready to collaborate with you? Is there a course you teach that seems particularly ripe for partnership? Would it feel safer to do this with a smaller class of students in the first instance? Over the next year or two, perhaps you can identify a time and a context that might be more flexible to try out a new pedagogical approach like this.

Why change my practice if I'm an effective teacher and my students are already learning what they should?

The goal of student-faculty partnership work is not change for change's sake but rather to achieve a deeper understanding of teaching and learning that comes from shared analysis and revision. It may be that partners reaffirm and clarify why a particular course design or pedagogical approach works well, and the outcome might be that the faculty member makes his ongoing practices more explicit to the students. It may be that a student partner makes a suggestion that the faculty member does not act upon but the faculty member is then better able to articulate sound pedagogical reasons to students about decisions made about the course. In some cases, faculty and student partners produce minor revisions, and in others they completely overhaul a course, assignment, or approach. What kind of change is made and how rapidly should be carefully considered. Indeed, too many changes made too quickly can be disruptive and might even be detrimental, so partners need to think carefully about what kind and extent of change is advisable for all involved.

Regardless of the scope and pace of change that takes place, there is reciprocity in the process: both faculty and students learn from their interactions, are more informed and thoughtful as a result, and carry their deepened awareness and more developed capacities into other contexts and relationships. As you will see in the statements by faculty and student participants we include throughout the book, the biggest impact that change has is upon attitudes: understanding teaching and learning as shared responsibilities rather than responsibilities distinguished and divided between students and faculty. These changing attitudes have broad implications for higher education, including for the best teachers and students.

What if I teach a really big class?

You can take different approaches to partnership in large classes. You might invite students who had previously taken a course to conduct group interviews with current students to investigate a particularly challenging dimension of the curriculum, as Mary Sunderland does in her ethics class in the College of Engineering at the University of California, Berkeley. You could invite experienced students to experiment with collaborative redesign of existing course materials, as Francis Duah and colleagues have done in mathematics at Loughborough University in the United Kingdom. You could invite all students enrolled in the course to come to a class consensus about what they need to do to achieve the learning goals of the course and to earn course grades, as Mano Singham, a physics professor at Case Western Reserve University, and his students do. Or you could use examples of student work from a large class as the basis for class discussion and curricular content, as Niamh Moore and Mary Gilmartin at University College Dublin did for their very large, first-year geography program. These and other examples are discussed in Chapter 3.

Won't students think I'm just experimenting on them?

If you invite students into partnership but do not really take up the premises of respect, reciprocity, and shared responsibility, then yes, students might well think you are experimenting on them. And they might be right. Faculty should be wary of claiming partnership without allowing real opportunities for students to collaborate. If, however, you present the opportunity as one in which you are truly willing to share—not give up, but share—power and responsibility in conceptualizing, implementing, or assessing some part of the class, and if you stay in open and honest dialogue with students about the processes as well as the outcomes, then they are not likely to think you are experimenting on them. Students may see the experience as experimenting *with* them, and that often is exciting for all involved. In our research at diverse institutions, we find that students are generally open to faculty being honest about the classroom serving as a site for coconstruction of ideas and outcomes, as long as the process is genuine and does not seem haphazard, ill conceived, or the result of bad (or no) planning. Students are more likely to be open to collaborative experimentation when they have choice in the matter and when choosing to work in partnership does not make them more vulnerable than they often already feel in situations where faculty grade their work.

If I decide to try developing a student-faculty partnership, what's the first conversation with a student or students like? I'm not clear about how I get started after I've identified potential partners.

At the initial meeting with potential partners or in the first class session when you discuss partnership, you will want to establish rapport, discuss the focus for your work together, and begin to clarify the roles students and faculty will play in the collaboration. For instance, during your initial meeting, you might talk briefly about your interests, questions, and hopes for a partnership, and ask students about what their interests, questions, and hopes are. Then you might discuss the project or question that will be the focus of your partnership—you might have a clear project in mind, or you might brainstorm with your partner(s) about how best to direct your work. Finally, chat about the process of partnership. Some faculty will want to approach this broadly, discussing characteristics of positive partnerships each of you have experienced before. Some will prefer to start with nitty-gritty considerations. Will the partners cofacilitate meetings? How will you organize your project time and how will you share the work? Ensure that students have a chance to respond and ask questions about what their role might be. Throughout this conversation, and the many that will follow, be patient. Many students (and faculty) may not have undertaken anything similar before, so give everyone time to imagine what the partnership will involve and to ask plenty of questions. Try to build in flexibility so you can adjust roles and responsibilities to suit individual and group skills and interests in the early stages of the partnership.

Conclusion

In this chapter, we have offered responses to the kinds of questions we often hear from faculty or faculty developers who are intrigued by but also cautious about developing student-faculty partnerships. We hope that they reassure you and affirm that your questions are important to pose and further explore. If you have other questions, or if you want to see what other kinds of questions faculty colleagues have asked, go to Chapter 8, in which we pose and address further questions that often arise as partnerships develop.

In the next chapters we provide a number of concrete examples of this work, starting with partnerships developed by individual faculty and then exploring broader program-level partnerships.

3

Partnerships with Students

Examples from Individual Faculty

This chapter examines individual faculty-driven and faculty-developed approaches to partnerships. Faculty have set up partnerships with students in a wide range of ways. This work can include many or just a few students, focus on narrow inquiry into student learning or broad exploration of pedagogical practice, involve large undergraduate courses or graduate-level seminars, and enjoy substantial or no institutional support (Bovill and Bulley, 2011). The examples we provide here are not comprehensive. Instead, we highlight diverse approaches across different disciplines and institutional contexts that share a commitment to engaging students in ways that align with our three guiding principles of respect, reciprocity, and responsibility. You might easily identify ways to adapt some of these examples to your own work, while others might seem difficult or even unsuitable in your context. We believe that each example can help reveal the complexities and possibilities of partnership.

In these examples, you will notice that in many instances, even in the most participatory approaches to learning, we as faculty are in control of the early decisions that guide these partnerships, such as which students to work in partnership with and what questions we will explore with students (Bovill, 2013a; Heron, 1992). Ideally, partnerships develop reciprocally from the very start. However, the time lines and habits of higher education make such grounded partnerships difficult. Students often move quickly through our institutions, and faculty reward structures typically focus our attention away from the cultivation of reciprocal relationships. While imperfect, authentic partnerships can and will emerge from the kind of faculty-initiated efforts we describe in this chapter, some of which just begin to approach partnership whereas others are highly collaborative. In Chapter 4 we will explore ways of enhancing the potential impact of partnerships by looking at how to develop broader institution-level and program-level student-faculty partnerships.

We have organized the examples in this chapter into three overlapping sections, featuring student-faculty partnerships focused on

1. Designing a course or elements of a course, including assignments
2. Responding to the student experience during a course
3. Assessing student work

While we use these categories to organize the examples, we do not mean to suggest that the groupings are at all fixed. A case we have included in one section might also fit into another section. Our goal is not to present a typology or a set of prescriptions about which kind of project fits into which category but rather to offer a handful of illustrative models for you to consider and use as a jumping-off point for your own ideas and approaches.

Furthermore, this organizational structure is not presented as moving from least to most desirable; rather, different pedagogical goals, disciplinary habits, and institutional contexts will influence which of these approaches is most promising to you. In all three of the sections in this chapter, we present a cluster of brief examples in each category to hint at some of the variety and levels of partnership that are possible and one more detailed case to illustrate the steps commonly involved in doing this particular kind of work. Some of the examples have been undertaken and have concluded, some of the examples are ongoing, and some of them are just beginning. You will therefore see different verb tenses used to describe these programs. All of this variation demonstrates the evolving and dynamic nature of student-faculty partnerships across time and context.

"I have become even more convinced that students are experts in learning and essential partners in the task of creating and developing new courses and refining existing ones."

Faculty partner

---

1. Designing a Course or Elements of a Course

Course design is perhaps the most important step in effective teaching (Fink, 2003). The design process is ripe for partnership because it allows for planning and deliberation, affording faculty and students an opportunity to develop comfort with, and confidence in, the shared work. Many faculty begin by codesigning elements of a course with students; others cocreate entire courses.

You might still be asking yourself, "How can students contribute to course design when they do not know the content?" As we have argued in previous chapters, partnership does not assume that all partners contribute the same things. In student-faculty partnerships focused on designing a course or elements of a course, you as faculty member remain the disciplinary expert. Students bring important perspectives as those who experience many, various courses and assignments—perspectives that we as faculty, unless we are students ourselves, no longer have. Bringing into dialogue the disciplinary expertise and pedagogical knowledge of faculty with student expertise and insight as learners can generate more engaging and effective courses, course components, and learning opportunities.

Courses comprise not only disciplinary content but also teaching approaches, schedules, reading lists, assessment, and many other elements. Our examples here illustrate how students and faculty have worked in partnership to explore these different areas, including: creating approaches to helping less advanced students understand difficult concepts; redesigning a virtual learning environment; deciding which cases and content will be studied; developing a class consensus on what students need to do to achieve the learning goals and to earn course grades; encouraging students to write their own essay questions; inviting students to choose assignment types, content, timing, and weighting of assignments; challenging students to author multiple-choice questions; and working with students to identify course objectives. For each example we provide brief information about participants, context, approach, and outcomes.

Brief example 1a: Francis Duah, a PhD student at Loughborough University in Leicestershire, in the United Kingdom, in collaboration with his supervisor Tony Croft and a Senior Lecturer in mathematics, Steven Kenny, invited a group of mathematics students to design teaching materials to help second-year students understand difficult concepts.

Duah has been researching student-faculty collaboration in mathematics course design under the supervision of Croft. Duah, Croft, and Kenny collaborated on the SYMBoL Project, which was a second-year mathematics curriculum-development project. Duah began his research into student-faculty collaboration in course design because he had a strong interest in significant problems with student performance, engagement, and satisfaction in undergraduate mathematics.

Four second-year mathematics students were employed as paid interns to experiment with collaborative redesign of existing materials for two second-year courses. The students had previously taken and passed the courses. After a series of discussions between the faculty and students, the four undergraduates developed a new set of supplemental materials to complement class lectures. These include video screen-casts of theory and examples and handouts on specific topics that were particularly difficult for many students in the class (see Duah and Croft, 2011). The student-faculty collaboration also involved the development of peer-assisted learning (PAL) sessions, to which the interns contributed resources and two interns also became PAL leaders.

The outcomes of this project are consistent with those of other such collaborative efforts. Not only did the students in the targeted courses demonstrate deeper understanding of difficult material, but the partners also changed. For instance, one of the interns reported that, "most importantly, my confidence in my mathematical ability and myself has grown so much since being a student intern, especially through working directly in partnership with lecturers." One of the faculty members involved reported that they were "quite impressed with the student [interns]. They seemed to make a lot of progress during the six weeks in getting a deeper understanding of the material."

Brief example 1b: At University College Dublin, in Ireland, two faculty, Niamh Moore and Mary Gilmartin, invited a group of three third-year undergraduate students to redesign the structure and the virtual learning environment of a first-year geography module, Introduction to Human Geography. This first-year course enrolls approximately 400 students each year.

The overall design was to be based around four case studies of relevant and contemporary issues within human geography— globalization, migration, contested landscapes, and power—and the three students were employed as interns to source and design new learning materials. The students were given complete freedom to innovate and were provided with access to computers, a digital video recorder, and a Dictaphone. During weekly progress report meetings with faculty, students were guided and advised on the work they were doing. They then produced written, audio, and video resources for the virtual learning environment that first-year students could interact with and use to support their learning, including short video clips, online quizzes, and assessment instructions. These case studies prompted discussion among small groups of students online and within the large class setting and provided structured themes for face-to-face tutorial activities.

Some of the outputs of these tutorials were then used by the faculty as lecture material within the large classes and examples of good student work. In this way, the current students' work directly influenced and contributed to the curriculum and the students demonstrated high levels of interaction, confidence, and responsibility for their own and others' learning. The assessment of the module illustrated significantly higher levels of student engagement across a range of indicators than other more traditional modules, and provided students with a much greater sense of identity as geographers within the general Arts program (See Bovill, 2013a; Bovill, Cook-Sather, and Felten, 2011; Moore and Gilmartin, 2010).

Brief example 1c: In an undergraduate environmental justice program at Queen Margaret University in Edinburgh, Scotland, delivered in collaboration with the environmental nongovernmental organization Friends of the Earth, Eurig Scandrett and colleagues provide the framework for the program by establishing the major themes, but students determine the specific focus of the curriculum.

An unusual aspect of the program is that students enrolling in the environmental justice program are required to be activists in their own communities involved in campaigns that are fighting environmental injustice. Scandrett and colleagues provide a curricular framework that includes key areas of study for examining environmental justice, including practical skills like using the law and practical organization and analytical modules on political change and understanding science. The students negotiate which cases and content will be studied, based on the specific examples of environmental injustice they are campaigning against.

One year the students explored a local community's fight over a nearby toxic waste dump and a controversial proposal to increase fish farming on the west coast of Scotland. These specific examples, which are rooted in individual students' own communities and experiences, provide the core content of the curriculum, which is therefore a negotiated outcome based on both academic criteria and the existing knowledge and learning needs of the students. Assignments are designed to encourage wider participation and collective learning in communities and to be useful for furthering the aims of the students' campaigns. (See for example Bovill, 2013a; Scandrett, 2010; Scandrett et al, 2005; Wilkinson and Scandrett, 2003.)

Brief example 1d: Mano Singham, a physics professor at Case Western Reserve University in Cleveland, Ohio, takes this kind of collaboration one giant step further.

After increasing frustration with what he called a "monster syllabus" that implied a legalistic contract between his introductory students and himself and that he perceived to be a barrier to student engagement and learning, he declared "death to the syllabus!" Singham now talks with students about the goals of a particular course, and then explains to his students that he has ethical obligations to both his discipline and his institution to ensure appropriate learning and rigorous grading. Within those constraints, he and his students then develop a class consensus on what students need to do to achieve the learning goals and to earn course grades. Students also help him set the schedule for class assignments and determine the consequence for late work.

While this approach is not a panacea to all that ails undergraduate education, Singham reports (2005, 2007) enhanced student engagement and a stronger sense of community within the course. Students take more responsibility for their own learning and for the performance of their peers, thus creating not only student-faculty partnership but also student-student partnerships aimed at learning.

Brief example 1e: Peter Kruschwitz, a classics professor at Reading University in the United Kingdom, collaborates with students to develop essay questions.

Kruschwitz provides his students with six to eight key words relating to the course they are studying and asks them to use the words to construct their own essay question. He checks the questions students have written to ensure that the scope of each question is not too narrow or too broad, and he suggests amendments, where necessary, before approving the questions for use.

By writing their own questions, students have to consider carefully what they are particularly interested in and the impact of the kinds of questions asked upon the angle and focus of the essay that can result. Students are essentially able to shape both the style of essay they choose to write and the particular topic that most interests them while still addressing central course themes. Kruschwitz still controls the grading, but students report finding the essays "relevant," and they demonstrate a higher level of involvement in their learning.

Over the last five years, students on average have performed consistently better in this course than in comparable courses delivered in a more traditional manner. Kruschwitz reports that involving the students in designing their own essay questions has enhanced the quality of nearly all student essays (and their associated grades) and also has reduced the incidence of plagiarism.

Brief example 1f: Suzanne Hudd teaches sociology at Quinnipiac University in Hamden, Connecticut. She has invited students in her introductory sociology class to design assignments and grading criteria.

The introductory sociology course is typically taken by first-year students although it enrolls some more advanced undergraduates. Students are asked to consider a range of assignment types, the content of assignments, the timing of assignments, and the weighting of assignments. Through collaborative group work, initially outside class and then back in the classroom, students come to agreement about appropriate assignments for the class.

The assignments are finalized in the third class meeting; this ensures that students are clear about what the final version of their assignment is and that they have plenty of time to prepare for completing it.

Most students welcome this opportunity to be involved in assignment setting, and all students tend to perform well on assignments. Some students think that the negotiation of assignments takes up too much class time when they should be learning about sociology. However, overall, most students are positive about the experience and report enjoying taking a more active role in their learning. (See Hudd, 2003.)

Brief example 1g: Katherine Cameron and Andrew Grosset, medical students at the University of Glasgow, in Scotland, have undertaken a review of PeerWise, which is free online software created by Paul Denny at the University of Auckland.

PeerWise enables students to author multiple-choice questions. Students can then answer each other's questions, rate the questions in terms of difficulty and quality, and comment upon the questions. All this can be undertaken anonymously.

Cameron and Grosset investigated the implementation of PeerWise in three first-year undergraduate courses at the University of Glasgow in 2011. In each course, a different method of implementation was used:

- Students of medicine were offered PeerWise on an optional basis.

- Dentistry students were asked to participate on a compulsory basis, with no reward.

- Veterinary medicine students were asked to participate on a compulsory basis, and received credit of 5% toward their overall grade.

Cameron and Grosset found that students in all cohorts engaged with the software most frequently at times close to both formative and summative assessments. When students were forced to participate, they tended to engage more in all aspects of the tool: in writing, answering, and commenting on questions.

Where faculty chose to make it compulsory for students to use PeerWise, students rated the software more highly, with many commenting that they planned to use this software in the future. One student commented, "PeerWise has enabled me to develop a greater understanding of the ins and outs of questions I am likely to face in my future career, and in exams. It has provided me with something I do not feel was covered in teaching; overall it has been a thoroughly worthwhile experience." Faculty have considered using some of the high-quality student questions that were contributed to expand their multiple-choice question "banks" for use in future exams.

Brief example 1h: Laura Gibson at Vincennes University in Indiana invited her second-year sociology students to design some of their course learning outcomes and assignments to be personally meaningful.

Gibson worked with 13 second-year social work students to set course learning objectives. However, she was concerned that to simply ask students what objectives they wanted to set might lead them to feel a bit lost if they had not had experience doing this before. She thought they might be unsure about what was meant or what kinds of objectives might be considered suitable. So she provided students with a list of possible course objectives to consider and asked them to select some objectives that they were most interested in aiming to achieve. They selected eight objectives and then Gibson provided them with 22 forms of possible assignments to choose from—assignments through which they could demonstrate achievement of their selected objectives.

Some things were nonnegotiable; for example, the assignment had to match the course catalog description and any written work had to meet the style conventions of the Department of Sociology/Social Work. They decided on assignments as a class, as well as the due dates for submission. Finally, they determined the relative weightings of the assignments.

When students are given more responsibility for their learning, they tend to engage more deeply in that learning and as a consequence are both surprised and inspired. This was the case for Gibson's students. One student commented: "I have been taking [university] classes now for 2 years and this is the first time a professor has asked what the students wanted to get out of the class. I loved this process!" (Gibson, 2011, p. 97). Another student commented: "The idea that you trust us is awesome. We are adults" (Gibson, 2011, p. 97). Gibson herself commented: "Students understand when the university environment has requirements that cannot be breached. They appreciate the professor's willingness to share the design of the course with them to make it personally relevant to their lives and to their future careers" (Gibson, 2011, p. 98).

Case Study 1: Student-Faculty Course Design

Background

Omri Shimron, a faculty member at Elon University in North Carolina, had successfully taught foundational music theory courses multiple times at two institutions, but he felt unsatisfied with his ability to teach students to hear complex musical patterns and chord progressions. This foundational skill, often called "ear training," is essential for students to excel as music students and as musicians, but many of his students found it to be devilishly challenging to learn. Shimron long ago had mastered this skill, and he struggled to remember what it was like to not know how to do it. The gap he felt between himself and his students over this capacity was compounded by his perceived lack of understanding of his students' musical experiences; while he grew up overseas and studied classical music from a young age, most of his students spent years performing in high school bands and choral groups in the United States. To try to bridge these gaps, Shimron deliberately designed his student-faculty partnership project to create an environment where he could interact with select students outside the classroom to engage in a frank, inclusive, and nonthreatening dialogue. He hoped that the exchange of ideas would foster a new sense of relevance and immediacy for students and would more effectively bridge the divide between expert and novice that he found so vexing.

Process

Shimron invited three former students to spend a semester studying student performance in a course he was teaching that term at Elon University. Shimron and his partners first had a few long conversations about the goals of the course, his various strategies for ear training, the background and musical habits students typically bring to this first-year course, and students' experiences in the course (including both the student partners' experiences and those of past students, as captured by course evaluations and written reflections). Based on those conversations, the three student partners periodically interviewed his current students to gather real-time impressions about what was and was not helping develop ear-training skills. Shimron and his partners met regularly to talk about what they were learning and to collaboratively develop new activities aimed at enhancing ear training. At the end of the semester, he and his partners spent several hours together redesigning the syllabus for the next time he taught the course, applying the lessons they had learned through the semester of partnership.

Outcomes

The redesigned syllabus maintained much of prior course structure and assignments, but it wove ear training more systematically through the semester, beginning with a challenging but fun activity on the first day of class. The new course also had progressively more complex ear-training assignments for students to complete outside of class, and daily short exercises to reinforce what already had been learned. His student partners additionally encouraged him to have students practice ear-training exercises in small groups, starting with music that was somewhat familiar to them, before they were required to work individually on more difficult tasks. They also prompted him to be more intentional about the in-class feedback he gave students during exercises to balance comments about their emerging strengths with areas that needed further development.

When Shimron taught the new version of the course, he noticed significant gains. All of his students advanced considerably beyond his former target for basic ear training, and a larger proportion of students than in any past semester met his stretch goals for this skill. Students also expressed less frustration with the demanding task of ear training, and many commented on their increased confidence in their ability to hear different aspects of complex and unfamiliar music. Although he has made minor revisions to the syllabus that resulted from this partnership over the past two years, he continues to follow the blueprint that he and his former students developed collaboratively.

Review of Designing a Course or Elements of a Course with Students

Across these different examples, the outcomes are strikingly consistent. Students develop greater confidence in their capacities, achieve deeper understanding, and make meaningful progress in their learning. They demonstrate significantly higher levels of engagement and a stronger sense of community within the course. Students take more responsibility for their own learning and for the performance of their peers, thus creating not only student-faculty partnerships but also student-student partnerships focused on learning. They find the work that they produce more "relevant," and they feel inspired by the trust faculty place in them. Consistent with the outcomes we discuss in Chapter 5, the findings from these faculty members' efforts to work in partnership with students have powerful implications in terms of students' actively engaging and effectively learning.

_____

> *"If we don't start involving students, and, more importantly, acknowledging when they do make a contribution, students are just going to be turned off. When exactly are their opinions supposed to be good enough to listen to? They have to practice to gain confidence."*
>
> Faculty partner

_____

2. Partnerships Responding to the Student Experience during a Course

Faculty routinely make revisions as class sessions or courses unfold. After a quiz we return to material that students are struggling with; during a seminar we learn which kinds of questions spark student engagement, and then we use those questions to prompt deeper discussion; in a lecture we evaluate body language and eye contact to monitor the pace of our presentation. Some faculty take one step further, collaborating with students in decisions about the evolution of the course as it progresses.

The following examples include having students select photos as prompts for discussions in class; inviting former students to interview current students to access their experiences in a challenging course; supporting students in the development and trying out of problem-based laboratory experiences; drawing on students' social bookmarking to shape course content; collaborating to create course content; and regularly gathering and responding to feedback from students. As with the examples discussed in the previous section, this set of examples represents a range of kinds and extent of partnership.

Brief example 2a: Mary Gilmartin teaches geography at the National University of Ireland, Maynouth. She asks students in an introductory class to take photographs that sum up their vision of contemporary social and cultural geography in the 21st century.

Gilmartin compiles the photos taken by the students, removing student names and other identifiable material. She then asks her students to vote for their favorite four pictures. These pictures are then used as prompts for discussions in class focused on contemporary social and cultural geography. Gilmartin also selects one of these student photographs to use as part of a prompt for an essay question in the students' final class exam.

In the spirit of partnership we advocate in this book, Gilmartin takes this approach as a way of trying to engage the students more deeply in the topic, but also as a way of emphasizing the legitimacy of students' own contributions and perspectives within the curriculum.

Brief example 2b: Mary Sunderland, in the College of Engineering at the University of California, Berkeley, has begun to invite student curriculum consultants into her engineering ethics class.

This initiative is supported by a National Science Foundation grant from the Ethics Education in Science and Engineering Program. The consultants took the engineering ethics course in a previous semester, and their role is to visit the class to conduct three group interviews with the students (without the teacher or teaching assistant present) during the 14-week-long semester. Sunderland worked with the students to develop questions aimed at assessing how students are engaging with this challenging dimension of engineering education.

Explaining why she took this approach, Sunderland (2013) writes about the challenges to curricular reform and the various barriers to making change. She emphasizes that "students...should not be additional barriers. Students should be partners." Summarizing her discussion of this work, Sunderland (2013) argues "that a student engagement approach to ethics education can help to relocate ethics to the core of the engineering curriculum. More importantly, empowering students to participate in curriculum reform has the potential to achieve unforeseeable, transformative results."

Brief example 2c: Mary Tatner and Anne Tierney teach large undergraduate biology courses at the University of Glasgow. One summer they asked six first-year students and six Graduate Teaching Assistants to work in partnership with them to revise an important microbiology laboratory.

Most first-year biology laboratories are short, recipe-driven experiments with a single outcome, which offer little opportunity for the students to actually solve a problem by doing a range of tests, collating the results, finding additional information from published resources, and then discussing the findings with their peer groups. Tatner and Tierney designed a problem-based learning exercise to take place over several consecutive weeks of laboratories, based on the diagnosis of six patients who had recently returned from abroad.

Working in groups, the students were provided with mock clinical samples, along with patient histories, vaccination status, risk factors, symptoms, and fever charts. Students carried out different tests on the samples, which were treated in the same manner as in a hospital diagnostic laboratory. The results of the tests themselves were not sufficient to provide a definite diagnosis without researching additional information. Each group of students then presented the results and conclusions for their patient and suggested appropriate treatment.

Tierney obtained funding from the UK Higher Education Academy, which enabled Tatner and Tierney to invite six of the first-year students who had already taken this class and six graduate teaching assistants to try out the labs to ensure optimal timing for the different stages of the experiments and clarity of laboratory instructions. The student group offered feedback and suggestions for change to optimize the student learning experience for those who would be taking the class. For those in the large first-year class who have undertaken the laboratory, student feedback has been very positive.

Brief example 2d: Derek Bruff uses social bookmarking tools to enable students to create and share course content in writing seminars and statistics lecture courses at Vanderbilt University in Nashville, Tennessee.

Bruff began working in partnership with students to generate and share course content in a first-year writing seminar on cryptography. Because he knew the course could never cover all of the possible topics that might interest students, from abstract mathematics to espionage, he created a social bookmarking assignment for the course. Each student found and tagged ten websites, news articles, or other resources that sparked their interest and that connected to ongoing course work. Bruff created a feed on the course web page to display the tagged items, and he regularly integrated them into class discussions. As students engaged with the assignment, more and more of class time focused on analyzing and learning from the content generated by social bookmarking—allowing student research to shape the course content. Bruff has adapted this assignment to other courses, including a larger statistics lecture class.

Bruff has found that social bookmarking helps students understand that they are contributing members of an authentic learning community. Partnership emerges as students come to realize that each person in the class, not just the professor, has important knowledge, perspectives, and questions to share. (See Bruff, 2012.)

Brief example 2e: Ignacio Canales taught an Entrepreneurship and Business Planning course at the University of St. Andrews in Scotland. He asked his students to collaborate in presenting and discussing key readings and in identifying key concepts and content needed during the course in order to be able to fulfill their group project requirements.

In this course, the students were required to undertake a group project to create a business idea that they developed to the point that it could be ready to launch. All students were expected to have to read several relevant articles from the reading list for every lecture. Each group was then given 30 minutes to present the assigned reading to the rest of the class.

All students were encouraged to ensure that their presentations were engaging and entertaining and that they highlighted key points of interest from the literature. Groups were also encouraged to facilitate an engaging learning activity for the rest of the class based on the readings. Meanwhile, Canales asked students to identify topics about which they needed more information and support to be able to successfully complete their group project. He then adapted his lectures to focus on the student-identified topics and concepts. This meant that the students had to actively engage in demanding the content they needed in order to develop their business plans.

Case Study 2: Midcourse Feedback as a Part of Sustained Dialogue and Collaboration with Students

Background

During the early years of her teaching at Bryn Mawr College, Jody Cohen was concerned by the fact that, although she regularly talked informally with students about what was and was not working for them in her courses, she did not have more regular structures to ensure their participation in those discussions about their learning experiences. She therefore developed a flexible and multipart strategy that includes several key moments at which she and her students establish and reinforce a collaborative approach. Cohen uses this technique in all of her courses, sometimes more formally and sometimes less so. She teaches two or three courses per 15-week semester, generally with enrollments of 25 students, ranging from second-year students to senior (final-year) students, as well as a writing and critical thinking seminar for 15 first-year students. Some of these students are pursuing a minor in education or certification to teach at the secondary level; others plan to major in fields unrelated to education.

Process

Early in her teaching career, the first moment at which Cohen invited students in her courses to enter into collaboration with her was in the third class meeting. She asked her students to write and share their aspirations for the course, she put these on the board, and she and the students organized them together into broad categories. Then she asked students to consider whether they all shared the same aspirations for the course, a process that sometimes prompted students to develop a consensus around certain goals, often rephrasing existing categories to better articulate the ideas students had developed. Other times this helped students, as well as Cohen, to recognize the diversity of motivations and purposes students brought to the class. Following this conversation, the group agreed upon guidelines for participation in the course, and Cohen typed these up and gave them to all students in the class. This set the tone and precedent for dialogue and shared responsibility in the course.

At about week five of the semester, Cohen asked the students to revisit the guidelines they generated as a group. Were they still useful and reflective of what the group wanted? Did they need to be revised? This was a moment for reflection and revision: an opportunity, after the class had established itself and students had worked together and with Cohen for several weeks, to reassess and either affirm the guidelines or make changes as needed. This reminded students of their original expressions of hope and expectation, their shared responsibility for the course, and Cohen's commitment to working in partnership with students in pursuing these.

Over time spent working with this process, Cohen took note of how differently classes came together—in terms of their pace, their level of listening and speaking, and their manner of dealing with differences. For some groups, the aspirations exercise came too early, before differences had truly emerged, and for others it was too general to address the particular classroom dynamics.

So Cohen began adapting the process, sometimes moving to the aspirations exercise when issues began to bubble up in class, other times creating specific process-oriented questions for the class to address, such as sharing their individual positions in relation to an issue with the evident potential to be divisive.

In all classes, at about mid-course, Cohen generates a set of questions upon which she wants somewhat more formal, written, anonymous student input, including questions about the classroom environment, the assignments, and the activities she has designed for the course. These mid-course questions themselves are usually broad, something like: "Consider our aspirations, our classroom environment, activities, assignments, etc.: What's stretching/challenging/compelling you at this point in the course? What suggestions do you have for how we might do things during the second half of the semester?" She asks students to respond to those questions and then she analyzes the responses and gives the students verbal feedback, open for discussion. Together, they talk through what is working well, what is not working well, and what could be changed to improve the learning experiences in the course. As a group, they agree upon what will be changed and how. This more formal moment of stepping back and analyzing together how the course is unfolding both builds on and deepens the collaborative dynamic established through the first moment of identifying hopes and expectations and the second moment of revisiting them.

Outcomes

Both formal end-of-course surveys and informal mid-term feedback from students confirm that Cohen's approach makes students feel like partners in their learning process with her. Students report that they have a voice in, and responsibility for, how the course unfolds, and they are more engaged and committed as a result. Cohen concurs, noting that student learning in and from the course is greater when her students engage in the partnership process more deeply. She also indicates that through this and other approaches of working in partnership with students, she connects with students "more fully or intensively from the perspective that we are all learners and all teachers."

In addition, Cohen has become more conscious of the distinct needs of different students, and she now is more intentional in her efforts to ensure that the class is a rich learning experience for each individual student and for the class as a whole. She acknowledges that this approach makes teaching more complex and unpredictable, but it also makes teaching more engaging and rewarding for her, as well as for the students. Her hope and intent are that these early and mid-course exchanges create trust and practice for a kind of dialogue that then can just become part of what she and her students do together and how they talk together, both in one-on-one meetings and in the class.

Review of Responding to the Student Experience during a Course

The examples we include in this cluster focus more on process than on outcomes. Despite the differences in particulars, however, all build on the principles of respect, reciprocity, and shared responsibility. Students' input, their analysis of learning experiences, and their active participation in revising courses as they unfold are demonstrated in a range of ways in these examples. Students' own contributions and perspectives are valued within the curriculum; past and current students collaborate with faculty to identify how best to support students in engaging with challenging courses; student feedback and suggestions regarding how to optimize the student learning experience are taken seriously and acted upon; and students become active partners in analyzing and revising how the course unfolds. Again, consistent with the outcomes we discuss in Chapter 5, the findings of these faculty members' efforts to work in partnership with students have powerful implications in terms of students' actively engaging and effectively learning.

"I work with students more as colleagues, more as
people engaged in similar struggles to learn and grow."

Faculty partner

3. Assessing Student Work

Collaborating with students to assess their learning often seems like the most risky approach to partnership for many faculty. We are ethically obliged to uphold the standards of our disciplines and our institutions, and we have spent many long years developing the expertise that permits us to do that. Will working in partnership with students who have less (sometimes much, much less) disciplinary and professional knowledge dilute their learning and diminish our obligations? Not necessarily. If we set up partnerships focused on assessment, we can acknowledge established standards in our fields while helping students to better understand and act within our disciplinary contexts. We can also contribute to enhancing their understanding of assessing learning outcomes in ways that are crucial to developing their knowledge of learning how to learn.

Some of the examples we include in this section focus on faculty opening up discussion of grading processes in an attempt to make assessment more transparent or to help students cultivate what Sambell et al. (2012) describe as "assessment literacy," enabling students to "better appreciate the standards, goals and criteria required to evaluate outputs within a specific disciplinary context" (p. 120). Other examples involve students engaging in deeper partnerships in which they negotiate with faculty their essay questions, grading criteria, or even their own grade. Still others focus on identifying the skills and approaches that will help students be most successful in engaging with and demonstrating mastery of course content. This variety demonstrates just some of the different possible types and levels of student-faculty partnership that faculty have attempted.

These examples align with a separately emerging discussion of designing "assessment *for* learning" in contrast with typical forms of "assessment *of* learning." Some faculty are moving away from forms of assessment that are just testing what a student has learned, and instead are embracing methods of assessment that test what a student has learned in addition to being assessment through which students learn (see for example Sambell et al., 2012). One of the more important things students can learn from this approach to assessment is that their own capacity to self-assess is essential to their future learning and development (Kaplan et al., 2013). Partnership, therefore, helps change the nature of assessment in a course.

Brief example 3a: In Dan Bernstein's large general psychology courses at the University of Kansas, students often struggle to understand what is expected of a college-level essay.

Bernstein developed a detailed rubric to articulate his assignment expectations to students. While the rubric helped with the grading that he and his teaching assistants carried out, many students still complained of not fully grasping his goals for their work. In response, about one week before the first exam, Bernstein brings to class the rubric and three examples of unmarked student essays from past semesters (written on questions that will not be on this semester's exam, and with all names removed). He has students read and score these essays using the rubric, and then he leads the class in a discussion about his expectations for student writing, with students pointing to specific places in the examples where students met, or fell short of, the standards in the rubric.

Students report that they now understand his goals for their writing, and Bernstein finds that the overall quality of student essays has improved substantially within groups of students that do this exercise.

Brief example 3b: Susan Deeley teaches public policy at the University of Glasgow in Scotland. In one of her honors courses, Ideological Concepts and Values, she invites students to generate grading criteria for their final essay. In another course focused on service-learning, she invites her students to co-assess, with her, their own end-of-course oral presentations.

In her Ideological Concepts and Values course, Deeley encourages her students to use their collaboratively generated grading criteria as guidelines for their essay writing. Then, as a formative self-assessment exercise and as an appendix to their essay, students submit a reflective statement focused on the extent to which they feel they have met the criteria. Deeley uses the criteria to mark their essays and give students written feedback, which takes into account their reflective and formative self-assessment statements. Reflecting on this experience, one student commented: "Being involved in the [grading] criteria helped to make clear in my head what exactly it was I needed to produce . . . it allowed me to look a bit deeper into the [grading] procedure."

In Deeley's service-learning course, students give a summative oral presentation where they critically reflect on the skills and attributes that they have acquired or enhanced by integrating a voluntary work placement with academic coursework. Using preset criteria on the content and delivery of the presentation, students self-assess their presentation and write reflective comments on it. Deeley also assesses the presentations. Immediately after the presentations, she meets individually with each student to discuss their presentation and their written comments to agree on an appropriate grade. This discussion is open to students' negotiation and a defense of the grade, which also helps to enhance their skills. In the event that an agreement cannot be reached, Deeley retains the responsibility for determining the final grade.

Students seem to benefit from this timely feedback, not just on their presentation, but also on their own assessment of it. One student commented, "I believe [grading] my own work allowed me to be critical of my own work, a welcome shift from the humdrum of standard university [grading] guidelines."

Brief example 3c: David Ross teaches in the Economics Department at Bryn Mawr College in Pennsylvania. Among a number of projects related to enhancing assessment of learning within the major, he is working to develop an inventory of ways to structure student peer feedback to one another on their work.

Ross has worked with student consultants through the SaLT program at Bryn Mawr for several years, each time striving to shift his practice toward greater collaboration with students. He is interested in getting students more involved in providing feedback to each other on their work, and devising an inventory to support this. Student partners asked peers to identify strategies they use in group work or in studying on their own in an introductory course. They have shared the results within the department and plan to disseminate these approaches to new economics students and beyond his department.

Reflecting on these efforts, Ross explained: "I've been gradually expanding opportunities for peer feedback. But, the impetus for creating an inventory of student learning strategies and incorporating that into a resource for future students came from a student consultant who (a) observed in my economics elective the wide variation in retention of material students were presumed to have mastered in the introductory course and (b) heard from friends—both economics majors and students currently taking Econ 105, Introduction to Economics—about their struggles to master the material."

That student consultant took the lead on developing a guide for students. She explained that the guide "aims to provide future students of Econ 105 with general information and learning strategies that will draw from your 105 experience. It will also be a great help to the professors, as the course guide will enable them to reflect on the course . . . [so that] changes can be made based on your suggestions. Last but not least, by helping in the creation process and looking back on the course, you may (hopefully) develop a deeper understanding and insight into introductory Econ."

Brief example 3d: Cathy Davidson at Duke University in Durham, North Carolina, invites students to collaboratively grade peer work.

Davidson teaches an interdisciplinary seminar entitled "This Is Your Brain on the Internet," which focuses on how technology is changing everything from business practices to cultural understandings of what it means to be intelligent (Davidson, 2012). The first time she taught the course, she included multiple opportunities for student-faculty partnerships to reinforce the seminar's lessons about "participatory learning" and "collaboration by difference." Her students responded with enthusiasm, yet noted that although she repeatedly said that *everything* was changing because of the Internet, she had retained exclusive control over grading in the seminar.

Since that first semester, the seminar's assessment is a combination of "old fashioned contract grading with peer review" (Davidson, 2011). She establishes a grading contract with each student to specify the nature and quantity of work the student must complete to earn a desired grade. Then she crowdsources grading by having pairs of students in the seminar determine whether each student's work has met the standards that the class itself has established.

Davidson reflects: "What this teaches my students is responsibility, credibility, judgment, honesty, and how to offer good criticism to one's peers—and, in turn, how to receive it. The beauty comes in the fact that those who judge one week are among those who are judged the next" (2009).

Brief example 3e: Netta Edwards teaches social statistics at the University of Alaska. She invited her students to take part in self-grading their homework assignments, as well as an exam.

Edwards usually has between 20 and 50 students in her classes. In setting out to work in partnership with her students, her motivation for implementing self-grading was partly an attempt to reduce the turnaround time for faculty to grade student work. It was also an acknowledgment that students could learn more from being involved in the grading of assignments. As Edwards describes, she explains to her students that she believes "they will learn statistics more easily if they can identify when and where they make mistakes" (Edwards, 2007, p. 73).

Edwards writes clear and explicit guides for the students to use when they are grading. She considers the time spent writing the grading guides to be more fruitful than that spent directly marking all the work herself. This is because the students are gaining a much greater insight into how to judge their own performance, where they are performing well, and why they have made mistakes, and they can also revisit the grading guides any time up to the final exam. In the case of an exam, Edwards checks all of the self-grading and adjusts grades if necessary. In most cases there is virtually no change to the grade awarded by the students.

Edwards is aware that many of her colleagues argue it would be easy for students to cheat in self-grading. She ensures that her students understand clearly that there are penalties for cheating: "such as receiving a zero on the assignment, getting kicked out of the class, and possibly being expelled from the university" (Edwards, 2007, p. 73). Students have overwhelmingly said they like self-grading, as they have the opportunity to understand more easily where they are making mistakes.

Case Study 3: Using Computer Software to Support Students to Peer Review Each Other's Work in Large Undergraduate Classes

Background

In 2004, John Hamer, Catherine Kell, and Fiona Spence, working at the University of Auckland, designed *Aropa*, web-based software to support students in undertaking peer assessment and reviewing each other's work. They supported faculty in implementing this software across different disciplines and courses, including computer science, software engineering, pharmacology, English, and photography. The idea behind *Aropa* was to create a tool that could open up the grading process to become more transparent and to help students develop a better understanding of how faculty grade their work. While many faculty support student peer assessment on a small scale, the software enables this process to be used within large undergraduate classes. Hamer has gone on to support faculty in the use of this tool in a range of other universities and disciplines.

Process

The software enables faculty to be relieved of some of the complexities of peer review in larger classes. *Aropa* manages the allocation of student submissions to student reviewers, enables students to enter their reviews (and, where appropriate, grades) online, and allows students to access feedback (and grades) on their own work. The software even can calculate grades. Using this tool, students are not only authors of their own work, but they also become reviewers of others' work and finally recipients of peer feedback. *Aropa* presents students with an online interface that enables them to view these roles simultaneously in different sections. Students can also change the settings easily to hide or show only particular roles. Students are provided with grading criteria, which are usually designed by faculty, although there is nothing to prevent these being negotiated between students and faculty early in the peer review process. *Aropa* also includes the option for students to be asked to complete an online questionnaire about their experiences of peer review at the end of the process.

One specific example of the use of *Aropa* within an English class of 80 students at the University of Auckland involved using the software to enable peer review on a course in Rhetoric in Public Culture. In this case, each student was randomly allocated three pieces of work to review, as well as being given the option to conduct a self-review of his or her own work.

Outcomes

In this example from the class on Rhetoric in Public Culture, students responded very positively to being involved in the review process. When asked what impact the peer review had upon their own work, one student stated:

It made me want to look at it more carefully . . . about the
argument I was making and see how much research other
people had done. I thought well, maybe I should go back
in, like I had done research but I hadn't included it in the
bibliography and everyone else had, it looked like maybe
I hadn't read anything and made all this up, so it made
me reassess what I'd done (Hamer et al., 2007, p. 8).

Another student described similar benefits:

The task of looking at one's own writing from an objective perspective in order to improve it or see things that
have been missed is a hard thing to do . . . The value
of both getting more than one set of other eyes on the
writing as well as the experience of analysing and cri-
tiquing someone else's essay gives a much better insight
in these aspects of one's own writing and writing in general (Hamer et al., 2007, p. 8).

Through this approach, students seemed to gain a broader perspective on what was taking place in the grading process:

You have to almost put yourself into their shoes, so you
have to think if I was going to grade this, these are the
things they would look at, I guess maybe look at the argument as a whole and kind of . . . when writing it you
feel you're really IN there and you're paying attention
to every small detail and even though it might make
sense in your own head when you read other people's
and then look at theirs and then come back to yours,
you're able to look at it with a slightly broader perspective (Hamer et al., 2007, p. 8).

Another student commented on the congruence between the
subject the students were learning, which requires the ability to

communicate well with an audience, and the aims of peer review in opening up work to the wider class audience. Overall, students seemed to be very satisfied with the experience of peer review using the *Aropa* tool. Where students were less happy, it tended to be because they had not received all three of their reviews because not everyone had fully participated in the exercise. Faculty thought that students seemed to see the peer-review process as having greater credibility through the use of the automated tool because it ensured anonymity and a certain formality to the process.

As Hamer comments, "Reviewing (i.e., coming up with comments) is where the substantive learning occurs, rather than in . . . coming up with [grades]. This reviewing aspect can be aided by designing the rubric to encourage the reviewer to present their own, personal perspective, rather than trying to come up with an impersonal, conformist review." Overall, peer review can open up mutual understanding between teacher and students of what is taking place in the process of grading and feeding back on student work. Hamer et al. (2007) state that students argue "assessment is the principal mechanism whereby [faculty] exercise power and control over students" (p. 10), so providing opportunities for peer review in large undergraduate classes has the potential to promote discussion between students and faculty and enhance the transparency of feedback and grading processes for mutual benefit.

Review of Assessing Student Work

When criteria for grading and other forms of summative assessment are negotiated, student learning and engagement deepen. Understanding grading and feedback criteria helps students meet expectations more effectively and comprehend more fully where (and why) they did not adequately demonstrate their learning. Like the students whose experiences we report in Chapter 5, these students describe becoming more critical—more intellectually engaged and capable. Taking students' self-assessments of the challenges of a particular content area and putting them into a guide makes assessment into a proactive process for future students, as well as a reflective one for current students. Similarly, having students engage in their own summative assessment makes them actively reflect on their understanding, not just focus on the right answer. These shifts make students far more active in, and responsible for, their learning.

Conclusion

The examples included in this chapter involve different numbers and types of people (e.g., a single faculty member working in partnership with a single student; a group of faculty members and a smaller set of students; a selected group of students collaborating with faculty; all students in a course and a single faculty member). They highlight different foci for faculty-student partnerships (e.g., students and faculty collaborating in the design of courses, labs, and criteria for grading; students sharing strategies, developing course material, and designing assessments). They also illustrate different structures for partnership (e.g., key moments during the semester designated for collaborative engagement; weekly meetings and consultations outside of courses to engage in meta-analysis) and different levels of partnership (e.g., students and faculty working in close partnership to design a course; students being given a say in how their assessments will be judged; students creating work that they share for the benefit of their peers; students commenting and giving feedback to their peers).

The set of student-faculty partnerships included in this chapter illustrates the range and scale of such partnerships, and the diversity of these examples underscores the flexibility of a partnership model. In different contexts and for different purposes, faculty might enter into partnership with one or many students to work on a single issue or to tackle a complex web of challenges. The next chapter elaborates on further examples of partnership by considering what becomes possible when student-faculty collaboration moves beyond the work of isolated faculty to become woven into the fabric of a program or an institution.

4

Program-Level Approaches to Student-Faculty Partnerships

In the preceding chapter we highlighted numerous ways individual faculty members might consider building student-faculty partnerships. Many successful partnerships rely upon the enthusiasm and creativity of individuals, but in some cases faculty have managed to embed and integrate partnership work on a larger scale or in more strategic ways across their institutions. If you are intrigued by the idea of developing projects that reach beyond a single classroom or an isolated faculty member, this chapter is for you. Perhaps you have seen the results of partnership in your work and would like to help other faculty and students reap the benefits. Perhaps you, like us, have found yourself shifting from a more traditional faculty role into a position with responsibilities tied to faculty development at your institution. Perhaps you have other reasons to think beyond individual partnerships. Regardless of your motivation, we hope this chapter will provide you with examples of practice and guidance for building and sustaining larger-scale partnerships.

The programs featured in this chapter have different purposes and unfold in different contexts in the United States, the United Kingdom, and Australia. As with student-faculty partnerships undertaken by faculty with little or no institutional support, partnerships that are supported by institutions can be large or small, they can range from short-term to longer-term, and they can adopt different forms or models of incentives or compensation. Like the examples we presented in Chapter 3, we do not see any of these models as preferable to the others. Rather, we offer a range so that individuals and institutions can make decisions based on their particular needs, context, and aspirations.

We have organized the examples in this chapter into three sections, featuring programs focused on

1. Designing or redesigning a course before or after it is taught
2. Analyzing classroom practice within the context of a course while it is being taught
3. Developing research partnerships that catalyze institutional change

These categories are not mutually exclusive. Our purpose with this structure is not to develop a typology or a fixed set of programmatic approaches but rather to provide diverse examples that might serve as inspirations for you and your colleagues.

Across all the programs discussed in this chapter, students are active participants in the work of constructing teaching and learning opportunities, they are equally valued partners with faculty members, and they are agents and "transformers" of their own and others' educational experiences. After presenting these model programs, we will explore the benefits and drawbacks of moving from individual to programmatic approaches. At the end of the chapter we have included a section for those in faculty development roles, highlighting some of the lessons we have learned in facilitating student-faculty partnership programs.

1. Programs Supporting Course Design and Redesign

Programs that support student-faculty partnerships focused on course design or redesign afford faculty and student partners the opportunity to collaborate in the process of cocreating engaging courses. Some such partnerships target particular courses while others consider a pair or cluster of courses within an academic program. Still other partnerships focus on the creation of an institution's curriculum or the forming of partnerships with other institutions. To give you a flavor of this range of partnerships and what might be possible, we list a few brief examples, and then we elaborate on a single program.

Brief example 1a: In 2009, the Geography, Earth, and Environmental Sciences (GEES) Subject Centre of the United Kingdom Higher Education Academy (HEA) piloted a year-long initiative to involve students in the planned revision of curricula in four GEES departments. This initiative applied some of the ideas developed by Change Academy, a collaboration program between the HEA and the Leadership Foundation for Higher Education in the United Kingdom.

The main feature of this initiative was a 48-hour retreat at which teams that included students were supported by discipline-based experts in educational development. Roughly half the time was spent working on their own projects, while the other half was spent working with other teams and in plenary activities that encouraged divergent and creative thinking and prioritizing of ideas to develop teaching and learning initiatives. All but one team had one or two student members. Participants involved in the GEES initiative came from the Universities of Gloucestershire, Manchester, Oxford, and Plymouth. Participants stated that "having the students with us has been immensely helpful, and frankly they have played as full a part as any other team member and have been just amazing" (Healey et al., 2010, p. 38). Faculty suggested that students had exceeded their expectations in the way they had taken the work seriously and contributed meaningfully. Indeed, students exceeding faculty expectations within partnerships is documented elsewhere (see for example Bovill, 2013a).

The number of students and faculty within any partnership team, as well as their attitudes to partnership, can have a huge impact on what is possible. One faculty member admitted to including students: "because you [sic] told us to. I was doing what I was told. But they were an incredibly helpful part of our team" (Healey et al., 2010, p. 13). Time and attention may need to be spent in the early stages of partnership to ensure that students feel they are legitimate and equal members of partnerships with faculty, particularly where senior faculty are involved. In the end, faculty involved in this initiative considered inclusion of students as one of the key features that had contributed to the project's success.

Brief example 1b: At University College Dublin, in Ireland, Geraldine O'Neill and Áine Galvin in UCD Teaching and Learning supported faculty across a range of different disciplines to redesign their courses to include student choice between two summative assessments. This initiative emerged from a broader effort to enhance students' control of aspects of the learning process.

While not setting up explicit student-faculty partnerships, this process aimed to enhance student-faculty dialogue about different types of assignments and the whole feedback and grading process, thus taking a step toward partnership. Three faculty ran the following course with the assignment choices for the first time in 2009–2010: Development and Advanced Pharmacology (third year, 65 students, choice between group poster or group oral); Environmental Biology (third year, 50 students, choice between continuous problem solving or an end-of-semester open book exam); Human Rights Law and Equality (fourth year, 33 students, choice between group presentation or individual essay). In 2010–2011 these three faculty repeated their courses for a second year and were joined by other faculty who implemented the courses, including Computer Science-Data Mining (fourth year, 66 students, choice between tutorial assignment or project); The Making of Early Modern France (first year, 40 students, choice between individual audiovisual assignment or individual essay and, for another assignment, choice between a group poster or group oral); Forensic Radiography (fourth year; 24 students, choice between a wiki or an applied essay).

All faculty completed a "student information and equity template" that set out information about the two assignments students were choosing between. It provided information including: the weighting of the assignments; why assignments might suit particular students; learning outcomes relevant to the assignment; grading criteria to be used; equity in terms of support students could expect for the assignments and for the way the assignments would be graded; student workload expectations; and whether samples of the assignment type were available to students (particularly where the method might be new to students). Providing this information required faculty to consider seriously the potential fairness of different assignments. Importantly, this information also ensured that students were able to make an informed choice about the assignment they preferred.

Often faculty are concerned that if students are given choice about the assignment methods to be used, they will automatically choose the easiest option. However, this is often not the case; in fact, students will frequently choose to challenge themselves. O'Neill (2011) reports that the most common reasons for the students choosing their assessment was "they wanted to try a different type of assessment" and the "timing of it suited their organization skills" (p. 9).

Brief example 1c: The Writing Fellows Program at St. John's University in New York City creates partnerships between experienced undergraduate Writing Center consultants and faculty who assign extensive writing in a course.

Each year since 2009, St. John's University faculty have been invited to apply to be Faculty Fellows who will work in partnership with an undergraduate writing consultant to enhance a particular aspect of writing in a course. At the same time, undergraduate Writing Center consultants at the university are invited to apply to become Writing Fellows who will act as consultants to Faculty Fellows. After both sets of Fellows are selected, the faculty and student participants in this program read one another's applications and have at least two or three interviews in different pairings. These one-on-one meetings offer opportunities for undergraduate writing consultants to influence faculty thinking and teaching even if they are not paired with the faculty they initially meet.

Once paired, Faculty Fellows and Writing Fellows collaborate on course planning for a spring semester course. In past years, Writing Fellows, who attend all meetings of the spring course, have codeveloped and codelivered in-class workshops with their Faculty Fellows, worked with their Faculty Fellows on rethinking writing assignments and feedback to student writers, and helped faculty learn more both about the students in their courses and about their own pedagogical goals. The pairs develop written job descriptions for their roles and expectations of one another. Programmatic assessment has shown that the more detailed the job descriptions are, the more successful the pairs will be when they work together.

In spring 2013 all eight of the classes involving Fellows, representing six disciplines, added a set of shared questions to the standard university course rating form. Eighty-five percent of the respondents agreed or strongly agreed that the writing they did helped them to learn in the course, and 75% agreed or strongly agreed that the undergraduate Writing Fellows had helped them learn in the course.

Brief example 1d: Olin College aims to radically transform engineering education by making student-faculty partnerships foundational to the institution.

Olin College opened in 2002 in suburban Boston, Massachusetts, with the goal of creating a new model of education that would prepare students to be "exemplary engineering educators." From the start, Olin positioned students as codesigners of the curriculum, which is built around hands-on engineering and design projects. Through a program that was called "Invention 2000," Olin hired its first faculty members and invited 30 students, known as "Olin Partners," to help them form the first curriculum. These students spent their first year at Olin exploring possibilities for assessment and grading methods, considering how to establish the kind of student culture the college hoped for, and experimenting with different approaches to engineering education.

The curriculum at Olin sustains this student-driven approach. It is built around project-based learning that begins in a student's first year and culminates in two final year 'capstone' projects. In the engineering capstone, Senior Consulting Program for Engineering (SCOPE), student teams are hired by corporations, nonprofit organizations, or entrepreneurial ventures for real-world engineering projects. In the Arts, Humanities, and Social Sciences or in the Entrepreneurship capstone, students work on a self-designed project relating to their focus (for more information, see Kearns et al., 2004).

Brief example 1e: At University of Ballarat in Australia, a suite of "Student Led Learning Programs" called "Succeed @ UB" have been codeveloped and codelivered with students.

One of the programs is UBReady, a crash course in academic skills development. The online teaching materials were developed by students over a summer break and the face-to-face component is codelivered by faculty and students. One semester, 150 students attended and 10 student leaders assisted.

A second program, the Mentor Program, assists with transition to university life. Each student who participates is assigned a student mentor who is in the second or third year of the new student's academic program. Having already experienced life at the university, these mentors can provide first-hand support to new students in the first few weeks of their study. During one semester 110 student leaders worked with 1,000 to 1,500 students.

Finally, the PASS program assists students studying in courses with traditionally high failure rates. The program provides Peer Assisted Study Sessions, in which students work together to reinforce key concepts and develop effective study strategies. The website emphasizes that this program is for everyone, not only students who might be struggling. It reinforces the notion of partnership in learning as beneficial to all.

All three programs are overseen by one faculty member. She has six interns reporting to her (i.e., student leaders employed 8 hours per week for 40 weeks). The interns are also working on some introductory videos and resources to teach some basic transition and study skills. (For further information, see University of Ballarat, 2013.)

Case Study 1: Course-Design Teams at Elon University

At Elon University in North Carolina, faculty, students, and academic development staff have experimented since 2005 with a variety of approaches to working in partnership in course design teams (CDT) that cocreate, or re-create, a course syllabus. Each team's process varies, but typically a CDT includes one or two faculty, between two and six undergraduate students, and one faculty developer from the university Center for the Advancement of Teaching and Learning; the student members nearly always outnumber the faculty members of the CDT. Faculty members initiate the redesign process, inviting the students and developer to coconstruct a team. Students usually apply to participate in a CDT, motivated by a desire to contribute to a course they have taken or that is important to the curriculum in their disciplinary home.

Once the CDT is assembled, the CDT uses a backward-design approach (Wiggins and McTighe, 2005), first developing course goals and then building pedagogical strategies and learning assessments on the foundation of those goals. Often the teams take as a starting point a significant teaching problem that the instructors identify and choose to treat as an object of scholarly inquiry (Bass, 1999; Delpish et al., 2010). The first CDT at Elon, for example, focused on an education course that students routinely criticized as unhelpful, but which faculty believed to be essential to the students' development as future teachers (Mihans et al., 2008). Other teams have focused on pedagogical challenges or learning bottlenecks in courses ranging from statistics and developmental psychology to Spanish literature and ethical reasoning. Some teams have even expanded the partnership to include not only faculty and students but also community representatives from service-learning sites (Moore et al., 2010).

Participants in these course design teams have found that time often is the most important element in the success of a CDT. Teams usually meet weekly for two or three months, providing ample opportunities to both accomplish the CDT's practical purpose of redesigning the course and, perhaps more important, to develop a true partnership that not only welcomes student voices but balances faculty and student contributions to the design or redesign process (Delpish et al., 2010). Students sometimes doubt that they will be taken seriously in the process, and they also need time to develop the language and the confidence to express pedagogical ideas clearly. Many CDTs experience a liminal moment when everyone present recognizes that a fundamental boundary has been crossed, either by a faculty member ceding significant authority for the course design or by students claiming power in the process. In one case, students on a team led a process to identify books for a course from a long list that had been created by the two participating faculty; after a thorough review of all of the titles, the students began discussing each and then eliminating some from the list. Students were surprised when the faculty did not object: "Wow! We [the students] really just cut those books" (Mihans et al., 2008, p. 6). Of course, the students did not simply delete books without the knowledge or consent of the faculty; if the faculty had thought that students did not have valid reasons for excluding a book, they would have spoken up. In this case, however, the partnership created a space where students could clearly and meaningfully contribute to the reading list and faculty came to see some familiar books from new perspectives.

As the book episode illustrates, one of the biggest challenges for the course design teams is rethinking and redistributing power. In interviews after the completion of a CDT's work, both faculty and students typically bring up the struggle of adjusting to new power dynamics. At Elon, the teaching center plays an important role in helping all team members navigate these potentially stormy waters. Since a teaching center colleague is present in the group from the start, neither faculty nor students need to facilitate the first meeting, thus allowing students and faculty to come to the table more like peers. The teaching center representative also intentionally models various behaviors early in the team process by, for example, gently but firmly challenging faculty assumptions and by playing devil's advocate to any idea that easily finds consensus around the table. Over time, students and faculty become more comfortable and skilled in these roles, allowing the teaching center representative to play a smaller part as the process unfolds. As one faculty member recalled after one course design team: "[I became] more willing to trust student partners by sharing power with them, not exerting it over them" (Delpish et al., 2010, p. 98).

While not all of the redesigned courses are transformed, nor are they all immediately successful, faculty consistently report that the new courses are substantially better than the prior versions. Probably the most significant outcomes, however, are those identified in Chapter 5, particularly the enhanced engagement and metacognition that both students and faculty develop in the process. (For other discussions of this program, see Bovill, 2013a; Bovill et al., 2011; Delpish et al., 2010; Mihans et al., 2008.)

2. Programs Supporting Explorations of Classroom Practice While a Course Is Being Taught

In this section we outline some larger-scale institutional-level and program-level initiatives that support student-faculty partnerships focused on analyzing classroom practice while the course is being taught. These shift our attention to how a curriculum that is already planned, or partially planned, can be navigated while a course is unfolding. In most of these examples, students adopt a role that is often described as "consultant" or "observer." This is one step (and occasionally many steps) beyond the common ways faculty solicit feedback from a course that invite episodic student engagement but stop short of more sustained partnership. These examples require student and faculty partners to think through how they will each contribute to the process of inquiry and negotiation, and how they will draw on their perspectives and expertise. We offer below several brief examples and then an extended description of one program.

Brief example 2a: The Students Consulting on Teaching program (SCOT) at Brigham Young University in Utah trains students to visit faculty members' classes in various roles to provide faculty with feedback on how to maximize the student learning experience.

This program was developed in the 1990s and has been sustained since then. The director of the program invites faculty to participate via email or flyers and visits classes and student organizations and asks faculty for recommendations in order to recruit student consultants. The SCOT program provides an introductory meeting for student consultants to give them an overview of the program and asks them to complete a practice observation, write up a report, and role play a follow-up consultation. As consultants, the students participate in bi-monthly seminars and are mentored by more experienced student consultants.

Faculty members may request that students in the SCOT program take on one of the following roles: Recorder/Observer: the student records, in writing, what went on in the classroom and gives the record to the instructor; Faux Student: the student takes notes as though he or she were a student in the class and returns the notes to the instructor; Filmmaker: the student films the class and creates a DVD for the instructor; Interviewer: the instructor leaves the classroom for fifteen minutes while the student conducts an interview with the class; Primed Student: the student meets with the professor prior to class to receive instructions on what to watch for (e.g., How often are students getting involved in the discussion? Which activities are most engaging?); or Student Consultant: The instructor asks the Student Consultant for feedback and suggestions about classroom activities or particular areas of interest.

Faculty feedback suggests that participating in the program adds "a new dimension" to the process of analyzing a course that is "conducive to improving the quality of teaching" (Sorenson, 2001, p. 182). Faculty members have been encouraged by the "great feedback and encouragement," which they describe as being "almost priceless" (p. 182). One faculty member reported that through participating in the program she was able to "learn from mistakes and build on strengths as a teacher" (Sorenson, 2001, p. 182). Student feedback has also been positive. One student consultant stated that working with a faculty member who was "interested in my ideas . . . was a valuable experience for me," and a student in a course that the student consultant observed asserted: "I'm impressed that he cares enough about us and our learning to do something about it" (Sorenson, 2001, p. 182).

Brief example 2b: The Students Consulting on Teaching (SCOT) project at the University of Lincoln in the United Kingdom invited students and teachers to work in partnership and take shared responsibility for the enhancement of democratic pedagogies.

This project involved six student pedagogic consultants and a student coordinator, who were employed on an hourly basis, offering student observations and perspectives on specific episodes of teaching and learning. The students undertook an explicit and mandatory short training program. The activities in this program were designed to be teacher driven, with the interaction between the teacher and the student consultant remaining completely confidential. The feedback that teachers received was from an impartial student perspective as the student consultants were not, and had not been, members of that course. Ten faculty members participated and sometimes requested more than one consultation, resulting in over 15 consultations in a six-month period.

This program explicitly aimed to challenge traditional academic hierarchies and habits. Describing Lincoln's SCOT program, Crawford argues that "commonly used often managerialist performance-led approaches to gaining feedback on the student experience . . . are at best impersonal, untimely and ineffective and at worst de-skilling and devaluing of professional practice in higher education" (Crawford, 2012, p. 52). SCOT offers a fundamentally different way of working with students and academics as partners in a community of scholars.

Brief example 2c: Carleton College's Student Observer Program invites students to be trained to become classroom observers who sit in on classes, provide faculty with feedback, and discuss insights and observations about learning and teaching in a course.

Through this program, professors request an observer for a particular course. A student is assigned to attend that professor's class and provides feedback on areas in which the teacher wishes to receive more information. Observers are carefully chosen by the faculty director of the program. Students must apply in writing and also have an interview, and they are trained (as part of an overall orientation session and then as "mock observers" in a situation with a faculty member who has agreed to help in the training process). Finally, the observers meet with the director on a biweekly basis throughout the year to give them a chance to talk about their work, share perspectives and ideas with one another, and troubleshoot any issues that may arise.

Professors often ask observers to provide feedback regarding student-teacher interaction, such as how long he or she waits for a response after asking a question or whether or not questions seem to be inviting open responses. Both lecture and discussion classes can be observed for clarity of presentation and levels of energy and enthusiasm expressed by students and the teacher. In other cases, observers are asked to comment on issues ranging from the physical set-up of the room and whether it could be altered to improve the effectiveness of the teacher, the way class time is used, or the quality of student-student interaction. In addition, the observers are sometimes called on to facilitate midterm or end-of-term course feedback sessions. Typically, the instructor provides the observer with a set of questions to pose. The student observer conducts an oral assessment session of 15 minutes, takes careful notes, and then presents the results to the instructor afterward. About this aspect of the program, the director states: "Our sense is that students provide more feedback, and more candid feedback, when they don't have to write out their responses."

As stated on the program website, "The point of the program is to give faculty the benefit of a trained student's perspective on a course as the course is developing." The program has worked successfully for faculty members from a wide variety of disciplines and at various stages of their careers, although the director indicates that the program has been used disproportionately by faculty who are pre-tenure or in visiting appointments. According to participants, taking part in the program not only improves their teaching but also their motivation and capacity to analyze teaching and learning. A faculty member explains: "I had specific goals for how to make the class more interactive . . . with the help of my observer, they worked so well that we've gone on to new issues!" And a student observer asserts: "Now I'm a student observer in all my classes…I'm gaining skills in identifying what works and learning how I learn best" (Carleton College, 2013).

The director suggests that the program "has proven to be of tremendous value to the faculty, including those who were originally somewhat skeptical about it." He suggests that this is because of the quality of the students they recruit to be observers and partly because the program is entirely confidential: "No faculty member has to share the information that they are using the program with senior faculty in their department, with the administration, or even with the other students in the course."

Case Study 2: The Students as Learners and Teachers (SaLT) Program at Bryn Mawr College

As we explained when we introduced this program in the Preface and Chapter 1, Students as Learners and Teachers (SaLT) is the signature program of the Teaching and Learning Institute at Bryn Mawr College, supported by a grant from The Andrew W. Mellon Foundation. We expand in this case study on the semester-long partnerships between faculty members and undergraduate students at Bryn Mawr and other nearby colleges through which these partners explore questions of classroom practice, each bringing a unique perspective and deriving different benefits from the exchange.

The program has a layered set of goals. The most basic is to support faculty and students in generative explorations of pedagogical questions and issues with the aim of affirming, improving, and further developing effective classroom practices. Beyond the immediate classroom focus, another goal of the program is to foster open, critical, and constructive dialogue, supporting faculty and students in becoming partners in the work of teaching and learning, not only through this program but also more generally. Finally, through striving toward these goals, the program aims to change the culture on campus to one in which dialogue about teaching and learning among faculty and students is a common, desired, and desirable practice.

Participation in the SaLT program is entirely voluntary; these opportunities are not tied to processes of review, unless individual faculty members choose to include their work through the program in their review dossiers. Any faculty member, part time or full time, may apply to work with a student consultant. The student consultants are sophomore (second-year) through senior (fourth-year) undergraduates. Students apply to take on the paid position of student consultant. The application includes a statement of their qualifications and why they want to be a consultant, and it requires two letters of support: one from a faculty or staff member and one from a student. Consultants are paid by the hour, sign a confidentiality agreement, and commit to a very active partnership with faculty members. There is an orientation for new student consultants, cofacilitated by experienced student consultants and the director of the program. There is no additional training; rather, student consultants are mentored by one another and the director through weekly meetings.

One of each consultant's key responsibilities is to make weekly visits to his or her faculty partner's classroom. During the visits the consultant takes detailed observation notes focused on pedagogical issues the faculty member has identified. The notes include a column for time, a column for observations (with no commentary or interpretation), and a column for reflections, questions, and suggestions. The goal of this note-taking format is to provide faculty members with glimpses from one student's perspective of what is happening in the classroom and how that student interprets those happenings. One faculty participant described these notes and the program itself as a deeply self-reflective activity, "only better."

Consultants meet weekly with their partners to discuss what they have observed in the faculty members' classrooms. These forums offer participants an opportunity to engage in dialogue, investigate one another's perspectives more deeply, and articulate both tacit and evolving understandings. These dialogues unfold, as one faculty partner put it, "outside of the normal relationship" between faculty and students. As this faculty partner continued, the student consultant is "not responsible for the content" and is "free of the grading," and the faculty member can discuss "what I am struggling with in ways that I would NEVER talk to a student." The liminal space provided by these partnerships allows both faculty and students to develop ways of communicating and interacting that inform, and sometimes directly carry over into, faculty interactions with other students.

Consultants are supported in all these collaborative activities through attending and participating in weekly, semi-structured, one-hour discussions with the director of the program and other consultants. These meetings focus on what is happening in faculty partners' classrooms and how to support faculty exploration, affirmation, and revision of pedagogical practices. This forum includes a great deal of discussion of how to perceive what is working well in a classroom, as well as what could be improved and how to develop language appropriate to capturing and conveying those insights.

Since 2006, 175 faculty members from Bryn Mawr, Haverford, and nearby Swarthmore College, Villanova University, and Ursinus College and 105 student consultants have participated in a total of over 250 partnerships. Other institutions, both like and unlike Bryn Mawr, have developed versions of the SaLT program, including Ursinus College, a selective independent, coeducational, four-year liberal arts college that secured funding from The Andrew W. Mellon Foundation and developed a student consulting program; Widener University, a private, metropolitan university emphasizing academics and community service with 3,300 undergraduates and 3,300 graduate students (see McHenry et al., 2009); and Community College of Philadelphia, which ran a year-long pilot program on the same model.

The feedback from faculty and students who participate in this program is included throughout the chapters of this book. But here we include two more general statements, one from a faculty member and one from a student, which reflect the power of partnership. One faculty member captured what many participants learn through working in partnership with students: "I don't have to teach alone. The burden of the learning experience is not just on me. It was freeing and liberating to come to that awareness. I can share the responsibility for what happens in the classroom with students." Students also realize the power—and responsibility—of partnership. As one student put it, "In past discussions I've always been talking about what the profs do to us and it's been a one-way street. And now I am able to look at it as a relationship in the classroom; if we're complaining about something that is going on,

it's also the students' role to step up and say something about that."
(For further information, see Cook-Sather, 2008, 2009b, 2010,
2011a, 2011b, 2011c, 2012, 2013b.)

3. Programs Supporting Research on Learning and Teaching

Many faculty work in research universities or schools that consider themselves research focused or research intensive, and
these faculty may worry that student-faculty partnerships focused on learning and teaching will not be rewarded within their
institutions. Those concerns are valid, of course, but there are
opportunities even in these environments to work in partnership
with students on research into disciplinary learning and teaching, which often is called Scholarship of Teaching and Learning
(SoTL). Although much SoTL takes place at an individual level,
our focus here is on the student-faculty partnerships in SoTL at
the institutional and program levels. An increasing number of
institutions are providing opportunities for student-faculty partnerships focused on research into learning and teaching, and, in
some cases, they involve significant change and transformation
to existing higher education processes and structures (Healey and
Jenkins, 2009; Hutchings et al., 2011).

Some SoTL projects recognize students "not as objects of inquiry . . . but as co-inquirers, helping to shape key questions, gather
and analyze data, and then push for change where it is needed"
(Hutchings et al., 2011, p. 79; see also Werder and Otis, 2010;
Werder et al., 2012). Students within this kind of SoTL project
are positioned as partners with faculty members in dialogue and in
action. This kind of SoTL has in common with action research a
commitment to exploring "practical questions evolving from everyday educational work" (Altrichter, Posch, and Somekh 1993,
p. 5), but action research has a set methodology of iterative and
reflective stages, while SoTL is less methodologically specific and

has tended to be seen as somewhat less politically charged (Felten, 2013). While it emphasizes making necessary change, SoTL typically does not use the more actively political language of integrating action and research to challenge the routines of the status quo (Somekh and Zeichner, 2009). We acknowledge, however, that views of the political nature of SoTL may be shifted by the move toward involving students in researching learning and teaching, thereby challenging our accepted notions of who carries out research and scholarship.

Brief example 3a: The Wabash-Provost Scholars Program at North Carolina A&T State University was initially developed as a way to "dig deeper" into Wabash National Study results through student-based focus groups, and it has expanded from there.

The Wabash-Provost Scholars Program, started in 2007, trains undergraduate students to conduct focus-group sessions with their peers, obtain and analyze qualitative and quantitative data, develop written summary reports, and lead scholarly presentations on their work and experiences. Wabash-Provost Scholars directly contribute to knowledge regarding the student-learning environment at North Carolina A&T, while participating students develop research and presentation skills. Composed of students from a wide variety of majors, the program illustrates how "high-impact practices," such as undergraduate research experiences, can be made available to all students, regardless of discipline, while also providing valuable service to the university. The students work alongside faculty and administrators in guided campus inquiry. Approximately 15 to 20 new Scholars are trained each year.

Initially launched as a volunteer activity, the Wabash-Provost Scholars Program is now organized as an academic course (1 semester credit hour) that meets once per week throughout a semester. The course is offered each semester, and students may enroll for multiple semesters. During the semester students participate in Institutional Review Board (IRB) training, mock focus-group sessions with debriefings, and qualitative research methods training, in addition to the activities outlined above. Scholars typically carry out one project per semester, culminating in a written report of their findings and recommendations and a presentation to the campus community and institutional leaders, including the chancellor and provost. All Wabash-Provost Scholar activities are carried out under IRB approval.

Wabash-Provost Scholars have given presentations about their work at national and international conferences and have served as assessment consultants on other university campuses. In addition, their work has been featured in a variety of publications (Hutchings et al., 2013; Baker, 2012; and Hutchings, Huber, and Ciccone, 2011).

Students in the program frequently report powerful outcomes, as one Scholar reflected:

> What has surprised me most about this program is how much of a role we play as a student. Although we were told on numerous occasions that this was our project and our research I truly did not understand it until we were put directly in the midst of everything. From the forming of questions, to conducting the focus groups, and even to the summarization of the data and the final presentation (to the department), we truly were in charge of this research project. . . . I believe that I can use the skills I learned to not only develop better relationships with others but also to apply those skills to other 'real world' situations and settings in my career.

Brief example 3b: The Undergraduate Learning and Teaching Research Internship Scheme (ULTRIS) at the University of Western Australia invites undergraduate students to undertake authentic research into learning and teaching outside their chosen discipline.

The university has stated that learning and teaching are a priority, and student-faculty research is widely understood to be a good opportunity for students to be able to make significant contributions to this priority, informing future changes in policy and practice. While this approach has obvious potential benefits to the institution, to subject areas, and to the individual students, it also has a broader cultural impact—sparking greater levels of interest in research among diverse groups of students.

The students who are invited to be interns in the semester-long program are second-year undergraduates. They are then allocated a supervisor and required to attend an intensive training period focused on basic research methods. Each student selects a research question from a broad range of teaching and learning topics that are considered to be of strategic importance to the university. In previous years these topics have included faculty-student interaction outside the classroom, the first-year experience, sustainability, and internationalization. Students are responsible for developing their own research questions and research design, although they can ask for advice from their supervisor. The students collect and analyze data, as well as write an academic paper through which they can report their findings internally within the university and externally at a teaching and learning conference.

Partridge and Sandover (2010) report high levels of student satisfaction with taking part in the program. They argue that this program provides a valuable and unusual opportunity for students to interact with different students across disciplines within the institution and with a focus upon something of universal interest. One student noted that, "The lecturer-student gap really closed for me . . . I also found out some really interesting things about institutional constraints to improving teaching and learning and some of the troubles lecturers were facing" (Partridge and Sandover, 2010, p. 12). Another student commented on "how relevant educational research is for all disciplines. That it is useful for improving my own uni[versity] experience both through self reflection on what is useful to me as a student and through being able to critically analyse the institution that I'm supposed to be learning through" (p. 13).

Brief example 3c: At Capital University in Ohio, undergraduate research projects have been used for several years to bring about institutional change.

The research projects pursued by the undergraduates examine issues that are experienced on many campuses (e.g., academic advising and parking) and across many academic disciplines (e.g., assessment). Students have a complete undergraduate research experience, from reading the relevant literature and developing a meaningful research question and method for answering that question to collecting and analyzing the data and disseminating the results at campus and professional venues. Students communicate their work to both lay and professional audiences.

Students who participate in this project indicate that through these research experiences they develop the work and mental habits of a social scientist, build their academic skills, obtain career guidance and preparation for graduate school and careers, elevate their attitudes toward learning, and improve their sense of self-efficacy. When students conduct research within the context of their own institution, they also enjoy a deeper sense of personal satisfaction knowing that the work they are doing is directly benefiting their friends and classmates and future students at their institutions. (For further information, see Karkowski and Fournier, 2012.)

Brief example 3d: At the University of Worcester, in the United Kingdom, a team of three academics and three students led a collaborative project using appreciative inquiry (AI) to determine what constitutes good inclusive practice within Worcester's Institute of Education.

The students collected data on what students perceived to be the positive things about their experiences of the Institute from year cohorts and specifically from disabled students. They analyzed the information and presented it at a faculty development event in the Institute. AI is a strengths-based approach and this optimistic slant, along with this being a student-faculty partnership project, contributed to faculty reporting being very positive about the project and considering the findings to be particularly powerful. For example, faculty reported that AI was a motivator to further developing their strengths and to starting to integrate an appreciative tone into university meetings. Experience from having run this project over several years now has led colleagues to realize that it can be particularly powerful for faculty to hear students report participatory research that conveys appreciation of work undertaken by faculty members (Snell et al., 2012). Students involved in the project have stated that

> The initial training phase of the AI process was fundamental in setting the tone for the relationship between students and staff . . . the relaxed and interactive nature of the training session allowed many student/ staff barriers to be removed. Our input and ideas were valued and respected, enabling us to confidently share our thoughts and ideas. Subsequent face-to-face meetings were held, which improved team cohesion between ourselves and the academic staff, and saw the shaping and development of the project. (Kadi-Hanifi et al., 2013, p. 4)

Another student reported that

> As a student researcher I feel this whole process has supported my growth as a practitioner. The skills I have learnt both from an academic and communicative perspective have proved incredibly valuable as I have progressed through into my second year of university.

> The AI Approach itself has influenced my thinking and it will most definitely shape my practice as a future teacher. (Kadi-Hanifi et al., 2013, p. 7)

It is also worth noting that faculty have reported a range of changes as a result of these student-led research projects. Some have implemented small changes, such as improving readability of PowerPoint slides, while other faculty have explored longer-term policy changes such as requiring student participation on course validation and review panels. Finally, as a result of students modeling the use of AI methodology within learning and teaching research, some faculty have been inspired by the students to start using this methodology within their own learning and teaching research.

Brief example 3e: The Student as Producer program at the University of Lincoln in the United Kingdom is a radical project that aims to re-envisage higher education through the lens of critical social theory. The program is attempting to move away from predefined learning outcomes toward a variety of student-led research and teaching initiatives.

As Neary (2010) states, "Student as Producer, and the revolutionary pedagogical practice which it promotes, is designed to interrupt the current consensual discourse about teaching and learning in higher education" (p. 8). Student as Producer aims to make strong connections between research and teaching and to challenge traditional notions of students as the objects of the learning process rather than as subjects within a social process.

Drawing on the work of Marx, Vygotsky, and other critical social theorists, the Student as Producer program establishes a pedagogic model with less emphasis on teaching defined by set learning outcomes and instead focusing primarily on a range of innovative, student-led, research and teaching projects. These projects involve unfamiliar ways of working for students and faculty, leading students on an intellectual journey involving "interruption and astonishment" in an attempt to promote intellectual and emotional development and social awareness.

Neary (2010) explains that "the purpose of the Student as Producer project is to establish research-engaged teaching and learning as an institutional priority at the University of Lincoln. This means that research-engaged teaching and learning will become the dominant paradigm for all aspects of curriculum design and delivery and the key organizational principle that informs other aspects of the University of Lincoln's strategic planning" (p. 7).

Case Study 3: The "Students as Change Agents" Program at the University of Exeter

The University of Exeter's Students as Change Agents program is a student-led action research initiative that brings students and faculty members together to improve experiences of higher education. Established in 2008, the initiative supports students from across the University of Exeter to carry out small-scale research projects about their learning and teaching environments focused on concerns that have been raised and discussed within student-faculty liaison committees. The students have carried out research and then made recommendations and taken action in partnership with faculty to enhance these areas of the learning experience.

The project was conceived of when some Exeter faculty attended a U.K. Higher Education Academy event entitled Students as Agents of Change, which stimulated these individuals to go back to the university to consider how they might implement some of these ideas within their own institution. As two of the leaders of the program, Elisabeth Dunne and her colleague Roos Zandstra, explain, "Despite the genuine attention to student feedback and the efforts of the university to engage with students, there has been a missing element—and that is the direct involvement of students in actually bringing about change" (2011, p. 4). Dunne and Zandstra argue that

> What is different about the change agent's concept is
> that it takes the idea of students as researchers into a dif-
> ferent dimension from the discipline-based research usu-
> ally discussed in higher education, with a new focus on
> researching pedagogy and curriculum delivery. Students
> apply and develop their research expertise in the context
> of their subject, taking responsibility for engaging with
> research-led, evidence-informed change, and promoting
> reflection and review at a departmental and institutional
> level. (Dunne and Zandstra, 2011, p. 15)

The key drivers of the project started by gaining institutional
support for the idea of getting students to undertake research
into learning and teaching. After securing modest funding from
within the institution, the head of the Academic Development
Unit appointed a graduate project coordinator; they then pub-
licized the project to students and offered support at a drop-in
session at a café on campus for students to come to sound out
their ideas and be given guidance on completing the application form. Ten projects were then selected to move forward. The
students designed and carried out the research with the support
of the graduate project coordinator. The students disseminated
their findings at an institutional conference before developing
recommendations and an action plan based on the research outcomes. Students then contributed to making changes based on
the outcomes of the research.

Working from their theoretical model of students as change
agents, Dunne and Zandstra (2011) differentiated among (1) students as evaluators, involving processes through which the institution and external bodies listen to the student voice in order
to drive change; (2) students as participants, such as efforts that
emphasize institutional commitment to greater student involvement in changes to teaching, learning, and institutional development; (3) students as partners, engaging students as cocreators and

experts; and (4) students as agents for change, which requires a move from institution-driven to student-driven agendas and activity (p. 18). Embracing the fourth of these, all student research projects focused on topics that were taken from within existing faculty-student liaison committee discussions, so agendas were shared and often picked up on unresolved issues from the past. This also provided a formal feedback route for any changes and actions arising from the research.

As documented in the Students as Change Agents booklet (Dunne and Zandstra, 2011), student research at the University of Exeter has driven organizational change, contributed to student engagement in shifts of policy and practice within the university, and supported students' learning in the areas of research, project management and presentation of outcomes, leadership, and understanding organizational development. The pilot study was so successful that the initiative has been continued, with over a hundred projects having been completed to date. Projects have now involved undergraduate and graduate students in almost all subject areas from across the university's three campuses, investigating student-selected topics such as assessment and feedback, technology, intercampus teaching, employability, personal and peer-tutoring, digital literacy, sustainability, and academic writing. Outcomes have included research reports, study guides, student-led conferences, as well as students organizing and running sessions on writing skills and careers, a buddy system, and peer-tutoring. Overall, many hundreds of students have participated in the various studies and many more have benefited from the outcomes. The Students as Change Agents initiative has also grown from being a small-scale pilot project run by enthusiasts to an initiative that is devolved to each of the university's five colleges and is largely funded and supported by them.

Feedback is consistently positive, as exemplified by a project where biosciences students researched issues of students' academic writing and created resources to help their peers to improve their written skills. One faculty member stated, "The Students as Change Agents project has revolutionized the way in which we develop tools for learning and teaching and is an excellent way of embedding student involvement through the curriculum." One of the students said, "Brilliant! [It] . . . covers all the problems that we're likely to come across. This will definitely prove very useful. Thank you." Finally, the university's student engagement manager stated: "Change agents has become so much more than a scheme. It is a culture and a way of thinking for our staff and students who overwhelmingly seek out opportunities to work together on new ideas."

Benefits and Drawbacks of Moving from Individual to Programmatic Approaches

The examples included in this chapter illustrate how faculty and students—as well as other academic staff and administrators—can work together, redefining traditional roles and changing the way pedagogical planning and practice are conceptualized, assessed, and revised. The role of facilitators, often teaching and learning center directors or staff, can be crucial in helping faculty and students not only rethink their roles but also move into the new and typically unfamiliar responsibilities those redefined roles bring. The liminal spaces that can be created by and within programs can provide an "in-between" space for innovation and experimentation that can then be carried into wider institutional forums.

There are both benefits and drawbacks to moving from individual to programmatic approaches to student-faculty partnerships. The benefits include the expansion in the number of partners, thus building student and faculty "partnership capacity" within an institution; the potential to secure financial support; and the possibility of beginning to transform campus culture.

Moving Further from Pedagogical Solitude toward Teaching as Community Property

Working in partnership with individual student consultants, collaborators, or co-researchers certainly moves faculty members out of pedagogical solitude by affording opportunities to cocreate curricula, collaboratively design pedagogical approaches, or contribute to institutional change with students. Participating in or developing a programmatic approach expands that collaboration to include faculty colleagues and other students. Through working with other faculty members engaged in partnerships with students and in explorations and revisions of educational practice, we can build communities of practice that expose teachers to others' insights and approaches. These communities afford the opportunity to share what is otherwise often individual work. Shulman (2004a) has argued that if we resituate teaching within "the community of scholars," we can move from "pedagogical solitude" to "teaching as community property" (pp. 140–141). Programmatic partnerships are one way of moving toward shared learning and teaching conceptualizations, discussions, and practices.

Securing Institutional and Financial Support

Another benefit of scaling up is that you may be able to draw inter- or extra-institutional support for your partnership work. Institutional support can be an important factor contributing to the success of student-faculty partnerships (Bovill, 2013a), not only because of the financial resources but also because the backing of senior administrators and colleagues brings positive energy and attention to your work. Good ideas grow, and when nurtured by passion and small successes, larger, even transformative, efforts can evolve.

Most often, funding and support for partnership programs increases over time, sometimes slowly and occasionally rapidly, as positive outcomes become apparent. This internal funding typically provides compensation, expert training, food, or other tangible benefits to participating faculty and students. In some cases, individual faculty members or teams secure external funding that allows partnership programs to be established and gradually to become integrated into the culture of an institution. Many programs also operate on a shoestring, perhaps tapping limited resources from an existing teaching center or student union budget. While some excellent partnership programs thrive without significant funding, large-scale sustainable initiatives typically require ongoing resources.

Successful partnership programs sometimes connect their work to other institutional priorities, such as student engagement, outcomes assessment, or graduate attributes. Although this might appear at first to be driven by policy makers' and administrators' agendas, building student-faculty collaboration into funded projects has the potential to spread partnership practices further and question the continuance of projects about learning and teaching where students are not involved meaningfully. This has happened in the United Kingdom, where the Higher Education Academy now explicitly funds "students as partners" programs and projects as a way of informing debates, enhancing the research base, and embedding partnership activity across universities.

Shifting Institutional Culture

A third benefit of moving from individual to programmatic approaches is that by expanding the community of practice focused on student-faculty partnerships and securing one or more forms of support for this work, there is the potential for institutional transformation—for moving toward a culture that embraces a notion of shared responsibility for teaching and learning (Cook-Sather, 2009b). As we discuss in Chapter 5, student-faculty partnerships are, to quote a Bryn Mawr faculty, making a difference "to the level of awareness at the college—of pedagogy, of roles, of possibilities—and also to the teaching and learning going on in all kinds of spaces here." Speaking specifically about the potential for institutional change, this particular faculty member, who participated in the SaLT program, continued: "As time goes on and more and more faculty and students experience this program, I believe that it will really change the language and content of our conversations here about what it means to teach and learn in and across our disciplines at the college." Through the successful processes and outcomes of one partnership, students can gain confidence and an increased trust in partnership processes that can lead to greater likelihood of their engagement in future partnerships.

Another potential benefit, particularly to new faculty members (and in the longer-term, for the institution), is the enhanced support new faculty receive for learning and teaching through institutional support for student partnership programs. Although no systematic study has been conducted, the provost at Bryn Mawr College has noted that the new faculty members reviewed for reappointment over the last several years—the first cohorts of new faculty to have participated in the SaLT program—have experienced fewer problems adapting to their new roles as professors and they have enjoyed more positive assessments of their teaching at their first reviews than was the case for previous cohorts.

While these benefits are real, neither partnership nor program-level work is a panacea. The drawbacks of moving from individual to programmatic approaches include the potential for loss of freedom and spontaneity, the potential for ossification, and the potential for imposition.

Potential Loss of Freedom and Spontaneity

Moving out of an individual partnership approach and into a community of practice might cause faculty to experience some loss of freedom and spontaneity. Faculty can more easily experiment with curriculum and pedagogical design within the actual or virtual walls of their own classrooms. So it is possible that becoming part of a larger program might compel some faculty and students to move in directions that are not of their own design or choosing, with larger programs structuring and guiding the explorations they undertake more than they would like.

Potential for Ossification

Like the institutions that house them, when programs become established, they can lose some of the flexibility, innovation, and responsiveness of pilots or individual efforts. The very stability that supports ongoing efforts can also stifle the development of new ones. This drawback can be avoided if those involved in developing a program embrace an explicit goal of committing to growing and changing in response to faculty and student interests and needs. Regular review of programs is another way to stop and check whether original aims are still being met or whether mainstreaming has led to dilution of the principles underpinning partnerships, with the need for revision to reinvigorate and rebalance initiatives.

Potential for Imposition

Another drawback is the potential for imposition. As some scholars have warned about student voice efforts in primary and secondary school contexts, when a practice becomes an initiative or a mandate, it can be used to compel participation or compliance. As we emphasize in Chapter 7, we believe that participation in student-faculty partnership programs should be voluntary. One excited participant in a student-faculty partnership program stated: "Somehow, everyone should have a chance (I would even say 'should be required,' even if it sounds a bit dictatorial!) to have this experience." This exclamation illustrates the danger that even well-intended enthusiasm can lead to imposition.

Recommendations for Those in Faculty Development Roles

Those with formal or informal faculty development roles are likely to be aware that the vast majority of professional development models assume that either faculty colleagues or the staff of professional teaching and learning centers should be responsible for supporting the development of faculty learning (Cook-Sather, 2011c). Some embrace or advocate reflective and collaborative approaches (Cowan and Westwood, 2006; Huston and Weaver, 2008), faculty learning communities (Richlin and Cox, 2004; Cox, 2003), and peer observation models (Peel, 2005) that put faculty into constructive dialogue with one another about what is and what could be happening in their classrooms and online. But because student involvement has in general been a small component of faculty development practices across universities—indeed, Cox and Sorenson (2000) claim "it has been virtually invisible" (p. 99)—many faculty developers may not have considered or may just be beginning to consider creating opportunities for faculty to work in partnership with students in professional development opportunities. As we have suggested, we have "an ethical obligation to involve our students more actively [in faculty development]" (Zahorski, quoted in Cox and Sorenson, 2000, p. 98), and this section of the book is for those who want to move toward such involvement.

Faculty developers work with many disciplinary differences and needs across a campus (Jenkins, 1996). Someone in a full-time faculty development role may have only indirect contact with students, unless he or she continues to teach in a discipline. It is possible, nevertheless, to intentionally seek out opportunities for developing relationships with students and to help colleagues to encourage hesitant students to become partners in pedagogical planning and exploration. In working with faculty who are supporting students to take their first steps toward or into partnership, it is helpful to offer constructive feedback and advice about what may feel like an alien process to some students and faculty. Such efforts enact and make visible a more democratic approach to supporting learning (Hutchings and Huber in Werder and Otis, 2010), with responsibility shared among students, faculty, and faculty developers.

Another productive approach is to share with faculty the benefits of working in partnership with students such as those we outline in Chapter 5. Some colleagues may not realize that simply having an observer in the classroom allows them to gain perspectives and insights that are otherwise not possible to gain (Cook-Sather, 2008, 2009b, 2010, 2011b). Other colleagues might be intrigued by the possibility that partnership provides for developing new understandings of both teaching and learning (Feiman-Nemser, 2012). Still others may see partnerships as an opportunity to increase awareness, confidence, and willingness to take risks and recognize the importance of transparency, explicitness, and communication and of seeing students as partners in the educational process, rather than as adversaries on the opposite side of the desk.

Drawing on our experience and previous work (see for example, Bovill et al., 2011), we provide the following recommendations for those in a position to support and guide others in developing student-faculty partnerships. Directors or coordinators of teaching and learning centers, faculty members in liaison roles, or faculty developers can all facilitate and support student-faculty partnerships by

- Serving as intermediaries

- Building on existing commitments among faculty

- Promoting and practicing cocreative approaches in professional development forums

- Acting as a bridge between different parts of the university and influencing policy

Serve as Intermediaries

Directors, coordinators, faculty developers, and administrators can facilitate the development of new relationships between students and faculty who may not be accustomed to approaching one another and building these kinds of partnerships. When the institution sends a clear message that such partnerships are valued and desirable, faculty will be more likely to be inclined to embrace such partnerships and seek support for them. For instance, you might adapt existing small teaching grants from your teaching center to allow, or perhaps even to encourage, student-faculty partnership. You also might connect faculty who seem interested in pursuing partnerships with those who have some experience of running partnerships. You even might approach members of your student government association or representative council to discuss their views on (and possible support of) students becoming involved in learning and teaching partnerships.

Build on Existing Commitments among Faculty

Many faculty have been working in partnership with their students for years. Some faculty already collaborate with students in research and others are informed by literature on critical pedagogy, popular education, and liberatory practices that place active student participation at the center of teaching and learning. Faculty members, faculty developers, and others can build upon these practices and find places where student partnership work aligns with teachers' disciplinary and philosophical approaches. Sometimes existing classroom techniques can be the catalyst for new forms of collaboration if they are viewed from a slightly different perspective; midcourse feedback, for example, can be gathered and used in ways that foster partnership. By building on existing practices and habits, you can help faculty and students to become more aware of, and intentional about, the kinds of self-authorship in which they are mutually engaged (Baxter Magolda, 2009; Cook-Sather, 2006).

And if you do not know about current partnership activities or you do not see many opportunities for such work on your campus, you can begin by asking colleagues if they have ever considered collaborating with students on teaching and learning. You, and they, might be surprised where that conversation goes.

Promote and Practice Cocreative Approaches in Academic Development Forums

In many universities across the world, a large proportion of new faculty undertake preparatory teaching programs and courses such as Postgraduate Certificates in Learning and Teaching. These programs emphasize the importance of reflection on, and critical analysis of, one's own teaching practice. Professional development workshops and seminars and other regular university-level learning and teaching forums are settings where faculty developers may be able to pose questions about the place of student-faculty partnerships within pedagogical planning processes. These spaces also provide opportunities to engage in significant dialogues about learning and teaching where pedagogies that engender greater expectations of students can be explored further. Faculty developers can also ensure that their practice is congruent with the learning and teaching research that espouses the importance of faculty developers practicing what they preach (Swennen, Lunenberg, and Korthagen, 2008; Brew and Barrie, 1999) through using cocreation in their own approaches to teaching.

Act as a Bridge between Different Parts of the University and Influence Policy

Faculty developers have a difficult role within universities and colleges, where they sit in a middle layer between faculty and administrators (Little and Green, 2012). Their role involves support, liaison, advice, investigation, quality assurance, as well as teaching and learning. All of these roles involve being both encouraging and constructively critical to faculty members, as well as to senior administrators within the university. In this sense, faculty developers can be perceived as a bridge between faculty members and administrative staff within higher education. This positioning provides a range of opportunities for faculty developers to support student-faculty partnerships, including, for example, influencing the nature of learning and teaching strategies and policies on campus. Faculty developers may also be in a position to influence the institution's public commitment to student-faculty partnerships.

Conclusion

Based on our analysis of student-faculty partnerships across different contexts, we note that the kinds of partnerships institutions seem to support reflect the primary commitments of the particular university. For example, liberal arts institutions, such as Bryn Mawr College and Elon University, focus their efforts on curricular and pedagogical projects, and research-intensive institutions, such as the University of Exeter, focus on student-faculty partnerships that involve students in research. This is not to suggest that the kinds of student-faculty partnerships that develop need only reflect specific goals of an institution, but rather that the kinds of student-faculty partnerships that initially emerge are likely to mirror institutional aims in that way. As institutions of higher education continue to ponder the question, "What are universities for?" (Collini, 2012), student-faculty partnerships may expand our perspective to see beyond existing horizons and, perhaps, student-faculty partnerships may expand our existing horizons and, perhaps, allow us to glimpse new possibilities for the purposes and practices of higher education.

In the next chapter, we examine some of the research that demonstrates the outcomes of partnerships—the ways in which both faculty and students experience enhanced engagement, motivation, and learning; develop metacognitive awareness and a stronger sense of identity; and contribute to the improvement of teaching and the classroom experience.

5

Outcomes of Student-Faculty Partnerships

Support from Research Literature and Outcomes for Faculty and Students

I f you have read straight through the book so far, you will have read about both individual and program-level examples of student-faculty partnerships across a wide variety of contexts. Those examples offer you glimpses of how some partnerships are structured and, in a few cases, some of the results of this work. In this chapter we delve much more deeply into the outcomes we have seen across partnerships, drawing on our own research findings as well as those of other scholars. We also link these outcomes to some of the most pressing themes in discussions and debates about higher education today, most specifically student engagement and learning. After brief mention of those themes and a note about the research methodology used in our own and others' studies, we move into a review of the research on student-faculty partnerships. We then explain the three primary sets of outcomes for all participants. We conclude by discussing implications of this research for individual faculty and for institutions.

Partnership as a Means to Reach Our Goals in Higher Education

Decades of research indicate that close interaction between faculty and students is one of the most important factors in student learning, development, engagement, and satisfaction in college (Astin, 1993; Baker and Griffin, 2010; Chickering and Gamson, 1987; Kuh, Kinzie, Schuh, and Whitt, 2005; Light, 2004; Farley-Lucas and Sargent, 2010). Indeed, frequent and meaningful faculty-student interaction is a central characteristic of all high-impact educational practices (Kuh, 2008). Because this kind of interaction is the foundation of student-faculty partnership, we believe that the practices we describe here are one of the most effective means to achieve the broader aims of higher education.

Partnership is a highly flexible practice. It provides faculty and other staff with a way to productively view *all* of their interactions with students—through a partnership lens—in the classroom, as well as in the many other spaces where rich collaborations are possible, including faculty mentoring undergraduate research, facilitating service-learning, designing and leading study-abroad experiences, and advising living-learning communities. We believe that putting partnership at the heart of educational interactions is essential to helping students learn and develop.

Authentic partnership, however, is not automatically or easily accomplished. As we have discussed in previous chapters, challenges arise when attempting to balance faculty and student voices in a way that fosters genuine partnership. The bottom line, as we have suggested, is constituted by the assumptions and expectations students and faculty have for their roles and relationships. After analyzing several case studies of partnerships, Delpish and her colleagues (2010) conclude:

> Students are accustomed to, and often comfortable with, assuming a relatively powerless role in the classroom, just as faculty are trained to believe that their disciplinary

expertise gives them complete authority over the learning process. When faculty or students challenge these
habits, students and faculty must confront fundamental
questions about the nature of teaching and learning.
(p. 111; see also Felten, 2011; Glasser and Powers, 2011)

This chapter focuses on these two interrelated realities—that
partnership work between students and faculty can be transformative and that such work is, at the same time, profoundly challenging of "the inherited routines of academic life" (Hutchings et al.,
2011, p. 6).

A Note About Research Methodology

Those of us who study student-faculty partnerships typically em-
ploy a range of qualitative research methodologies and methods to
access and analyze student and faculty experiences and outcomes.
Many studies are framed using evaluation research methodology,
case study methodology, action research, or participatory action
research. These are approaches that are consistent with the kinds
of critical theoretical questions being raised in work that challenges our accepted ways of understanding student and teacher roles
within learning and teaching (Bovill, 2013a; Seale, 2010). And, as
you might expect, many of these studies have been conducted in
partnership with students.

The outcomes of student-faculty partnership included in this
chapter, like the examples of partnership included throughout the
book, are drawn from programs we run or that we have studied as
part of our research and also from examples colleagues have shared,
both formally in print and more informally at conferences and in
conversation. In our research we ask participants to complete questionnaires and surveys, we conduct interviews and focus groups, and
we analyze the feedback faculty and students offer during their participation in these projects and programs. We often use a constant
comparison approach as outlined by Creswell (2006) or elements

of grounded theory (Glaser and Strauss, 1967) in order to analyze the data we gather. We typically start by engaging in open coding: "the process of breaking down, examining, comparing, conceptualizing, and categorizing data" (Strauss and Corbin, 1990, p. 61) before identifying key and emerging themes within data. Colleagues on whose work we are reporting often use similar approaches. These research approaches are established and appropriate for the contexts of partnerships. More quantitative and experimental methodologies, while essential in many areas of educational research, are not necessarily well suited to inquiry into partnership practices and similar nuanced pedagogical innovations and negotiations (Huber and Hutchings, 2005).

Drawing on the findings of our own and others' research, in this chapter we include statements from students and faculty to introduce sections of our discussion, and we weave some of these statements into our discussion to give you a sense of the outcomes from the perspectives of those who experience them. If the quotations come from work published by others, we indicate that. If there is no name attached to the quotation, it has been drawn from our own data, and to preserve confidentiality, we have not included names.

What Are the Outcomes of Partnership?

Research suggests that partnerships tend to produce similar outcomes for both students and faculty (Bovill, Cook-Sather, and Felten, 2011; Cook-Sather, 2011b, 2011c; Cox, 2001; Sorenson, 2001). Since students and faculty are so different, these shared outcomes might seem surprising. However, partnership's roots in reciprocity and shared responsibility create a solid foundation for all participants to learn and grow in similar ways.

There are three clusters of outcomes from this work, and we use these to form the next three key sections in this chapter: (1) *engagement*—enhancing motivation and learning; (2) *awareness*—developing metacognitive awareness and a stronger sense of identity; and (3) *enhancement*—improving teaching and the class-room experience. These outcomes typically are expressed and ex-perienced differently by students and faculty, but the resonance be-tween groups is striking. In short, partnerships tend to make both students and faculty more thoughtful, engaged, and empathetic as they go about their work and life on campus.

Outcome 1: Engagement—Enhancing Motivation and Learning

"I discovered that I could contribute important insights instead of withholding my thoughts. This dialogue was a transformative experience for me, and it boosted my confidence to share my thoughts in my adult education classes as well, which added an excitement to my learning experience."

Werder et al., 2012, p. 35

Shevell Thibou made this observation while reflecting on her experiences as a graduate student participant in Western Washington University's Teaching-Learning Academy (TLA). In the TLA, faculty, staff, community members, and students meet to deepen individual and collective understanding of the campus learning cul-ture. Thibou's words mirror what research tells us: engagement is crucial to student success in higher education. Engagement means serious interest in, active taking up of, and commitment to learning (Ahlfeldt et al., 2005; Barnett, 1997; Bryson and Hand, 2007; Freire 2003; Kuh et al., 2010; Mann, 2001; Webber, 2004). Autonomy and agency are also important factors that contribute to students' taking more responsibility for their own learning (hooks, 1994; Rogers and Freiberg, 1969). Although sometimes students and faculty hesitate to embrace this more active role for university students, research dem-onstrates that independent engagement makes students more likely to adopt deep approaches to learning. Students "become adaptive experts who both recognize and even relish the opportunity and necessity for breaking with traditional approaches and inventing new ones" (Bain and Zimmerman, 2009, p. 10). Having the opportunity to engage in dialogue with other students and faculty inspired Thibou and gave her the confidence to more actively and intentionally learn.

Research reveals that this experience is widely shared. Student-faculty partnerships consistently deepen student engagement, motivation, and learning (Bovill et al., 2010, 2011). Specific outcomes for students include enhanced confidence, motivation, and enthusiasm (Cook-Sather, 2010, 2011a; Little et al., 2011; Sambell and Graham, 2011); enhanced engagement in the process, not just the outcomes, of learning (Bovill et al., 2010); and enhanced responsibility for, and ownership of, their own learning (Bovill et al., 2010; Cook-Sather, 2011a; Manor et al., 2010). On a larger scale, Barnes et al. (2011) describe student-faculty partnerships leading to students gaining a better understanding of the university and their place within the university community. Similarly, Sambell and Graham (2011) report students becoming aware of their potential to be more active and meaningful contributors to the academic community.

While the evidence for student engagement and motivation is compelling, students are not the only ones who might experience such shifts. Indeed, Thiessen (2010) calls student-faculty partnership a "pedagogy of mutual engagement." Faculty have described partnership experiences as leading to a transformation of the way they think about teaching and how they practice as teachers (Bovill, 2013a). They describe a profoundly changed understanding of learning and teaching through experiencing different viewpoints (Cook-Sather, 2008, 2011b; Werder and Otis, 2010). They also talk about reconceptualizing learning and teaching as collaborative processes (Bovill et al., 2011; Cook-Sather, 2009b, Cook-Sather, 2013b). These are big changes from how many faculty experience teaching and learning, and for some faculty, such changes come as a surprise.

In the following subsections we focus first on engagement outcomes for students in terms of

a. Enhanced confidence, motivation, and enthusiasm
b. Enhanced engagement in the process, not just the outcomes, of learning
c. Enhanced responsibility for, and ownership of, their own learning
d. Deepened understanding of, and contributions to, the academic community

We then focus on engagement outcomes for faculty, including

a. Transformed thinking about and practices of teaching
b. Changed understandings of learning and teaching through experiencing different viewpoints
c. Reconceptualization of learning and teaching as collaborative processes

These are complex, interrelated sets of outcomes, and we attempt throughout our discussion to link as well as clearly delineate them.

Engagement Outcomes for Students

"Participating in this program has given me the push I didn't know I needed back in the direction of hard work and taking college seriously as a learning experience."
                                        Student partner

Scholars in the United States and internationally have noted that many of today's college students seem adrift in their education, taking a passive and disengaged approach to learning (Arum and

Roska, 2010; Mann, 2008). This orientation may arise in part from institutional structures and individual expectations that implicitly encourage students to float along without serious challenge or engagement as learners (Green and Popovich, 2012). While we do not minimize the challenges facing faculty, institutions, and students, research into student-faculty partnerships in different contexts with diverse students has convinced us that students are neither naturally inclined nor happy to experience their education in this way. If afforded the opportunity, students are capable of, and enthusiastic about, becoming engaged and motivated learners. Partnerships are one way to create chances for students to engage in ways many universities describe eloquently in their aspirational mission statements and that faculty hope for—to make our classrooms and online teaching spaces more engaging and effective places to be, and to ensure that students' learning is meaningful and enriching to them.

a. Enhanced Confidence, Motivation, and Enthusiasm

Research suggests that students in partnership with faculty experience enhanced confidence, motivation, and enthusiasm (Cook-Sather, 2010, 2011a; Little et al., 2011; Sambell and Graham, 2011). Students also carry their engagement and motivation into their own ongoing learning. These outcomes are the result of students having a range of opportunities: the opportunity to be taken seriously as collaborators in explorations of teaching and learning; the opportunity to develop the language to name what they know about those processes and deepen that knowledge in dialogue with faculty; and the opportunity to then apply that understanding with their faculty partners, influencing teachng practice as well as enhancing their own educational experiences.

The intersection of confidence, motivation, and enthusiasm is important because it leads to productive action. One student both captures a change in her behavior and points to her participation in a partnership program as the inspiration for that change:

"Recently, I met with one of my own professors and explained why I was feeling uncomfortable/anxious about the class. I know I would not have had the confidence or language to do something like that before becoming a consultant." We have seen this kind of change over and over, both in our own programs and in other scholars' analyses. As a result of their partnership work, students become excited, motivated learners—the kinds of students we most want to teach, the ones we would like to see shaping the intellectual culture of our campuses, and, as we have learned, the kind of students the majority of students themselves want to be.

b. Enhanced Engagement in the Process and Not Just the Outcomes of Learning

Our research also suggests that the opportunity to work in partnership with faculty helps students shift their focus from outcomes, often in the form of grades, to processes that focus on learning itself. Within partnerships, extended dialogue between students and faculty opens up access for students to begin to analyze faculty members' perspectives and practices and to develop their own critical views of learning and what facilitates it. Students can then apply their developing perspective and the understanding it yields to their own and others' learning. They learn, as one student partner put it, to "look at the big picture," and they come to understand "the aim for each exercise from an instructor's perspective." Crucially, through thinking about teaching as well as learning, they come to see learning as a process in which to actively engage as opposed to a prescribed set of hoops that they must jump through to reach their real aim.

Virtually every student partner in our many studies describes the experience, in one student's words, of becoming "more conscious of my learning process in all courses." Another student described how this "elevated consciousness" allows students to analyze the way a particular professor is teaching and, in another's words, "adjust my own learning accordingly." Thus, this elevated consciousness adds a layer of awareness as well as engagement to a student's participation in her courses, making learning both more intentional and more enriching. We expand on this point in our discussion of the development of metacognitive awareness as an outcome of this work (under Outcome 2: Awareness—Developing Metacognitive Awareness and a Stronger Sense of Identity).

c. Enhanced Responsibility for, and Ownership of, Their Own Learning

Many students who have worked in partnership with faculty describe in passionate terms the enhanced responsibility for, and ownership of, their own learning that results from their partnership experiences (Bovill et al., 2010; Cook-Sather, 2010, 2011a; Manor et al., 2010). While a multitude of studies and stories carry a certain weight, a single, slightly more expanded example might make this point more clearly. Christopher Manor began working in partnership with another student and two faculty members at Elon University late in his first year in college. In his second year, he reflected on how his thinking about his own role in his education changed as a result of this experience:

> I grew up thinking what I assumed every other student thought and the majority of students still think—what do I want to get out of this class? An A. The thought of actively trying to learn something never crossed my mind. Then one day . . . we happened on the subject of teacher and student responsibility and then *wham!* The realization hit me: What were my own responsibilities for my education? It was such an odd question. Why had I not thought of this before? (Manor et al., 2010, p. 5)

After asking that apparently simple question, Manor had a fundamentally new orientation toward and motivation for his studies. While he still cared about the grade, his focus became learning and his own responsibility for and ownership of that learning, rather than primarily satisfying expectations and standards that others had created for him.

We have heard similar stories over and over from students who have been engaged in partnerships. Having the opportunity to talk with faculty members about teaching and learning leads to: gaining perspective on learning and teaching processes; developing a deeper understanding of the value of their own learning; and a clearer picture of what kind of active role they can take in pursuing their education. All of these yield not only to better teaching experiences for faculty but also to better learning outcomes for students.

d. Deepened Understanding of and Contribution to the Higher Education Community

When students gain a deeper understanding of learning and a better understanding of the university and their place within it (Barnes et al., 2011), they can become more active and meaningful contributors to that community (Sambell and Graham, 2011). One student captured this change in her perspective and participation this way:

> Nothing is more powerful than seeing a professor take your ideas seriously, to have rich discussion about them and possibly see them implemented into a class. When I see a professor open to my ideas as a consultant, I feel that I am truly making a difference and becoming an important leader in this community. (Cohen et al., 2013)

This change embodies what we are defining as respect, reciprocity, and shared responsibility. When faculty listen to students and revise pedagogical practice as a result, students have the sense that they are contributing to the learning of other students as well as deepening their own learning. In other words, the learning goes in multiple directions and benefits all involved.

Taken together these engagement outcomes encompass enhanced learning experiences for students as individuals, both in their courses and as members of the wider academic community. The confidence, motivation, and enthusiasm students develop help them build the capacity to be active, engaged, and effective learners. This kind of engagement expands students' notions of learning to include the process, not just the outcomes. In turn, students develop a deeper sense of responsibility for, and ownership of, their own learning and the importance of supporting others' learning. And finally, all of these lead students to experience a deepening understanding of, and a desire to make a deeper contribution to, their academic community.

Engagement Outcomes for Faculty

"My student partner did a good job of reconnecting me to the students. She was a bridge back to me being an advocate for the students and serving them well. She reminded me of how much I care and made me refocus my attention on helping students as opposed to simply setting up challenges and obstacles that I expect them to meet."

Faculty partner

Many of us did not have meaningful pedagogical preparation when we began our teaching careers. The common expectation is that if we know our discipline, we can teach it. In many cases this assumption leads us, quite reasonably, to reproduce the teaching practices that we remember working for us, and to avoid the ineffective ones that we experienced. Faculty who have had the opportunity to work in partnership with students realize that using ourselves as a reference point for student learning is not necessarily effective. Our students are not who we were, and in order to challenge, engage, and motivate them, we need to respond to who they are as learners. As one faculty member wrote after collaborating with a student, "Rather than always privilege what worked for me as a student, I work to draw out how different pedagogical practices can illuminate the space of a classroom for all those around the table."

Engagement outcomes of student-faculty partnerships for faculty complement outcomes for students. Again, faculty members' version of enhancing their motivation and learning include (a) transformed thinking about and practices of teaching, (b) changed understandings of learning and teaching through experiencing different viewpoints, and (c) reconceptualization of learning and teaching as collaborative processes.

a. Transformed Thinking about Teaching and Our Practice as Teachers

Because we as faculty have so many competing responsibilities for our time and focus, we may not always give our teaching and our students' learning the careful, critical attention that they deserve. Instead, we may fall back on "tried and true" practices that we have used or seen before. Often it can be difficult to try, or even to imagine, other ways to teach. When we add to that the pressure many of us feel to be cautious shepherds of our time and reputations as we strive toward review and promotion, it is understandable that some faculty shy away from what might seem like more risky, unconventional, or demanding pedagogies.

And yet we have heard from faculty who have participated in partnerships that they are often pleasantly surprised at how much more engaging and effective it is to work *with* students rather than *against* them. Partnerships can illuminate how to move from inherited routines to more thoughtful and more effective practices. Indeed, some faculty partners suggest that partnership frees them from patterns in which they feel stuck: "'It was liberating,'" claimed one faculty member, because she moved from teaching "'that just didn't work'" to classroom practices that were "'put together in ways that

I never even imagined were possible"" (Bovill, 2013a). This faculty member reported that "'it's really transformed how I think about teaching and how I teach.'" Like many of their peers, both this faculty member and Thibou, the former Western Washington student we quoted earlier, evoke the notion of transformation to describe the profound changes experienced by engaging in dialogue about learning and teaching and the impact upon their thinking and practice.

b. Changed Understandings of Learning and Teaching through Experiencing Different Viewpoints

One of the most consistent research findings in this field is that faculty and students alike expand their perspectives on one another's and their own work (Bovill, Cook-Sather, and Felten, 2011; Cook-Sather, 2008; Manor et al., 2010). This finding substantiates calls for the inclusion of students in Scholarship of Teaching and Learning (SoTL). As Werder and Otis (2010) argue, "While students have much to gain from teachers in a SoTL exchange, faculty and institutions have just as much to gain from students about how learning works" (p. 29). Scholars who seek to "understand students' perspectives on what makes learning enjoyable and engaging" (Wood, 2012) recognize that such perspectives are essential to their own practice. Faculty involved in student-faculty partnerships regularly comment that having access to student perspectives enriches their understanding of learning.

Through partnership faculty gain new angles of vision—insights that students offer and that we as faculty cannot gain without student input. This might seem like a minor difference, but it has major implications for how we understand and facilitate what happens in our courses. If we look at the classroom from only a single angle, we cannot, by definition, have perspective. Students have, as one faculty member put it, "a line of vision that I do not," both literally and metaphorically. Adding those new, student angles of vision not only means seeing differently, it also means that faculty can act and interact differently.

c. Reconceptualization of Learning and Teaching as Collaborative Processes

We have found that when faculty transform the way they think about and practice teaching through experiencing different viewpoints, many of them reconceptualize learning and teaching as collaborative processes. Rather than thinking of teaching as something they do for or to students, and thinking of learning as something students do in response to what a course and faculty member offer, faculty begin to think of all their students as partners in both teaching and learning. This does not mean that faculty relinquish their responsibilities as experts in their fields and as an authoritative presence in the classroom, but it does mean that they have adapted their approach to teaching and their understanding of learning (Breen and Littlejohn, 2000). Indeed, it implies changes to our traditional understandings of the roles of students and faculty.

This collaborative process involves drawing on students' very different expertise and sharing the responsibility for teaching and learning with them. As we noted in Chapter 4, one faculty member commented, after collaborating with students for the first time, "[I] see students more as colleagues, more as people engaged in similar struggles to learn and grow." This new perspective reflects the shift in attitude and approach: the shift from the student-as-consumer view of learning and the sage-on-the-stage model of teaching to a conceptualization of both students and faculty members as learners as well as teachers. Taken together, these engagement outcomes represent a revision of the ways faculty think about learning and teaching.

Outcome 2: Awareness—Developing Metacognitive Awareness and a Stronger Sense of Identity

Research demonstrates a second cluster of outcomes from partnerships: both students and faculty make significant gains in developing deeper metacognitive awareness connected with a stronger sense of identity.

The importance of metacognitive awareness in learning is well established (Azevedo, 2009; Flavell, 1971, 1979; Pintrich, 2002; Underwood, 1997). Substantial evidence highlights that developing awareness of one's awareness—"thinking about one's own thinking" or "cognitions about cognitions"—can help us make better informed and more intentional decisions about practice. However, much of our understanding of what we think and do remains tacit, just underneath our conscious awareness, unless we are required to make it explicit to ourselves or to someone else. Put differently, having to articulate our thinking makes that thinking clearer and open to analysis, revision, and changed behavior; when we become aware of our thinking, we can act in more intentional and informed ways.

Partnerships between students and faculty provide a unique opportunity to develop metacognitive awareness of learning and teaching because, through dialogue, partners articulate different experiences with, and perspectives on, pedagogical practice. Through discussion of a particular learning activity or assignment, students and faculty develop greater awareness and insight into how to make that educational experience most effective.

When learners, both students and faculty, make the transition from simply enacting what is required of them to learn to consciously analyzing what constitutes and enhances that learning, they change "not just what the learner knows . . . but also who the learner is" (Dreier, 2003, in Wortham, 2004, p. 716; see also Cook-Sather, 2010). Through this change, one's sense of identity can be strengthened and intentionally pursued. Baxter Magolda (2009) calls this self-authorship, a process of actively creating a self: an identity and way of being. Students are engaged in this process all the time, and at a fast pace. They are expected to change, grow, and master all kinds of new information virtually daily. For faculty, the expectation is different. Although we are no longer formally students, many of us see ongoing learning as an integral part of our identities as teachers and scholars, even if we do not expect to change as rapidly or as thoroughly as our students do.

The process of creating a self—an identity and way of being—is the process of internally coordinating one's beliefs, values, and interpersonal loyalties rather than depending on external values, beliefs, and loyalties (Kegan, 1994). Such self-authorship is informed by three dimensions of development—(1) how we know or decide what to believe (the epistemological dimension), (2) how we view ourselves (the intrapersonal dimension), and (3) how we construct relationships with others (the interpersonal dimension)—that intertwine to contribute to self-authorship (Baxter Magolda, 2001, 2004, 2008). Students and faculty not only bring their existing complex identities and ways of being into student-faculty partnerships, but they also develop their values, beliefs, and loyalties through their partnership experiences.

In the following sections we unpack and explore this set of student outcomes in terms of

a. Developing metacognitive awareness
b. Developing a stronger sense of identity

We then mirror this exploration of student outcomes by examining faculty outcomes in terms of:

a. Developing metacognitive awareness
b. Developing a stronger sense of identity

Awareness Outcomes for Students

a. Developing Metacognitive Awareness

> "My involvement [as a student consultant] has allowed me to view the experience of learning when I am not engaged in that role [of learner] myself. If I don't understand something that the professor is explaining, I try to figure out why I don't understand it, as opposed to struggling with how to write the course content in

> *my notebook. This feeling provides a clear space for*
> *me to think about how a professor teaches and I learn,*
> *as opposed to what is being taught and learned."*
>
> Student partner

Students with the metacognitive capacity described in this quote are often our best students (Bain, 2012). And when we as faculty can step back from the day-to-day tasks to critically analyze our own teaching, we also are at our best (Bain, 2012). Through assuming an observational and analytical role and perspective toward the learning that is happening in classrooms, students and faculty develop "awareness of their awareness." As one student partner explained:

> You really don't understand the way you learn and how others learn until you can step back from it and are not in the class with the main aim to learn the material of the class but more to understand what is going on in the class and what is going through people's minds as they relate with that material.

Sambell et al. (2012) argue that opening up to students processes of critical analysis of their learning through self-assessment is a key step in the development of metacognition. The awareness that students can develop of the learning process itself, of how they are engaged, or not, in that process, and of the progress they are making through it, can make them better learners. By taking on the role of partner, students gain distance from the learning process and from "what is going through people's minds as they relate with the material." This not only creates the space for reflection but also makes it the student's responsibility to analyze learning in this way.

Gaining new perspectives within the context of their partnerships, students can apply the insights they have to their own work as learners. Across different partnership projects, students regularly describe how their critical analyses of their learning and their engagement in that learning increase because of their heightened awareness. As one student partner put it:

> As a student I am more conscious of my own goals for taking a particular class and the big cohesive ideas that emanate from the individual lessons in the class. I constantly evaluate the level to which I engage with the material I learn. I may not necessarily change my strategy for engaging with ideas, but I realize that I have become much more conscious of my level of engagement. I realize that I have become more aware of my own learning patterns.

This metacognitive awareness produces a greater capacity and inclination to become an active participant in the educational process. While this expanded perspective and empowerment are often positive, they occasionally can lead to student dissatisfaction with some educational practices; student partners sometimes report frustration in other courses: "Now that I've seen what's possible, I'm not just bored. I'm mad." In our experience, the benefits of enhanced student metacognitive awareness far outweigh the risks, but faculty need to be ready for students who are passionate and knowledgeable about teaching and learning and who want to have an impact in other courses and elsewhere in the wider university community.

b. Developing a Stronger Sense of Identity

> *"Participating in the [student-faculty partnership]*
> *program changed the way I see myself as a student*
> *and [the way I see] my professors."*
>
> Student partner

Many students who have the opportunity to work in partnership with faculty develop a sense of capacity and agency that moves them further along the path to self-authorship. When students feel disengaged, they tend to mentally check out. However, once they have experienced a deeper sense of engagement through working in partnership with faculty members, they often eschew such resignation and re-orient their approach to learning, taking steps to become the selves they want to be. As one student partner explained:

> When a class isn't working for me, instead of just resigning [myself] to the idea that it's a bad class, I work to understand why I am having a negative experience and what would need to happen to make it a positive one.

Not only has this student demonstrated the sophisticated capacity to act as an adaptive expert in her learning (Bain and Zimmerman, 2009), but she has also recognized the need to "take responsibility for crafting [her] own identity" as a student (Baxter Magolda, 2008, p. 49; Cohen et al., 2013).

The clarity students develop regarding their own role as learners, as individuals, and as social beings contributes to their developing a sense of responsibility, which informs how they participate in their own classes. These developments reflect students' changing understanding of learning and teaching as well as their stronger sense of identity, and students understand themselves differently as a result of their insights. As another student partner explained: "I feel more capable and aware as a student, and I feel more connection and compassion for my professors and the type of work they do." That is the kind of engagement we hope to see in all of our students.

Awareness Outcomes for Faculty

a. Developing Metacognitive Awareness

"What you get is looking in a mirror, only better."
Faculty partner, quoted in Cook-Sather, 2008, p. 473

Through partnership with students, faculty see themselves reflected back, but the image is inflected by the students' perspectives. The purpose of such reflection is not to replace faculty members' perspectives or authority with students' perspectives or displace students' respect for faculty expertise. Rather, the goal is to bring all perspectives into student-faculty relationships in ways that make them explicit, through articulating them to ourselves and to our student partners. The insights and action that follow may be reaffirmation of existing practices or revisions of those practices, but in either case, they are more informed and intentional: students and faculty have a clearer sense of what they are doing and why.

Faculty describe how, through working in partnership with students, they develop a greater awareness of their pedagogical goals, an enhanced ability to analyze those goals, and an increased capacity to name what they intend and how they strive to achieve it. The raised awareness that faculty develop through dialogue with their student partners leads directly, as one faculty member put it, to being "better able to point out and articulate (to myself or others) what is and is not working the way I want" (Cook-Sather, 2011a, p. 35). Faculty members clarify their sense of themselves as teachers through partnership with students. The combination of what is familiar and what might be new or surprising prompts faculty to develop what one faculty member called his own "3rd person perspective" (Cook-Sather, 2011b, p. 34), a more distanced and more informed perception of his practice.

b. Developing a Stronger Sense of Identity

> I have not merely transferred my habits and comportment in my disciplinary research to my teaching, I have successfully eliminated any distinction between the two domains and the research I do in both (Manor et al., 2010, p. 9).

The preceding quote is from Stephen Bloch-Schulman, a faculty member at Elon University, who writes about how his work with students as partners helped him to eliminate the distinction between teaching and research domains that often causes significant stress for faculty members. As he describes, one of the most important ways that partnership can support the strengthening of faculty identity is through at once affirming and challenging faculty members' sense of who they are and how those selves interact with and affect students.

At first, faculty may find this shift in awareness to be highly uncomfortable. One faculty member, for example, who self-identifies as white and was working in her partnership with a student of color on creating a more culturally responsive classroom, reflected on how her student partner's "highlighting of the issue of how I bring myself into the classroom made me conscious of myself in an unaccustomed and uneasy way." That kind of uncertainty and instability in your identity as a teacher might tempt you to retreat to familiar ways of being. But one of the benefits of student-faculty partnership is that such increases in metacognitive awareness can be supported and affirmed by student partners, allowing faculty to embrace rather than avoid ambiguity. As this faculty member realized, through dialogue with her student partner, she "needed to not only be myself but to name and claim that self in terms of a privileged social location but with active, forward-moving recognition rather than effacement or guilt" (Cook-Sather and Agu, 2012). In other words, she needed to acknowledge and embrace her identity as a privileged white woman but to do so in a way that allowed her to move ahead without needing to apologize or feel guilty for who she is. Such naming and claiming her classroom identity is a change not only to what the teacher knows but also who she is; it is a strengthening of that self.

One of the most important identities we have as faculty is that of scholar. Most of us maintain research programs and publish our findings. While many faculty with whom the three of us have worked experience their identities as teachers to be in conflict with their identities as scholars, we have found that student-faculty partnerships can help to reduce, or at least soften, this tension.

Like Stephen Bloch-Schulman, many faculty we have interviewed comment that partnership in their teaching made them better scholars as well, helping them to integrate the various dimensions of their professional identity.

Outcome #3: Enhancement—Improving Teaching and Classroom Experiences

---

"Participant enthusiasm and motivation was no-ticeable within the classroom where students were animated and keen to discuss the findings of their [collaborative] evaluation exercises."

Faculty partner quoted in Bovill et al., 2010

"My experience as a student consultant has provided me with more critical thinking towards my other classes. I pay more attention to my professors' teach-ing styles and adjust my own learning accordingly."

Student partner

This third cluster of outcomes emerges from the previous two. When engagement, motivation, and learning are deepened, and when faculty and students develop greater metacognitive awareness and a stronger sense of their identities, teaching and classroom experiences are enhanced.

In the following sections, we describe how students

a. Become more active as learners
b. Gain insight into faculty members' pedagogical intentions
c. Take more responsibility for learning.

We then move to examine how, as a result of their partnerships with students, faculty consistently describe

    a. A deeper understanding of students' experiences and needs

    b. A reconceptualization of students as colleagues

Enhancement Outcomes for Students

—————

"I ask myself what I could do differently to improve my own classroom experience, rather than complaining about the professor or the course in general."

                                 Student partner

—————

Through their partnerships with faculty members, students rethink their roles as learners, becoming more aware of classroom dynamics and the effect of their own participation. As they come to understand the diversity of learners in the classroom, they recognize the ways that faculty might try to engage those diverse learners and become, as one student put it, "a bit more patient" with the professor and classmates. This shift in attitude is characterized by some student partners as becoming "more conscientious." This active, engaged, and more responsible approach improves the classroom experience for students and teachers.

a. Becoming More Active as Learners

Through partnerships, students develop approaches to their studies that make them a joy to teach—and learning becomes more joyful for them. Blair Kaufer, a Western Washington University undergraduate, describes the energy and drive he developed through collaborating with faculty and staff through the Teaching and Learning Academy. He asserts that he has "become a more adventuresome learner—eager to investigate new territory" (Werder et al., 2012, p. 36) as a result of participating in regular dialogue with faculty. He explains that by this he means he has a "yearning for investigative learning" and the confidence to say, "'Hey, I don't know this, but I want to,' and then persevere until I do" (Werder et al., 2012, p. 36). Such a shift in orientation and such critical self-examination constitutes a radical rethinking of what it means to be a student in college or university. Kaufer is not willing to sit passively through his education; instead, he is actively engaged in learning—seeking out opportunities to be engaged and developing the confidence necessary for that quest.

b. Gaining Insight into Faculty Members' Pedagogical Intentions

Through their dialogue with faculty, students learn about the challenges we face as teachers. As one student explained: "I think my partnership has showed some of the difficulties of being a professor/teacher." By multiplying their own angles of vision, students are better able to discern and analyze professors' pedagogical intentions and the reasons that we as faculty do what we do. As one student partner put it, "[I now am] much more aware of the work behind the scenes for creating lessons." This makes students much more empathetic toward the work and experiences of teachers. Some students even describe becoming "teacher advocates"—they defend faculty when other students complain, asking, "What have you done to improve your own learning?" One student in a study of student-faculty partnerships in sociology even stated, "I am glad that I am not, nor will I ever be, a teacher/professor, because deciding what to do, when to do it, and when items need to be turned in is very difficult" (Gibson, 2011, p. 98). These new perspectives and commitments allow students to develop greater confidence, capacity, and agency as learners (Cook-Sather 2010, 2011a, 2013b). That confidence translates into increased motivation and engagement (Little et al., 2011; Sambell and Graham, 2011), and these benefits transfer from the partnership into other student courses and experiences in higher education.

c. Taking More Responsibility for Learning

When students become more active and aware, when they reconceptualize learning and teaching as collaborative processes (as we explained earlier in this chapter), they assume considerable responsibility for their own learning. Faculty often lament that students are too passive, that they do not seek help when they need it, and that they need to take more initiative. Collaborating with faculty members in explorations of teaching and learning helps students build the capacity and confidence to do all of those things. One student captures what virtually all student partners assert: "Participation in this program has really made me feel more responsible for my own education." By "responsible," students mean that "it is up to the entire community to make learning spaces function, so that means students have just as much responsibility as professors." The productive sense of obligation and accountability inspired by student-faculty partnerships carries over into students' work across other courses.

When students become more reflective about their learning, they are more likely to think about their responsibilities as students. As one student partner put it, "I've started thinking about ways I can help make the discussions better for everyone in the class, including the professor, instead of just for me." This shift away from a focus on "just for me" is a highly significant one, countering a tendency some faculty worry about—that students are being driven toward an increasingly self-absorbed consumer mentality. Students positioned as partners not only perceive, but also embrace, the possibility of working collaboratively with faculty and other students to make classrooms and online spaces into places of engaged and meaningful learning for their own and others' benefit.

Enhancement Outcomes for Faculty

> *"I am more committed to creating a classroom environment for collaboration and teacher as learner. To create an open transactional classroom like that, you have to really redefine your role, really redefine."*
>
> Faculty partner

While improvement in classroom teaching and learning does not happen overnight, there are many reasons that you might be inclined or impelled toward partnership in the hopes of such improvement. Some faculty participate in partnerships with students after they realize that a particular course or program is not as effective as it could or should be. Students might be learning in superficial ways, skimming across the surface rather than diving deeply into the material; or students might be engaging just enough to get by, satisfying the basic requirements without committing to their learning. At other times, faculty initiate partnerships because a class feels broken and they want to reinvent it from the ground up. Still others find external pressures, such as institutional priorities or changes in the higher education landscape, to be a catalyst to move toward partnership. Others may hold strong views about the importance of creating democratic classrooms.

Whatever the motives, many faculty report that working in partnership with students helps them improve their practice. The partnership process allows them to see the familiar with new eyes by giving them access to student experiences in the classroom. We have already discussed the ways in which faculty gain new perspectives through dialogue with students, but here we want to emphasize how this specifically improves classroom experiences. In partnership, faculty members can make teaching decisions that are informed by evidence from their students because they gain understandings and insights from discussing their own and students' perspectives on classroom experiences. In other words, faculty do not need to guess what students are experiencing and understanding; they are in dialogue with students about those things.

These revisions improve their teaching and positively affect the classroom experience for them and for their students, expanding the teaching strategies faculty use to engage students (Sorenson, 2001; Werder and Otis, 2010). The dialogue in which student and faculty partners engage provides a forum for reflection and analysis that is often otherwise missing from our daily lives as teachers (Cook-Sather, 2008, 2011, 2013b). Some faculty also strive to create more democratic classrooms (Hutchings and Huber, 2010; Manor et al., 2010) in which partnership is practiced as the norm.

a. Becoming More Reflective and Responsive

Being reflective "encompasses both the capacity for critical inquiry and for self-reflection" (Larrivee, 2000, p. 294), but in higher education, opportunities for reflection are not generally built into the "structure of teaching" (Elbaz, 1987, p. 45; Felten et al., 2013). Many faculty lament the lack of time and opportunity to contemplate their teaching approaches and discuss them with colleagues. Indeed, in the absence of opportunities to reflect on our "knowledge in action" (Schön, 1987, p. 12), we run the risk of "relying on routinized teaching" and "not developing as a teacher or as a person" (Reiman and Thies-Sprinthall, 1998, p. 262; see also Hunt, 2007; Klenowski, Askew, and Carnell, 2006; Zeichner and Liston, 1987).

The traditional notion of reflective practice has the practitioner tacking between analysis of assumptions, on the one hand, and how those apply in practice, on the other (Imel, 1992). Working toward a more dynamic notion of reflection, Lesnick (2005) uses the image of a "mirror in motion" to argue for "an understanding of reflection that admits of ongoing movement, change, and interaction, so that 'success' in reflective practice is a matter of agility, mobility, flexibility, and, importantly, of the interdependence of one's movements with those of others on and beyond the reflected scene" (p. 38). Integrating students into the "cycle of interpretation and action" (Rodgers, 2002) that constitutes reflective practice provides participants with a unique forum within which to access and revise their assumptions, engage in reflective discourse, and take action in their work (Cook-Sather, 2008, 2011a; Lawler 2003; Merriam, Caffarella, and Baumgartner 2006; Mezirow, 1991).

Roxå and Mårtensson (2009; 2013) demonstrate that academic departments that produce the greatest student learning outcomes tend to engage in more dialogue about learning and teaching than other departments do. Such dialogue requires and inspires reflection. We suggest extending the idea that dialogue about learning and teaching can be beneficial to university departments, by suggesting that these dialogues could be enriched further by including students as meaningful contributors and partners within these conversations and reflections.

Partnership provides a focused forum for reflection and analysis that can create space and time for critical reflection on teaching and learning. One faculty member explained that her student consultant "asked me each week what I would like her to pay attention to, forcing me to constantly ask myself what I was working on in my teaching practice." She therefore had to think more carefully about those pedagogical practices herself. She explained that "it felt like the difference between working out on your own, and working out while your coach is observing you to provide feedback: it kept me focused." The intensified focus on pedagogical practice that student-faculty partnerships afford allow faculty to perceive and respond to student experiences that otherwise might remain invisible. One faculty member asserted that his student partner "alerted me to students' confusion, affirmed and/or challenged my choices of activities, and helped me identify the pedagogical practices that worked, even for the most withdrawn students."

b. Creating More Democratic Classrooms in which Partnership Is the Norm

Prompted by heightened awareness of the issues in teaching and learning that are of importance to students, faculty think "about classroom collaboration in more democratic and self-directed ways" (Manor et al., 2010, p. 9). By answering Hutchings and Huber's (in Werder and Otis, 2010) call for "shared responsibility for learning among students and teachers" (p. xii), faculty partners come to understand and approach students as colleagues. They acknowledge that students challenge them to consider issues they might not have identified themselves: "Many of [the questions I ask now] I would not have asked were it not for students' voices and students' collaboration with me" (Manor et al., 2010, p. 9).

They see themselves and students as partners in a "pedagogy of mutual engagement" (Thiessen, 2010); that is, teachers and learners together engaged in "intellectual collaboration" (Selover and Miller-Lane, 2011). Although we acknowledged in Chapter 3 that faculty often make a range of decisions prior to student involvement, such as which students to invite into partnership (Bovill, 2013a; Heron, 1992), if we are serious about creating democratic classrooms we should aim to invite students into partnership as early as possible within decision-making processes.

This shift in how faculty conceptualize and work with students can be seen in the language faculty use to describe their work with students. A common change in attitude and approach is signaled by a shift from "me" and "them" to "we" and "us" in the ways that faculty describe their interactions with students. For instance, one faculty member explained: "I have always strived to adjust course content and process to match student interests and needs, but I had always seen that as a process of *me* adjusting things for *them*." As a result of his partnership with a student consultant, however, this faculty member realized that he had begun to think about his course in a more collaborative way: "I was thinking about building the course *with* the students, as partners" (Bovill et al., 2011; Cook-Sather, 2009b, 2013b).

The shift in prepositions that this faculty member highlights— from "for" to "with"—also embodies the shift that partnership entails (Fine et al., 2007; Cook-Sather, 2006, 2013b). Faculty and students who partner to explore educational practices reconceptualize learning and teaching as collaborative processes, as reciprocal engagement and learning. Taking up this more collaborative approach does not constitute an abrogation of responsibility or a complete loss of control on the faculty member's part. As one faculty partner explained: "'It doesn't mean that you are giving over control of the course. But there are elements of the classroom that we are co-responsible for, that we are travelling through together'" (Cook-Sather and Alter, 2011, p. 48).

This set of enhancement outcomes highlights a significant shift in student and faculty thinking and practice. In short, partnership prompts students to be more conscious of and more intentional about the teaching and learning process, helping them to become better students. They come to see themselves as part of a learning community rather than individuals looking out only for themselves. This shift, coupled with faculty members' expanded awareness and more reflective and intentional approach to their teaching and their embrace of more democratic notions and practices, leads to enhanced teaching and classroom experiences.

Outcomes of Partnership for Programs and Institutions

"This was a transformative experience; it re-connected me with my love of, and investment in teaching; recharged my understanding of the connections between the classroom, my scholarship, and my work as a member of my college community; and reawakened my faith in the potential academic institutions have to be sites of innovative and vital work for all who are part of the community."

Faculty partner

"I was really surprised to realize how much more connected I feel to [the college] now that I have interacted with the community in a new and very different way . . . than a regular student usually would. I also feel like I have contributed something to the school as well and done my best to help future teachers and learners on the campus. I'm no longer just a student who takes classes here."

Student partner

Partnerships, even when not part of an institutional program, often make participants feel part of the larger campus community in new ways. Faculty and students describe being reconnected, reanimated, even transformed, by partnership work. Feeling such an integral part of the community inspires students and faculty alike to embrace more democratic approaches and to see teaching and learning as shared responsibilities within individual classrooms. It also inspires them to create these cultural norms across the institution.

Many colleges and universities aim to develop citizenship skills and democratic capacities in their students (Smith, Nowacek, and Bernstein, 2010). While faculty and institutions have developed a variety of effective practices in their efforts to reach this aim, student-faculty partnerships are an important, and often missing, piece in this puzzle. Stefani (1998) points out that "an educational process that is so determined by others cannot seriously intend to have as its outcome a person who is truly self-determining, self-motivated and committed to becoming a lifelong autonomous learner" (p. 340). Partnership work, however, gives students an opportunity to engage in democratic practices as well as democratic ways of being. Barnett (1997) has argued that it is crucial for students in higher education to engage in critical thinking, as well as understanding themselves critically and learning to act critically. He sees these elements as contributing to the realization of "critical being." This concept aligns well with many of the experiences described by students and faculty in the quotes we have included from a range of student-faculty partnership approaches.

For some faculty, the particular subject that they teach aligns well with the goal of reconfiguring the student-faculty relationship to become more democratic and less hierarchical. For example, colleagues teaching concepts such as citizenship, politics, and social justice often find that shifting their teaching approach toward a model of student-faculty partnerships is more congruent with the concepts they are teaching than more traditional, didactic forms of instruction. Similarly, many colleagues in educational disciplines such as those providing initial teacher education programs often find student-faculty partnerships a useful way of modeling alternative approaches to course design and student-faculty relationships.

Some faculty come to student-faculty partnerships with a strong desire to create more democratic learning and teaching spaces. Often this group of faculty have been influenced by the work of critical theorists (such as Freire, 1970, and Habermas, 1974), feminists (such as Maher, 2001, and Orner, 1992), advocates of student voice (such as Cook-Sather 2002b, 2006, Fielding 2004, and Rudduck, 2007), and advocates of critical pedagogy (such as Darder et al., 2003, Giroux, 1983, and Rogers and Freiberg, 1969). This broad-ranging critical literature informs the belief that students should have the opportunity to play a meaningful role in their own learning.

If you embrace one or more of these perspectives, you might be compelled by the "radical collegiality" that supports students as "agents in the process of transformative learning" (Fielding, 1999, p. 22). This is a model through which teachers learn "with and from" students "through processes of co-constructed, collaborative work" (Fielding, 2006, p. 311; see also Healey, 2012). Such an approach recognizes that students and teachers acting as partners "demonstrate essential skills for citizenship" (Manor et al., 2010, p. 12; see also Nussbaum, 1997). It also implies a change from often accepted teaching and learning practices where students tend to be subordinate to expert faculty. Instead, this approach implies a reenvisaging of students as agents and actors with relevant, meaningful, and diverse contributions and views that can ultimately transform learning into something more meaningful for individuals and the communities in which they live.

Student-faculty partnership programs have the potential to shift the culture of higher education toward a more collaborative, democratic context. Although as Shor (1996) noted, "Democratic practices in one classroom do not mean that school and society have been democratized" (p. 220), small-scale partnerships can help establish the foundation for more systematic change. Faculty who have participated in student-faculty partnerships that are part of larger programs regularly note seeing this work influence the culture and practices of their institutions. For instance, Barnes et al. (2011) describe student-faculty partnerships focused on developing inquiry-based learning resources at the University of Manchester and the University of Sheffield. They reported students gaining a better understanding of the university and their place within the university community through taking part in this work. Others talk of students becoming aware of their potential to become more active and meaningful contributors to the university academic community (Sambell and Graham, 2011). And Tierney (2008) reports her students' surprise that at a conference where they presented findings from their student-faculty partnership work, professors were asking them questions—a situation that provoked them to reconsider their identities as students and as members of an academic research community.

Once students realize their views matter and that they have valuable contributions to make within colleges and universities, they become more empowered and fuller members of our extended higher education community. There are both challenges and benefits in embracing the changes that come with partnership and with more engaged participation in the educational project. One student partner captured the challenge this way: "The risk of changing is that you constantly have to let go of what you previously believed to be true, causing yourself to know less before you know more." In crossing the threshold that student-faculty partnerships present (Cook-Sather, 2013a; King and Felten, 2012; Werder et al., 2012), this student illustrates a deep understanding of learning and engagement, not just partnership work. It is important to create opportunities for students to gain this significant insight into lifelong learning. There is little within the structures of higher education that supports coming to this kind of understanding and embracing this kind of change: "The [partnership] program allows students to take risks because it isn't directly associated with grades, and as we un-learn within the context of being a consultant, we learn to be less rigid and more human—really more democratic."

Faculty also embrace becoming more engaged, more human, and more democratic, both individually and institutionally. Like the student quoted above, a faculty participant in the same program asserted that the program is making "a profound difference to the level of awareness at the college, of pedagogy, of roles, of possibilities, and also to the teaching and learning going on in all kinds of spaces here." This faculty member sees long-term implications, suggesting that as more members of the college community participate in the program, "it will really change the language and content of our conversations here about what it means to teach and learn in and across our disciplines at the college."

These benefits that include changing mindsets among students and faculty have exciting and powerful potential to enable transformation of how higher education is conceptualized. Where these changes take place in the context of a department or an institution supportive of a democratic view of classroom practices and supportive of students taking greater responsibility for their learning in a university, there is potential for significant change to some of the underlying assumptions politicians and policymakers often have about the purpose of higher education. In this new vision, knowledge construction takes place not just in ivory towers, and not simply for economic impact, but also within new collective spaces where faculty and students' ideas and voices are acted upon in ways that create divergent forms of knowledge, new perspectives, and value to pedagogical practices.

This changing of mindsets and philosophy is also an encouraging indicator of the potential for sustainable change within an institution. Larger-scale program outcomes enable others to see what is possible and so have a further sustaining effect. Barnes et al. (2011) describe their student interns becoming key facilitators of new partnerships and thereby contributing to the sustainability of partnership work institutionally. They describe students moving into this facilitative role while, "at the same time, students have retained their 'expertise' as a student, allowing them to form a bridge between [faculty] and the wider student body" (p. 27).

Conclusion

To address the question of why faculty, students, and institutions should consider creating student-faculty partnerships, we have combined references to research literature on teaching and learning with discussion of several interrelated sets of outcomes for students and faculty who engage in partnerships. We have attempted to show how partnership work between students and faculty can be transformative although, and because, it is profoundly challenging to "the inherited routines of academic life" (Hutchings et al., 2011, p. 6). We feel that the themes that we have surfaced through our research—enhancing engagement, motivation, and learning; developing metacognitive awareness and a stronger sense of identity; and improving teaching and the classroom experience—are compelling enough to warrant taking student-faculty partnerships seriously as a way to strengthen and improve teaching and learning in higher education. But as we have stated previously, partnership is no panacea, and this work presents profound challenges, both to individuals and to institutions. It is to those challenges that we turn in the next chapter.

6

The Challenges of
Student-Faculty Partnerships

In the previous chapter, we provided evidence of the benefits of student-faculty partnership. In this chapter, we focus on some of the potential difficulties of partnership. A number of cautions are worth emphasizing when considering both individual efforts and larger-scale implementation of student-faculty partnerships. Of course, challenging the typical power dynamics within a classroom can be unsettling for all involved. Challenging traditional institutional structures and the power dynamics embedded within them can also be a daunting prospect. As you approach or create partnerships, we recommend that you

- Be aware of student and faculty vulnerability

- Consider in particular underrepresented students and faculty members

- Be careful and intentional regarding the language you use to describe partnership

- Directly address power issues

- Start small

- Be wary of adopting student-faculty partnership processes and programs uncritically

- Keep in mind institutional contexts and larger constraints

- Do not assume that all students and faculty will embrace a partnership model

Be Aware of Student and Faculty Vulnerability

As advocates of student voice in elementary and secondary settings have argued, we should be careful not to use students in disingenuous and manipulative ways (Fielding, 2004; Fine et al., 2007; Lodge, 2005; Thiessen, 1997). Both students and teachers who work in pre-college classrooms have cautioned against the ways in which students' voices are sometimes elicited but then ignored. This can happen, for instance, when a well-intentioned faculty member initiates a partnership project but then is unable to sustain it. In other cases, students are invited—and may feel coerced—to support a particular practice or agenda. This is a greater danger to students before college, when education is more strictly regulated by state and national standards, but it is also a possibility in higher education. Partnership approaches that do not have at their core the principles of respect, reciprocity, and shared responsibility run the risk of reproducing the ways in which students are already vulnerable in higher education.

However, students are not the only vulnerable individuals in any partnership. Many faculty experience significant challenges in their roles, particularly when they are in part–time, pre–tenure, or non–tenure track appointments. Even those of us who are fortunate enough to have stable, long-term positions may sometimes feel overwhelmed by the many people offering us advice and demanding our time. Adding student voices to that chorus may seem especially problematic, since doing so introduces new and potentially competing claims on our work. As we have indicated, within the partnership model as we advocate it, we do not see student voices drowning out faculty voices but rather engaging in dialogue with them. Indeed, we agree with Cousin (2010) that "we need a restoration of dignity for academic teachers by placing them alongside students and educational researchers rather than above or below them" (p. 6).

Consider in Particular Underrepresented Students and Faculty Members

Underrepresented students and faculty may be at particular risk for being left out of student-faculty partnership efforts if they are overlooked by those who run such programs or if they feel that, as with many structures and opportunities in higher education, these projects do not speak to their interests or needs (Felten et al., 2013). A good deal of anecdotal, and some published, evidence suggests that certain student voices are privileged while others are marginalized in partnership projects (McIntyre et al., 2005; Robinson and Taylor, 2007).

One example that illustrates this marginalization can be seen in the case of faculty of color, who are still underrepresented and often inequitably treated in many higher education contexts (Cook and Córdova, 2006; Fries-Britt et al., 2011; Patitu and Hinton, 2003), despite efforts to recruit more faculty of color for reasons of equity and for their important contributions to undergraduate education (Umbach, 2006). Partnership opportunities and programs have the potential to be "counter-spaces" for underrepresented students and faculty—spaces "where deficit notions of people of color can be challenged and where a positive collegiate racial climate can be established and maintained" (Solórzano, Ceja, and Yosso, 2000, p. 70; see also Solórzano et al., 2005). Such spaces can be "central to student empowerment and faculty learning" (Cook-Sather and Agu, 2013, p. 273) if they are intentionally structured in this way.

Be Careful and Intentional Regarding the Language You Use to Describe This Work

We strongly recommend that you give careful consideration to the language you use to describe and to invite people into partnership. Our often unconscious use of certain terms can send unintended but unfortunate messages to students and faculty alike about what the work is about. For instance, if you talk about "giving students voice" and "using" students as consultants, you may convey a message that students have voice only when we as faculty bestow it upon them and that students are a means to an end. We suggest, instead, using phrases like "seeking student perspectives on questions of teaching and learning" or "inviting students to consult on approaches to pedagogical practice" or "collaborating with students to design courses." These terms still indicate that faculty have more power and agency than students—we are doing the seeking, the inviting, and often the grading—but at least the intention is to work in partnership.

Paying close attention to our language need not be debilitating; you might invite students to collaborate with you to develop the most appropriate way to describe your work together. Some students and faculty, for instance, find "partnership" too formal a word, so they choose to call themselves a "team" or a "planning group" or some other label that resonates in a particular context.

Whatever language you use, we urge you to try to avoid communicating unintentional messages or reinforcing existing hierarchical and unequal dynamics. We are not suggesting that differences of power and position can be eliminated easily—or sometimes, at all; rather, we are suggesting that these differences be acknowledged and that by choosing language carefully in ways that convey respect, reciprocity, and shared responsibility, we can begin to question and change existing structures that separate and alienate faculty and students.

Address Power Issues

These points evoke what might be the most critical dimension of this work: the complicating of traditional power dynamics in higher education. We advocate striving to find a balance of participation, power, and perspective. As we have asserted previously, collaboration between students and faculty does not require a false equivalency, nor does it mean placing students higher than faculty; instead, it means that the perspectives and contributions made by partners are appropriately valued and respected. This is relatively simple to state, yet it can be vexing to enact. Kothari (2001) claims that often "participatory approaches simplify highly complicated social relations. Thus participatory techniques can conceal inequalities and in certain circumstances reify them" (p. 152). Kothari's warning reminds us that power can be exerted within and among groups that are considered powerless or marginal, even though we often focus on the power being exerted by more privileged and powerful groups. Treating students as a homogenous group is dangerous as it blinds us to the complex interrelationships and power dynamics within groups of students.

As partnerships unfold, participants will find themselves negotiating concerns and conflicts that arise. Let's say, for example, a faculty member has entered into partnership with students to design a final exam for her course. In the past, she has used in-class essay tests because she believes that this approach best develops the learning skills that students will need in subsequent courses and professionally. The group of students with whom she has partnered, however, voice strong opposition to this approach, arguing that take-home essays both develop their skills in more lasting ways and are more realistic. Through dialogue and negotiation, this faculty member and her students might agree that they will have both forms of assessment or a single exam that has both components. Neither the faculty member nor the students simply assert power or succumb to the other's beliefs.

As we have indicated already, we recognize that teaching and course design have tended to be viewed as the domain of faculty, and consequently faculty are often responsible for creating opportunities for partnership (Bourner, 2004; Bovill, 2013a; Heron, 1992). This is a key acknowledgment because it emphasizes that partnership may rely on faculty motivations for initiating and pursuing collaboration with students. It also implies that as individual faculty, you may have to develop ways of working on course design or teaching that are new or unfamiliar to both you and your students. The nature of partnership is then also dependent upon how you conceptualize the idea of a partner. Indeed, some forms of partnership might still feel impositional rather than empowering to students (see Tabak, 2011).

When students are involved in faculty research, for instance, typically the faculty member's agenda dominates, although students benefit from being mentored and may well contribute in significant ways to the research. In this type of relationship, faculty and students are not partners, although they collaborate. In a meaningful partnership model, students and faculty would generate research questions together and engage cooperatively, or at least actively, in the research, analysis, and presentation process. Consequently students and faculty will learn different things from this experience that are individually significant as well as experiencing shared learning from collaboratively constructing and discovering new knowledge.

Start Small

As we have noted elsewhere, it is important to start small. Whether you are at an institution that fosters a culture of partnership or not, and whether you have experienced partnership work in the past or not, we recommend that you begin with a modest effort and allow time for the partnership to grow in depth and breadth. Because there will be surprises, good and bad, and because collaboration is more complex and demanding than solitary endeavors, give yourself and your partners time and opportunity to take manageable steps. If you go too far too fast from the outset, you may set yourself and others up for failure, disappointment, and aversion to future efforts.

Be Careful of Adopting Student-Faculty Partnership Processes and Programs Uncritically

As with anything related to teaching and learning, we caution you to be careful not to adopt processes and programs uncritically. Sometimes when initiatives have worked well on a small scale, we make assumptions about their potential for translation into larger-scale approaches. Similarly, when we see a colleague or another campus have success with a particular model, we are tempted to hop on the bandwagon. The complex and nuanced nature of student-faculty partnerships in different contexts requires deliberation and adaptation, rather than assuming a "one size fits all" approach. Even in programs or institutions where student-faculty partnerships are widely practiced or formally sanctioned, homogenization of pedagogical or partnership approaches is neither possible nor desirable.

Also, it's important that we are reflective about our own practices over time, checking to see whether we have fallen into bad habits about the levels of partnership we are facilitating, the language we are using, and which students are involved. In addition, we benefit from thinking regularly about our motivations for our partnership work. Why have we chosen to work with a certain group of students? Why do we focus our partnership on these questions or topics? Why do we see some elements of learning and teaching as nonnegotiable? Maintaining this critical stance makes us more likely to enact forms of partnership that are meaningful and inclusive. As Cooke (2001) highlights, "participatory processes never take place in an ideological vacuum. What is seen as a positive outcome from a participatory process, indeed what effectiveness means, will depend on an ideological position" (p. 119).

Keep in Mind Institutional Context and Larger Constraints

Another consideration is that institutional contexts vary widely in their receptivity to revisions of inherited routines and their capacity to support change. As Taylor (2001) asserts, "Participation can be used as a commodity or 'formula' by agencies which can be marketed as part of a corporate image to assist with reputation building" (p. 136). However, in other institutions, senior faculty and administrators conceptualize partnership in more meaningful ways. Colleges and universities that have a strong teaching mission often provide fertile ground for student-faculty partnership. Perhaps unexpectedly, research-intensive universities also have many areas where this kind of work can flourish, emerging from centers, institutes, or programs that focus on cultivating students as citizens or researchers, or developing students' graduate attributes, such as investigative, inquiring, and problem-solving skills. In some contexts, other faculty create space for pedagogical experimentation, or teaching and learning centers support innovative and effective practices.

In addition, forces outside higher education shape what seems possible on campus; in some places, such as Ontario in Canada, Scotland, and Northern Ireland, there is a growing public interest in student representation and student voice within primary and secondary schools and in university governance systems. These arguments are often based upon the notion of students' right to have their voices heard alongside faculty within university decision-making structures (Lundy, 2007). While we welcome these initiatives, partnership is too significant to be limited to student representation on committees and through the brokerage of student unions. This can be seen in the recent UK National Union of

Students Manifesto on Partnerships, where claims are made that student unions are core to understanding partnership, and student representation is considered the only real form of collective action and democracy (NUS, 2012). Student representation is a crucial element of student voice and partnership work, and in many contexts student unions play a significant role in student-faculty partnerships, but this perspective misses the enormous potential for partnership between students and faculty in diverse teaching and learning contexts.

Do Not Assume That All Students and Faculty Will Embrace a Partnership Model

Finally, even if we as faculty are eager to enter into pedagogical partnerships, students may have their own reservations. Some students seem particularly eager to explore partnerships, seeing them as an essential component of their education. Others might be hesitant or even resistant, expressing discomfort with the new demands that partnership places on them or wondering if this approach is a distraction from their primary goals at the college or university. We need to acknowledge that many students will be new to the idea of student-faculty partnerships and they may not have clear ideas to contribute to discussions and negotiations on the first day. Students, like faculty, will need time to adjust to what student-faculty partnerships are and the range of partnerships that might be possible. In the same way that some faculty will be resistant to engage with the idea of partnerships, so some students are also likely to be resistant to partnerships. We need to be careful in our partnership work. Kothari warns "there is an implicit notion of deviancy for those who choose not to participate" (2001, p. 148). So although we may want to share our enthusiasm for student-faculty partnerships and the compelling outcomes we have experienced and witnessed, it is essential to respect our student and faculty colleagues who choose not to participate.

Conclusion

Keeping in mind the benefits we outlined in Chapter 5 and challenges we have now outlined in this chapter, you may be ready to start thinking about participating in a student-faculty partnership or extending the partnership in which you are already engaged. The following chapter provides guiding principles and recommendations for concrete practices that can support you in experiencing the outcomes we have described here and also help you avoid, or at least address in an informed way, the potential challenges of partnership.

7

Practical Strategies for Developing Student-Faculty Partnerships

*"Come in with an open mind about how much you
can change your perspective, but do not get hung
up on a perceived need for a radical change in your
pedagogy: one of the most valuable things about
this work for me has not necessarily been learning
completely new ideas, but rather forcing me to think
through, articulate, refine, and put into a stronger
framework the techniques I have in place."*

—Faculty member

As the examples we included in Chapters 3 and 4 illustrate, student-faculty partnerships take many forms and can lead to a wide range of outcomes, from affirming techniques you already use to making minor changes or even totally revising pedagogical approaches. This chapter outlines practical strategies for starting and sustaining partnerships.

As you think about the nitty-gritty of this work, you might find it helpful to envision student participation as a ladder or continuum (see for example Bovill and Bulley, 2011, ladder of student participation in curriculum design in Appendix I). For instance, one end of a continuum might be anchored in full-scale collaboration across an entire course or program, while the other end rests on students being invited to make a meaningful choice about an element of a course, such as which reading or topic they would like to explore in more depth. A continuum like this is not intended to imply progress in moving from one end to the other, but rather describes some of the ways partnership can be practiced in different contexts. As you think about this work in your own circumstances, you may want to locate yourself in one place or another on that continuum, or you might start in one place for one course and in another spot for a different course. However you choose to think about your work, keep in mind the options that are available to you by shifting your orientation one way or the other.

In this chapter, we offer concrete strategies that we set out in three sections:

1. Getting started with student-faculty partnerships
2. Sustaining and deepening student-faculty partnership practices
3. Negotiating roles and power within partnerships

If you would like to see how two well-established partnership programs frame their guiding principles and general strategies, we have included as appendices statements from Bryn Mawr College in the United States (Appendix II) and the University of Exeter in the United Kingdom (Appendix III). The first of those, Bryn Mawr's Students as Learners and Teachers (SaLT) program, which we have discussed previously, supports semester-long, student-faculty partnerships focused on explorations of pedagogical practice undertaken while the course is being taught. The second, Exeter's Students as Change Agents program, which we presented in Chapter 4, focuses on developing student-led learning and teaching research projects across different disciplines and practices (e.g., using technology with large and diverse cohorts of students).

In Chapter 1 we discussed the guiding principles—respect, reciprocity, and shared responsibility—that we believe should inform all student-faculty partnerships. To help you keep these guiding principles in mind as you consider and undertake practical approaches to partnership work, you might ask yourself the following questions periodically:

- Is mutual respect central to my partnership with students?

- Is our partnership unfolding in a way that we are both/ all putting something meaningful into it and getting something meaningful out of it?

- Are we all being responsible to the other participants with whom we are working?

In the following sections, we offer concrete strategies that are infused with these principles.

Getting Started with Student-Faculty Partnerships

Some people will jump into the deep end right away, but most of us begin more slowly, wading in and getting used to the water as we go. If you are ready to dip your toe into partnerships, then this section can serve as your guide as you get started.

Getting Started Strategy 1: Start Small

Because student-faculty partnerships can be exciting and also sometimes overwhelming, starting small is both practical and prudent. Think of this as a long-term orientation rather than a quick fix. Begin with an approach that seems manageable in your particular context. Can you readily identify people or situations that seem open to partnership? For instance, you might consider expanding your current approach to gathering and responding to student feedback, integrating students into the process of collecting and making sense of that information, or collaboratively acting on the outcomes of this feedback. Or you might develop a partnership in one section of a course by, for example, inviting upper-level undergraduates or graduate students to decide the topics of study during several weeks late in the term. Or after a course is complete, you might sit down with a few former students to discuss possible revisions for the next time you will teach the course. While these might seem like baby steps lacking the benefits of full partnership, they can help you develop the expertise, and also the courage, necessary for you to extend the level of partnership with students, as suggested by the metaphors of "continuum" and "ladder" (see Appendix I).

> "My student consultant provided plenty of positive reinforcement (which was great, very empowering) and identified a couple of issues to work on and watch out for in the future. It's funny, it is so easy to think that only negative criticism will suggest change… but that really isn't true. Having something that works pointed out is just as effective, since it can lead you to think, 'Oh, I should do that more!' or, 'How can I work that into future classes/discussions?'"
>
> —Faculty partner

Getting Started Strategy 2: Be Patient

However well you prepare for student-faculty partnerships, things will not always go according to plan. This is a common experience with any form of teaching, and you should anticipate a few bumps as you begin with this approach. In our research, faculty have identified some surprising and, in some cases, difficult experiences that made them realize they need to take this work more slowly. Some have told us that their expectations of what students would bring to the partnership did not match what student partners in fact brought. Others have talked about thinking that they wanted to hear "constructive criticism," but then when their student partners offered it, they found themselves feeling defensive and vulnerable. Still others have reflected on the experience of realizing that they disagree with the student perspectives and recommendations their partners offer them and having to rethink their pedagogical commitments based on those discrepancies. All of these examples suggest that partnership is more challenging than simply proceeding with the teaching we are accustomed to and comfortable with, but the examples also lead to greater insight into that work and clarification of pedagogical commitment.

Even if you are ready for all kinds of changes, your students might not be so sure. If students initially seem hesitant or resistant to your efforts at partnership, they might be struggling because they may not have experienced many alternatives to didactic teaching, or they may feel they do not have enough experience with teaching to make a valuable contribution. Like faculty, many students find partnership a bit uncomfortable at first because it is outside of the norm in higher education. When your students are eager to engage, sometimes you might feel uncomfortable to proceed or you might stumble. Be prepared for the creation of a partnership to take longer than you initially expect, and be forgiving (of your students and yourself) when things do not go as smoothly as they could. Partnerships take time to develop. Try to be patient, because both you and your students will need time to adapt to new partnership roles and to think about new perspectives that emerge.

"When I first learned that my faculty partner would be transitioning from teaching lecture-style classes to a discussion based format, I was really excited about bringing in my knowledge of and experience with discussion tactics to facilitate his transition. I'm starting to realize that inherent in my excitement was the hope that my suggestions would be instantly well received and implemented. While my expectations may not have been met in the sense of integration into the

> *classroom, I'm realizing that this is not bad or unusual,*
> *and I need to give the process more patience and time."*
>
> —*Student partner*

Getting Started Strategy 3: Invite Students to Participate Rather than Requiring Participation

We believe strongly that partnership should be voluntary. Requiring participation creates a tension with the principles at the foundation of this work. However, someone needs to take the initiative, and faculty typically act as gate-keepers of curriculum design (Bourner, 2004; Bovill, 2013a) and are in control of many other teaching and learning processes within higher education. Whether you plan to work with a single student or a group of students, outside the context of one of your courses or with students enrolled in your course, inviting students to be partners challenges traditional hierarchies and roles, raising complex and sometimes troubling questions about power and agency (for more on this topic see the section called "Negotiating Roles and Power in Partnerships"). Therefore, being clear and welcoming is essential when broaching the possibility of partnership (see also our discussion under the subheading "Be Careful and Intentional Regarding the Language You Use to Describe This Work" in Chapter 6).

If you extend a broad invitation to students, you also should be prepared for the possibility that you will have an overwhelming response—that many students will want to work in partnership with you. Anticipate how you will structure and manage such extensive participation. Establishing partnership with a whole class is a different endeavor than working with one or several students, so you will need to be intentional to ensure that respect, reciprocity, and shared responsibility inform larger-scale partnerships.

Think through your goals for the partnership and be prepared to explain these goals to students and to others who may ask you questions about your work. Try not to be shy about expressing your hopes and enthusiasm, and encourage questions and ideas. This invitation to join a partnership is a process, just like all partnership work. If you are patient enough to allow the invitation to be considered and, ideally, accepted willingly, the result will be a more genuine partnership. Invitations that students read as requirements undermine the goal of partnership. Even with circumstances that aim to reduce or at least make explicit existing power dynamics, be honest with yourself and with students about why you are inviting them into partnership.

"Make it clear to faculty that student partners are resources for US. When I learned about the program, it sounded very watch-doggy. It was totally the opposite when I met my student partner, but it was a bit off-putting as I came to the program thinking that an 'agent' would be sitting in my class, watching over me."
—Faculty partner

Getting Started Strategy 4: Think Carefully about Whom to Involve in a Partnership

With whom will you develop a partnership? If you are only inviting an individual or a small group of students to be involved, think clearly about your criteria for selecting students. The goals of your partnership, of course, should be central, but since this is relational work you will also want to think about other assets that students (and you) bring to your collaboration.

Some faculty prefer to work in partnership with high-achieving students whom they know well already, while other faculty seek out students with particular subject knowledge, technology skills, or perspectives on relevant issues. In other cases, faculty foreground interpersonal dynamics, seeking out students who are inclined to engage seriously, to question critically, or to think creatively. Sometimes faculty are looking for students who know nothing about the subject and so can afford them candid insights into what it is like to try to learn the course material for the first time. Still others invite underrepresented students into partnership, both to gain their important insights and to begin to counter the sense of exclusion many of these students feel.

While all of these considerations might seem overwhelming, we have found that partnerships thrive when well-intentioned people work together across differences (Cook-Sather, forthcoming). Think carefully about the implications of choosing, and by implication not choosing, particular groups of students, and expect to be surprised as you learn more about your partners and yourself in this work. If you are not working with an entire class of students, you will need to consider carefully what criteria you will use to select students and be transparent about this. Carey (2013) reports students' disappointment at not having had an opportunity to contribute to collaborative work with faculty, while in our experience students are often still pleased that other students' perspectives have been influential in designing learning and teaching.

"Define for yourself what an ideal partnership will look like for your given situation early in the semester. Periodically evaluate if your ideal is being met, has changed, why/why not. Doing this will remind you of your purpose in the event that you feel lost. Periodically evaluate your goals for the classroom: Have they been met? Have they changed? How would your refine your goals?"

—Student partner

Getting Started Strategy 5: Work Together to Create a Shared Purpose and Project

After you have initiated the partnership, your first task might well be to give it away. For a partnership to succeed, it needs to become shared work: "our project," not "mine" or "yours." To develop this common purpose, all involved need to recognize themselves and the others as legitimate partners who bring valuable perspectives and expertise to the project. Sometimes, particularly with advanced and confident students, this is as simple as stating that fact: "Let's all participate actively and critically in this work, and together let's monitor our group dynamics to make sure we're as respectful, reciprocal, and responsible as we can be." More often, however, the partnership evolves as participants build respect and habits of reciprocity.

To encourage the development of trust and confidence, look for early opportunities for all to contribute, and consider ways to disrupt traditional hierarchies by, for example, having students take primary responsibility for important early decisions within the group. One of the challenges and benefits of partnership work is the opportunity it can provide to examine explicitly our everyday language. Think about the terminology you use that students might not be familiar with—both disciplinary terms and ways of talking about teaching. Often, students have insights and suggestions for how to clarify or complicate terms that have become so ingrained and accepted in our own minds that we forget to question them.

Avoid nonessential jargon that can confuse or alienate people, and shy away from overly broad claims about your partnership. Students sometimes have had negative experiences with projects and processes in higher education that promise more equity than they deliver. Just as inviting student feedback in a course that is then ignored or dismissed can be more detrimental than beneficial, inviting students into partnership but then keeping them powerless does more damage than we sometimes realize. To work against these too-common practices, build in regular moments, early in the partnership process and throughout the collaboration, where both faculty and student experiences and perspectives are acknowledged and affirmed. Revisit, revise, and reaffirm your goals in order for students to realize that their views and actions are being taken seriously and, where appropriate, acted upon and for you as faculty members to feel that you are also equal partners in the process.

Getting Started Strategy 6: Cultivate Support

Many partnerships take place in isolated pockets where individual faculty provide opportunities for students to participate meaningfully in decisions about learning and teaching. However, to enhance sources of information, support, and collaboration, try to identify faculty, administrators, and students on your campus who might be interested in your partnership. You only need one or two colleagues or a single person in a key role to make this work feel a lot more achievable.

Meet with these people to discuss both their experiences with this kind of work at your institution and their insights into possible campus resources that could be used to bolster your partnership. They may have discovered approaches and sources of support that you do not need to rediscover or recreate. In the process of seeking out such support, you might be surprised by the allies you have across campus, from senior administrative staff to your teaching center and student government or representative council.

"I think that having the opportunity to reflect with other people is crucial. It's difficult to find time for that and make a space for it, but I've tried to address particular questions about teaching in conversations with other faculty."

—*Faculty partner*

Getting Started Strategy 7: Learn from Mistakes

As you gain experience with student-faculty partnerships, you will discover some things that work well in your context and you will step in a few potholes that you will want to avoid next time.

Perhaps the most common problem we have heard about from faculty is having unclear or overly ambitious goals for a partnership, thus leaving faculty or students or both frustrated at a process that does not seem to be progressing as it could. Another common difficulty is getting carried away with the excitement of discoveries from your partnership, and changing everything in your course at once. This is rarely a recipe for success. A third concern is thinking that others will welcome the approach and the outcomes of partnership. In some cases, both faculty colleagues and students are suspicious of changes and offer negative feedback, at least initially.

If you build critical, collaborative reflection into the partnership process, you can avoid some of these challenges or at least have a mechanism for managing them. Some groups do this through discussion or keeping journals, while others adopt more formal assessment practices such as anonymous reflections, which all participants read and respond to, or interviews of participants by someone who is not part of the group. Your assessment practices should also model a partnership approach where possible by being collaboratively designed and carried out. This is probably not the first thing you want to work on as a new partnership unfolds, but before too long you should be considering how the group will know about whether it is making progress toward its goals in ways that honor the contributions of all members.

"Our different perspectives mean that we are seeing different things, and we have different biases, so we sometimes have some conflict when we meet about what's going on in the classroom. And that gets at the root of what [my faculty partner] wants to get out of the discussions, and what she wants her students to experience in class."

—*Student partner*

Sustaining and Deepening Student-Faculty Partnership Practices

As you become more experienced, you will want to plan for ways to make partnerships a sustainable practice and an even more valuable learning experience for you and your students. The strategies outlined in this section are designed to help you plan for longer-term work.

Sustaining and Deepening Strategy 1: Integrate Partnerships into Other Ongoing Work

Because time is precious to both faculty and students, integrating partnership practices into other ongoing work can be essential to sustainability. What activities do you or your students already do that could regularly involve partnership (teaching, pedagogical planning, course feedback, programs offered by your teaching and learning center)? Institutionally supported partnerships can be easier to sustain as they are often accompanied by support structures, guidance, and resources. If you are working without aid from a program or your institution, think carefully and creatively about how you can integrate the partnership into your existing work.

Regardless of the support you have, you'll want to plan for what comes after your partnership. Should you build in a review of student and faculty experiences at a later stage to measure the impact of the partnership and consider further intervention? If you design a course in partnership with current students, will this redesign be relevant to the next cohort of students or will you need to renegotiate the course every time you teach it? As we have mentioned, students have often reported that when another group of students has been involved in designing a course, that prior partnership has been appreciated; however, that is a very different experience from being directly involved themselves.

While you should aim to weave partnerships into existing activities, you may want to seek or create spaces for this work that are not part of any particular department. It is important that you feel that you have the freedom to explore and experiment without being under anyone's surveillance or judgment. Our strong conviction is that your partnerships should not be linked in any formal way to review for reappointment or promotion, unless you choose to make them so or your institution's criteria for reappointment and promotion specify and value this form of work. Partnership requires risk, but as one faculty member characterized his experience with a student consultant, "This project is making a safer place to be vulnerable and thus learn and grow and be out of your shell." When you feel safe enough to experiment with new ways of learning and teaching, you are much more likely to invite students into partnerships and dialogue about collaborative teaching and learning.

Where student-faculty partnerships are focused on designing courses, you will want to ensure that you meet the demands of your institutions' course design and curricular review processes. Typically, there is a great deal of flexibility for creative partnerships to flourish within the structure of learning outcomes and assessments. Where you feel structures are too constraining, try to make changes to these structures.

> "Don't limit your thinking and explorations to the
> course that is the focal point for your reflections;
> the opportunity to think and respond actively to the
> course under investigation can open up new ap-
> proaches in your other course(s), new avenues for
> discussions about curriculum in your department,
> division, and institution, etc."
>
> —Faculty partner

Sustaining and Deepening Strategy 2: Give and Get Credit for Working in Partnership

Because this is hard work, you need to think carefully about the benefits of your efforts for everyone involved in the partnership, including both your students and yourself. Partnership has many intangible outcomes, and for some people, the excitement and creativity that participants experience might be enough to sustain, or provide a rationale for pursuing further, partnerships. Others may want to consider more tangible outcomes, particularly for students who may need to set aside other academic or paid work in order to work in partnership with faculty.

Decisions about whether students will be compensated in some tangible way are likely to be influenced by your institutional context and also the nature of your partnership. If you are working in partnership with an entire class, then you might consider whether some portion of each student's grade could be earned through partnership activities. If you are working with small groups or individuals, then you might be able to provide other concrete benefits. Some institutions will provide grant support, work-study funding, or similar resources to compensate students, while others have formal structures (such as undergraduate research programs) that make course credit a possibility. Many successful faculty-student partnerships, however, do not offer any monetary or academic reward for participating other than the mutual benefits of the processes and outcomes of the partnership.

Of course, students are not the only ones who might appreciate or need recognition for this work. Institutional culture and practices vary widely in how they 'count' student-faculty partnerships. In some cases, faculty are able to document their partnership activities and outcomes as evidence of teaching excellence or leadership, and then have that evidence weighed in departmental and institutional review, promotion, and tenure processes. Even at institutions where this work is valued, you might need to raise awareness among your faculty and administrative colleagues about partnership so that they fully appreciate the processes involved and potential outcomes of your efforts. At many institutions, partnerships will yield less tangible benefits for faculty, although they can be personally stimulating and rewarding, something that many faculty consider to be more motivating over the course of an academic career.

"The most significant benefits of participating in this program were gaining understanding and insight from a student's perspective not just on what I do or do not do in the class, but also what her peers (fellow classmates) do and do not do to affect her learning experience."

—*Faculty partner*

Sustaining and Deepening Strategy 3: Include Varied and Diverse Perspectives in Partnerships

Student-faculty partnerships are fundamentally dialogues across differences of position and perspective, yielding fresh insights and deeper engagement in teaching and learning for all involved. Ideally, the partnership experience should both affirm and challenge participants to think critically, take risks, and develop new ways of talking with one another about teaching and learning. With such structured support, participants can build enough trust to talk honestly across differences. A range of voices within a partnership typically produces richer perspectives, so you may want to consider the diversity within your partnership. Some faculty attend specifically to race and gender, for example, while others may want to include other salient aspects of student or faculty identity (such as full-time or part-time status, years at the institution, and so on). The more that you and your student partners open yourselves to perspectives and insights that you cannot achieve from your own angles of vision, the more likely you are to be inspired to act on these new ways of seeing.

"One of my greatest realizations from this work is that there is a real difference between being a teacher and being a professor. Professors are experts in their field, but they are rarely given the opportunity to learn and discuss what it means to be a teacher.

> *[Partnerships between faculty members and students]*
> *provide a positive and incredible chance for the pro-*
> *fessors to wrestle with pedagogical issues and be able*
> *to get the perspectives of students and other faculty*
> *members alike. Not only does it make the class better*
> *for the students, it provides the faculty members with*
> *educational ideas they may have never developed*
> *otherwise because they are not usually given these*
> *opportunities as teachers."*
>
> —*Faculty partner*

Sustaining and Deepening Strategy 4: Consider Professional Development for Faculty and Students Involved in Partnerships

Even for faculty and students with experience in partnerships, this work often makes participants at least slightly uncomfortable because it shifts the traditional roles and habits of teaching and learning in higher education. To manage those feelings, and to think reflectively about other aspects of partnership practices, you may want to pursue (or create) professional development opportunities for you, your faculty colleagues, and your students. At many institutions, teaching centers and student representative bodies have relevant expertise or offer appropriate programs to support student-faculty partnerships. You might also talk with professionals in your institution's office of student affairs because they typically coordinate training for students on group processes, leadership, difficult dialogues, and similar topics. If you have this kind of expertise yourself, you might want to think carefully about whether taking on this role within your group will strengthen the collaboration or will reinforce traditional expectations about faculty expertise. You do not need to go into this work on your own. Many campuses have resources that can help you and your partners develop the capacity to have more productive relationships with your students.

Sustaining and Deepening Strategy 5: Value the Process

Value the processes of collaborative pedagogical planning and not just the products. Deepening student and faculty meta-understandings of learning processes and knowledge construction, changing the culture of higher education, and developing new approaches to teaching and learning are all important as potential beneficial outcomes in terms of enhanced engagement, satisfaction, and performance. Take time within projects to pause and share experiences of your partnership. Are people's expectations being met? Can anything be done to enhance the group processes within the partnership? What is working and what could be improved? What is everyone learning from the process of working together in partnership? How can this learning best be captured, celebrated, and shared with others? Encourage your students and colleagues to value the processes of partnership, too. Try to collaborate in learning how to effectively articulate these valuable process outcomes to others.

> *"It seems helpful to think of faculty-student partnerships as a kind of journey. It is a process with tremendous potential that relies on active and considerate participation from both partners."*
>
> —*Student partner*

Sustaining and Deepening Strategy 6: Formally End a Partnership When It Is Time

All partnerships end. The work is completed, students graduate, or faculty priorities change. These endings can be a time to reflect and relish, or they can prompt fear and frustration. To make the conclusion as positive and productive as possible, begin with the end in mind. Many partnerships take advantage of the academic calendar to set the boundaries of partnership work. For example, we will work together weekly throughout this semester, or let's plan to conclude by the close of the academic year. Being explicit about time lines often makes it easier for faculty and students to say "yes" to partnerships, since they usually have a good idea of their current time commitments and might feel less certain and more anxious about long-term obligations. When the appointed time comes, you can always decide to continue your work. However, it is more likely you will use your end point as an opportunity to think together one final time about your shared and individual accomplishments and learning experiences as well as the challenges you faced.

Negotiating Roles and Power in Partnerships

> *"To create a classroom environment that is more conducive to participation by all students, faculty members must work on methods that downplay faculty power and encourage co-operation."*
>
> Auster and MacRone 1994, p. 298

In the first two sections of this chapter we focused on strategies that we have synthesized from our own research and participants' perspectives. In this section, we more explicitly draw on some of the theory that is behind student-faculty partnerships, both to provide scholarly support for the approach and to encourage you as you grapple with the complex issues of power and roles involved in partnership work based on respect, reciprocity, and responsibility.

In most societies, traditional understandings and conventions place faculty in the position of expert and therefore as holding more power than the learner. Students assume a low level of agency and are usually subordinate to the expert teacher. Heron (1992) argues that this view of the faculty-student relationship assumes that because teachers are a disciplinary authority, they should also exercise political authority by directing students and making decisions for students. If you conceptualize power and authority in this way, you privilege and generalize a single source of expertise, denying or devaluing other sources, thus firmly establishing a hierarchy. Most educational institutions and their practices are premised on this hierarchical view of higher education.

Unbalanced power relations created and reinforced by institutions play out in multiple ways in classrooms. Students and faculty bring assumptions like these to their courses, and we often act on the assumptions without making them explicit, let alone calling them into question (Popovic and Green, 2012). There are multiple influences at work here. As Mann (2008) observes, individual student participation in classroom settings is influenced both by "the social relations they have with other students in the group" and with the teacher and by "their understanding of what is expected" of students and of teachers. Such understandings encompass norms regarding "forms of address and turn taking" (p. 59), and they contribute to the establishment of patterns that can be difficult to break.

Within the parameters either implicitly or explicitly set up for student engagement within classrooms, students actually have very limited agency. In many aspects of learning, structures and processes are organized in ways that prescribe to students what they must do, when they must do it, and how they should behave; in other words, students are encouraged to take on a passive role and voice in learning processes (Mann, 2008). This passivity then "constrains the student's autonomy and the capacity to take responsibility" (Mann, 2008, p. 61) while simultaneously reinforcing faculty power and authority.

Mann's analysis helps to explain why some faculty and some students might react negatively to the suggestion of student-faculty partnership. We have labored under expectations of ourselves as disciplinary experts and therefore sole authorities, and we have contributed to students' acculturation into an education system in which our shared expectations are based on a persistent view of the student as subordinate to faculty. Changing this model to one based on participation and partnership challenges the norms for both students and faculty. As Sorenson (2001) has argued, student-faculty partnership "narrows the hierarchical distance between professors and students" (p. 182), encouraging what Havnes called "shared responsibility between different, and potentially conflicting, partners" (1998, p. 1). Such a change positions students as agents "invited to participate in the process of transforming higher education" (Havnes, 1998, p. 1). Any significant repositioning tends to lead to discomfort or fear in some individuals; it is, therefore, important to recognize that partnership asks many students and faculty to step into unfamiliar territory that can initially lead to resistant responses.

This seems a somewhat negative view of the ways in which faculty and students relate to one another. There are alternatives, and many authors view power as a dynamic force rather than a fixed and clearly located one. This perspective emphasizes the potential for any power imbalance to shift. Mann (2008) states that "what we might take to be a 'natural' and 'objective' phenomenon such as 'learning' is in fact formed within particular discourse(s)" (p. 63). Among these discourses are psychological and educational ones that are themselves historically produced and socially constructed. Learning, Mann (2008) continues, is therefore not a decontextualized concept "out there" in the world; it is, rather "generated through discourse" (p. 63). What this understanding of learning reveals is that discourse is a form of power: "the power to construct reality in particular ways" (p. 63). Within this notion, there is both a negative and a positive aspect of power. The negative aspect is that discourse can create "realities that support the interests of powerful groups (as in hegemony and within ideologies)" (p. 63). There is also a positive understanding of power "whereby agents have the capacity through discourse to transform such realities" (p. 63).

When a teacher within a classroom takes a stance that only allows for his or her perspective and within which students are expected simply to accept and acquire that perspective, then you have hegemony. In contrast, when you have a classroom within which students are guided by faculty to develop a discourse through which they name and transform knowledge, then you have a classroom that fosters the development of agents. In short, the discourse that frames and forms learning has the potential to disempower or to empower.

If you accept Mann's argument that learning is generated through discourse, and if you wish to strive for a classroom in which students have agency, then students must have voice. As Alcoff (1995) has argued, it is often, though not always, the case that speaking for others leads to "a reinscription . . . of hierarchies" (p. 250). In contrast, within student-faculty partnerships, students speak for themselves, faculty speak for themselves, and each listens to the other. Simply speaking and listening does not automatically change the power imbalances that exist, but those are essential steps in shifting the balance.

In this and other ways, student-faculty partnerships call for a rebalancing of power; the rejection of a notion of authority as situated only in a single person or position. Dewey (1997) reminds us, though, that "when external authority is rejected it does not follow that all authority should be rejected, but rather that there is need to search for a more effective source of authority" (p. 21). The more effective source that we argue for is a form of shared authority—power with: "mutual teacher-student authority" (Shor, 1992, p. 16). This notion contrasts radically with most ways of thinking and interacting in higher education, but embracing a more democratic approach to learning and teaching premised on respect, reciprocity, and shared responsibility can lead to deeper, more engaging learning.

In Chapters 3 and 4 we presented examples that help to illustrate what this sharing of power might mean in terms of, for example, designing a course or deciding upon some elements of class content. Moving forward from those examples and the discussion in the first part of this chapter of practical strategies for developing and deepening partnerships, we present in the following sections some advice specifically focused on power that we hope can guide you in navigating power issues within partnerships.

*"Part of my interest in this program is the partnership
between professors and students that recognizes us
both as teachers and learners, which takes away some
of the traditional power dynamics. I think in my first
experience, my partner was already thinking about
less traditional student/teacher relationships and my
current partner is much more accepting of traditional
relationships between students and teachers. This has
been interesting for me to explore, because although
he is open to my advice, I think there is still a clear
divide between student and teacher (which to an
extent is understandable). I hope as the semester goes
on, I can work in conversations about power dynamics in the classroom and what the pros/cons are of
traditional student/teacher relationships."*

—Student partner

Negotiating Roles and Power Strategy 1: Before You Begin, Think about Your Own Attitudes

Student-faculty partnerships require a change to many people's conceptualization of teaching. You may feel comfortable sharing some control over decision-making with your students, or you may find this strange and unsettling. Try to prepare for partnership by considering in which areas of your practice you feel more or less comfortable sharing decision making. Faculty have a wide range of approaches, but three common places to begin are some of the same ones upon which we focused in Chapter 3:

1. *Designing a course or elements of a course:* Some faculty feel that students do not have the disciplinary expertise to select or design the most appropriate learning materials or to craft the best assignments for student learning, and so worry

that they might be doing students a disservice by sharing this responsibility. Other faculty see sharing control of assignments as a way of making students more accountable for the subject matter of the course and affording students an opportunity to learn that content more deeply, since having to craft questions or activities that assess learning is much harder than simply answering other people's questions.

2. *Responding to the student experience during a course*: One example of this approach involves faculty asking for feedback partway through a course. In order to enhance the likelihood of students feeding back anonymously, often faculty leave the room for students to have faculty-less discussions. This kind of sharing of control can feel, to some faculty, like losing the direct line of communication with students in the class. To others, it feels like letting conversation about, and perhaps critique of, the course proceed without faculty oversight, and some faculty experience that situation as threatening. Still others find it refreshing and inspiring, indicating that they trust the feedback much more because the students know that they were offering it anonymously, without the threat of faculty knowing who said what.

3. *Assessing student work*: For many faculty this is the most complex (and perhaps most exciting) approach since it not only challenges what has traditionally been entirely in the purview of faculty but also intersects with institutional accountability.

By identifying in which areas you are more and less open to sharing power with your students, you can anticipate some of the challenges you might face within partnership work before you begin. Do you consider any areas as unavailable for negotiation? In some disciplines governed by a professional body, for example, medicine, this might include a performance assessment that enables a student to demonstrate a particular clinical competence. However, even if assessing an area of clinical competence is mandatory, the method of assessment may be negotiable and other elements of the teaching and learning experience are likely to be more flexible. What is important is that you are clear about what is and is not in play, explaining and making transparent why some things are considered in or out of bounds.

Negotiation does not mean that you have to do everything that your students suggest or request, but neither does it mean that you can simply dismiss every point that students raise. The idea is not to defer entirely to the student perspective or substitute students' recommended approaches for your own, nor is it to simply reassert everything you already do. Rather, the aim is to engage in dialogue that stretches, reaffirms, and challenges your thinking so that you might teach as intentionally and effectively as possible. Through the partnership, if you integrate some of students' suggestions and offer cogent explanations of why you choose not to integrate others, students will understand that you have taken the process seriously.

"When I heard about the student-faculty partnership program, I thought I am too old to be involved. I figured that, unless you are able to change some things, don't do it. I wasn't sure of my capacity to change anything at this point. But what I've found is that some of my consultant's feedback has caused me to look at some of my classroom practices in a different light, and that's helpful. I think they will change, maybe not tomorrow, but I think they will change. For example, I had always thought of my taking notes on the blackboard as nothing but positive and supportive, whereas it struck her as fraught with a power dynamic. Do I write every word? Whose words? I think I'm still going to do it, but I am rethinking how I am going to do it."

—Faculty partner

Negotiating Roles and Power Strategy 2: Develop Ways to Negotiate within the Partnership

Both students and faculty may lack experience of negotiating within partnerships. When individuals are used to relationships based on an imbalance of power, students and faculty may take time to learn how to behave in more equitable conditions. Students and faculty will have good reasons why they may not agree with each other, but it may take time for them to develop effective methods of communicating wishes, learning to compromise, and learning to listen to others' wishes. One example might serve to illustrate this issue.

One faculty member who was shifting from teaching a large lecture course to teaching a small seminar chose to establish a partnership with a student to develop strategies for this new pedagogical context. For the first few weeks, they both experienced tension in their meetings, as the faculty member felt challenged and vulnerable and the student felt frustrated that her faculty partner was not taking her advice. Realizing that they were coming from very different perspectives regarding what enables good discussion to emerge within a course, they both took a step back and decided to refocus their partnership work, the student partner looking more at what was working well and the faculty member trying out a few approaches that he had not been comfortable with before.

Perhaps most challenging in terms of negotiation is learning to agree on how decisions will be made within a partnership. A range of possibilities exist, including majority vote or listening most closely to the voices of the least vocal and the underrepresented. Learning to compromise and to build consensus may require both faculty and students to develop new skills. Collaboratively setting ground rules can often be a useful opening exercise to discussions about what negotiation means and how decisions will be made within partnerships.

Learning to share power like this can be destabilizing for both faculty and students. For many faculty, sharing power feels unfamiliar, uncomfortable, and even, sometimes, irresponsible. Likewise, for many students, sharing power will also be unfamiliar and uncomfortable. However, if you and your students recognize this discomfort as part of a generative process, you will learn the kinds of valuable lessons faculty and students describe in the pages of this book. For others, sharing power can feel liberating and can reaffirm for students and faculty many of the reasons they came to the university. The emphasis on shared learning and cocreated processes and outcomes can be invigorating.

"I've found my partnership really generative in that I've learned how vulnerable-making the . . . process can be for both the student and the professor. This realization has led me to strive for more of a balance of affirmation and critique/suggestion in writing up my classroom observation notes."

—Student partner

Negotiating Roles and Power Strategy 3: Be Honest about Where Power Imbalances Persist

Student-faculty partnerships challenge hierarchical relationships and encourage greater dialogue, shared decision making, and pursuit of consensus. However, most faculty still have responsibility for grading students and therefore retain power over students even within partnerships. Leaving this unsaid rarely strengthens a partnership.

Be clear with students about what level of partnership is possible and whether faculty maintain sole responsibility for decisions over areas of the curriculum such as assessment. It is easy for partners to fall back into traditional ways of relating to one another when important issues that are central to student experiences, such as grading, are not explicitly addressed: for example, with faculty setting every agenda and students passively following along. Regularly monitor who talks the most and whose ideas carry the most weight, and try to make adjustments that enable new and different voices to be heard and acted upon.

Conclusion

The guiding principles—respect, reciprocity, and responsibility—that we discussed in detail in Chapter 1 and to which we have returned across the chapters in this book are evident in the three sets of strategies we have outlined in this chapter. Respect is particularly apparent in strategies that embrace patience, that constitute invitations rather than requirements, and that see mistakes as opportunities to learn (Tompkins, 1996). Reciprocity underpins strategies that support students and faculty in working together to create a shared project or approach, cultivate supportive relationships within the college community, consider ways of rewarding partnerships, and value the process. Responsibility is particularly evident in thinking carefully and critically about whom to involve in partnerships and how to involve them, seeking to include diverse perspectives in partnerships, developing ways to negotiate partnerships, and honestly acknowledging where power imbalances remain.

While we have laid out sets of strategies that aim to support and offer advice to those who might be new to partnerships as well as for the more experienced, we also want to suggest that these strategies and the process of thinking through the questions they raise should be recursive. The work of developing and sustaining partnerships is ongoing. That may sound daunting, but once you become more familiar with partnership, you might find, as has been the case for many faculty we have worked with, it becomes a way of life—a mode of being that not only challenges traditional student-faculty relationships and norms in higher education but also nurtures student and faculty participants in a wide variety of ways and contexts. Regardless of where you and your institution are located on the continuum from hierarchical to democratic, working in partnership, in small or larger ways, can be deeply rewarding and rejuvenating.

We offer a lot of practical advice in this chapter, but questions may remain or have arisen anew for you. You may still feel that you are not quite ready to jump into or extend your partnership work without a little more reflection and analysis. In the next chapter, we share additional questions faculty and students have asked us over the years and responses that, as in Chapter 2, attempt both to reassure you but also to affirm the importance of asking—and repeatedly addressing—such critical questions.

8

Further Questions about Student-Faculty Partnerships

This chapter addresses further questions that you may have about student-faculty partnership and reflects the iterative nature of partnership development. The work of exploring and attempting student-faculty partnerships rarely is a one-time activity; instead, the process of establishing and nurturing partnerships typically is part of a long conversation full of questions, some possible answers, more questions, and some more possible answers. In Chapter 2, we focused on issues that often arise when you are in the early stages of thinking about student-faculty partnerships. Here we pose and address some other questions that might take you deeper into an exploration of partnerships or provide an opportunity to revisit some of the persistent questions you have about this work.

Now that I have read about partnerships, I am eager to try this approach. But I have never done this before. How am I supposed to know what I am doing? Is there any training required?

Most faculty have no formal preparation in creating or participating in student-faculty partnerships. The three of us certainly did not. Rather, we and our colleagues who have undertaken this work either invented the particular approaches used, read about collaborative models in other people's work, or chose to join in a program that offered invitations to enter into structured spaces for dialogue and partnership. For most of us, even those connecting to ongoing programs, this meant that we experienced a messy (and often exhilarating) period of actively learning alongside our student partners and faculty colleagues about the work of partnership.

This suggests, once again, that it is prudent to start small. Is there an assignment or a project you could revise in collaboration with students, either within one of your own courses or in your department, as Mary Tatner and Anne Tierney did in their large, undergraduate, biology courses at the University of Glasgow? (See Chapter 3 for a discussion of this project.) Is there a particular pedagogical question you have that would be better informed by student input? Could you meet every other week for lunch with colleagues and students to talk about it, either informally or, as they do through Western Washington University's Teaching-Learning Academy, in more regular and structured forums? (See Werder, 2013, and our discussion of this project in Chapter 4.) Is there an innovation fund at your institution that might support a modest pilot program for a small group of faculty and students? Were there any examples in Chapters 3 and 4 that seemed particularly relevant to you or manageable within your own context? The models and citations in this book should be a good place to start.

If reading about projects feels too abstract, reach out to one of the people involved. You may know someone on your campus, in your professional network, or at a nearby institution who could sit down with you. Or you might email someone profiled in this book, even one of us. We have found the colleagues who do this work to be generous with their time and expertise.

It can't be true partnership if we as faculty are still grading the students, can it?

Yes, it can. The idea of partnership is not that all power or other differences are eliminated. Indeed, for partnership to function well, participants need to acknowledge explicitly that power exists within, and typically complicates, the relationships of those involved. For instance, as we described in Chapter 4 in the case study from Elon University, when Richard Mihans, his colleague Deborah Long, and several students redesigned an education course, student partners "had to adjust to the new power dynamics" and the faculty members of the team had "to trust student partners by sharing power with them, not exerting it over them" (Delpish et al., 2010, p. 98). This kind of candid discussion is essential whether the partnership develops in or out of classrooms.

If your partnership with students is outside of a classroom, for example, then grading typically is not an issue but power differentials remain. If your partnership with students is within the context of a course you teach and in which they are enrolled, then you need to have a different conversation about power and the structures within which you are working. Some of the examples in Chapter 3, such as Susan Deeley's approach to her Public Policy courses at the University of Glasgow, in which she invites students to generate grading criteria as well as co-assessing their own work alongside her grading, and Cathy Davidson's work at Duke University, where she has students collaboratively grade peer work, present alternatives to the traditional way of thinking about and approaching grading of, and with, students.

I'm concerned that only the brightest and most engaged students will take part. How can I engage my academically average, or even below-average, students, including those who don't regularly turn up to class?

This is not always easy, but the key to student participation is offering real partnership. As we discussed in Chapter 1, students are often disengaged because of institutional or faculty expectations that they will be passive recipients of our knowledge. And students sometimes bring habits of disengagement with them into our classrooms. To break this cycle, we should invite students to be more active and to take more responsibility for their own learning. Often faculty use engaging pedagogies to begin this process, and then later pursue partnership as students gain confidence and passion. As one student put it in Chapter 5, participating in a partnership program gave her the push she didn't know she needed "back in the direction of hard work and taking college seriously as a learning experience."

So if you offer a genuine invitation to students to work in partnership with you on some aspect of your class, to have some real input and to work with you in the process of the course's development in some meaningful way, you may find that previously apathetic students become more engaged. Note the words we use here: "genuine," "real," and "meaningful." These are consistent with the definition of partnership we offered in Chapter 1; the invitation must be guided by respect, reciprocity, and shared responsibility. Some students may be skeptical of your invitation, believing that they have heard this before or that you simply are trying to manipulate them into conforming. Be patient, be persistent, be authentic. In our experience, many faculty are able to develop partnerships with some students who might at first seem hard to reach. These collaborations typically have the positive outcomes that characterize this work in general, but also have the added satisfaction (for all partners) of seeing habitually disengaged students awakening.

I can only select a small group of students to take part in this work. What criteria do I use to choose partners? How will I identify the best students to work in partnership with?

Focus on the goals of the partnership. When redesigning a course, for instance, some faculty seek out students who have previously taken the course, and some look for students outside the discipline who will come to the material fresh, asking questions similar to those that novices enrolled in the course will have. In working on an ongoing course, faculty sometimes prefer to collaborate with a representative sample of students, and other times they want to connect with students who share certain characteristics such as high-achieving students or nonmajors. In course design or while teaching, some faculty invite students who are the presumed target population of a course, and others seek students who have traditionally been underrepresented, to better address their needs. For research projects, faculty make similar decisions: Do they want experienced or novice students? Successful or struggling? Well represented or underrepresented? In Chapter 3 we presented Niamh Moore and Mary Gilmartin's example of partnership from a large geography course at University College Dublin. When selecting students starting their third year, who were going to be designing materials for a virtual learning environment, they focused on technology skills, creativity, and a history of being involved in active community campaigning as some of the capacities they valued in the diverse students they interviewed and employed.

Once you have identified the partnership's goals, then you can formulate and share criteria that will help you and your possible collaborators make the best fit (e.g., "I am looking to work in partnership with students who struggled in this course so I can gain insight into the key challenges and help better support students in meeting those. I am defining 'struggled' broadly, so if you found this course to be challenging, then this might be right for you."). Invite students to explain, either in a formal application or less formally in conversation, how their experiences and perspectives prepare them for the partnership role. This helps them start thinking about their responsibilities in partnership. From what we have seen on many campuses, there is no particular profile of a "good" student partner; rather, any student who is willing to commit the time and attention necessary to collaborate can be a good partner because he or she brings a perspective and set of insights that we as faculty do not have.

The students did a great job of co-designing the course this year, but do I need to start from scratch again next year with the new cohort of students and redesign it all again? To what extent can I build on previous partnerships and to what extent to do I need to start over with each new group of students?

You might consider a combination of carrying forward some of what previous students cocreated with you and inviting a new group to modify or expand upon what had been done. In this way, you both honor the previous effort and invite the current group to share the ongoing responsibility for developing courses or course components. Students have often told us that they appreciate when other students have been involved in course design even if they personally have not participated. However, continuing to consult with new cohorts of students opens up the possibilities for deeper pedagogical development and also enhanced outcomes for both the new students and you.

Such sharing of responsibility demonstrates to students that this collaborative approach is a commitment, not simply a one-time experiment. We have found that it can take some time for students to really believe that they are being invited into partnership, since it is quite rare and, in many contexts, so countercultural. Therefore, seeing that you have collaborated in this way and want to continue to do so often proves to students that this is an orientation rather than some trendy new technique. And for some faculty, but not for everyone, partnership may be more than an approach, it is a mode of being that is congruent with a democratic ideology.

Beyond your motivation, a range of factors may influence your decision whether to start with a brand new approach to partnership or to build on previous work. For instance, are you doing this as part of an existing partnership program, which often makes starting anew less daunting, or are you working in isolation on your campus? In addition, are your teaching duties consistent year-to-year or do you experience lots of variation? A more stable teaching schedule may enable a course-based approach to partnership, working iteratively or periodically on the same course; on the other hand, faculty who rarely teach the same course twice in a row may want to focus partnerships on questions or themes that bridge across multiple courses. As with all partnerships, the best way forward is likely to be influenced by your own particular context and motivations.

What is the role and nature of change in partnership? Is change a necessary outcome of this work?

Change is at the heart of learning. What we mean by change, however, can vary widely. Some partnerships might yield a new awareness and also a reaffirmation of existing teaching. Others might open up the possibility of different practices or even entirely new approaches. Still others might prompt radical transformation, altering the foundational assumptions a faculty member has about learning, teaching, and students. One kind of change is not preferable to another in all cases. We see change on a continuum, without an ideal end point for all faculty and students. Because of this variation, we suggest faculty and students talk together about the kinds of change both partners hope and expect might result from the work, and that your work may not meet all of your expectations.

As we indicated in Chapter 2, the goal of student-faculty partnership work is not change for change's sake but rather collaboration and the deeper understanding of teaching and learning that come from that shared analysis and revision. How much and what kind of change results from working in partnership with students should depend on the context and participants.

We provide many examples of changes faculty and student partners have undergone—of attitude, relationship, and practice. In Chapter 5, one faculty member articulates what is perhaps the most common theme we hear from faculty: "I see students more as colleagues, more as people engaged in similar struggles to learn and grow." Students also frequently describe changes in attitude, relationship, and practice: they become "more self-reflective" about their learning, they think about their responsibilities as students, ways they can "help make the discussions better for everyone in the class, including the professor, instead of just for me."

What do I do when I cannot or do not want to do what my student partner recommends?

The point of partnership is not to defer to the student perspective or automatically substitute students' recommendations for your own existing, often well-thought out, practices. The idea is to engage in dialogue that stretches and challenges your thinking so that you might act even more intentionally in your teaching, regardless of whether that means continuing what you are doing but doing it more deliberately, tweaking your current practices in small ways or explaining more clearly to students why you do what you do, or perhaps even making major revisions. As one faculty member we quoted in Chapter 1 explained, "Taking student contributions seriously DOES NOT mean blindly or directly following their opinions and suggestions, but rather taking them seriously, carefully reflecting on and analyzing them, and then addressing the core concerns behind them in a way that is consistent with my overall goals and values."

We have seen a wide array of faculty responses to the ideas proposed by student partners. If a student recommends a change to an activity or assignment, a faculty member might explain the pedagogical rationale for it, and the student may rethink her suggestion, recognizing a logic and purpose of which she might not have been aware. For instance, if a student recommends an increase in student-to-student discussion, the faculty member might take the opportunity to pose classroom questions in a different way while still actively facilitating. Or the faculty member might discuss a bigger change with students, such as experimenting with a Silent Board Discussion, in which everyone writes in silence their associations with a term or concept and then discusses out loud the group's mapped out thoughts. We have seen these responses and more. You will want to figure out and discuss with your student partners what makes sense to change and why and what needs to stay the way it is and why. Just having that discussion clarifies a great deal for both partners.

Eurig Scandrett in his Environmental Justice program (Chapter 3) described how difficult negotiation is, because it is not about faculty maintaining the control they are used to, but nor is it about swinging to the other end of the spectrum and students being completely in control. The balance of partnership in between is far more complex. He described how both faculty and students found negotiation particularly tricky when students asked for one meeting without faculty present. While he welcomed this as a sign that students were taking more responsibility for course design, some of his faculty colleagues were uncomfortable with this development. He also reported that some of the students were surprised when they were allowed to hold a meeting without faculty, as they were so used to having to fight people in authority for what they wanted (Bovill, 2013a).

As that example suggests, you probably should take a pragmatic approach to change within your partnership. While you will want to think ahead about how you plan to make decisions with your student partners, you will need to be agile as the partnership unfolds. Having some different decision-making options in your mind and discussing these with students can be a helpful way of dealing with new roles and power relationships.

What do I do if my student partner seems inclined to question or challenge every pedagogical decision I make?

Sometimes students can respond overenthusiastically to a partnership opportunity. Some might be frustrated, carrying lots of pent-up passion or dissatisfaction, and others might think that constant criticism is what we are seeking. Partnership should provide an outlet for student frustration but, at the same time, make clear that collaboration is not possible in an environment that is too steeped in blame or praise. Respect and reciprocity require some responsibility from all parties, of course. Partners sometimes need to vent before they can get down to the central task of working together. The relationship, however, should evolve so that hyper-critical or overly defensive postures develop into more constructive stances and forms of engagement from all participants. If a meeting or a partnership seems to be going off-track, look for ways to remind everyone of the goals of your work together.

An excellent resource for this kind of recentering conversation has been created by Student Participation in Quality Scotland (SPARQS), an organization that supports student representation in higher education institutions across Scotland. SPARQS uses the visual metaphor of a sound engineer's control board in a recording studio to emphasize the importance of helping students to get the volume and tone just right—not so quiet or meek that students' views are unheard, but not too far into the "red" loud and angry zone that might prompt faculty to turn away (SPARQS, undated). This tool is not meant to imply that only students have a responsibility for getting volume and tone right, as faculty still have a responsibility for facilitating dialogue in partnerships in ways that ensure all voices are heard. But this metaphor, and its related tools, could be used as a starting place for dialogue between faculty and student partners.

How should participants and facilitators manage the intersection of different perspectives and the disagreements that can arise at those intersections?

Welcome them. Listen carefully to them. Learn from them. We are used to having differences and disagreements divide us

(Solomon, 2012), but a key goal of student-faculty partnerships is to elicit contrasting perspectives and then use those to foster deeper understanding and clarify or expand practice. Of course, this is easier said than done, but we encourage you to open yourself to different angles of vision, recognize that different words mean different things to different people, and engage in dialogue with the goal of deeper understanding (Cook-Sather, 2009a, pp. 223–224).

To do this, you may want to develop some strategies for stepping back from the intersection of different perspectives or from disagreements to ask yourself direct questions such as: What are the tensions here? What can we learn from them? How do they illuminate our shared project, and how can we put them to productive use? Working in partnership is rarely simple, and there is no one-size-fits-all response to some of the difficult contradictions and challenges that may arise. However, the complexities within partnerships can also be exciting and can offer new understandings. We recommend continuing to engage in dialogue with students and faculty colleagues to discuss possible steps and solutions, persistently trying different approaches to reaching agreement, consensus, or disagreement but with identified steps forward.

How do we prevent students from getting hurt in partnerships with faculty?

As in any relationship, it is impossible to ensure completely that students—or faculty—do not get hurt in such intensive, relational work. Sometimes participants might leave a partnership angry, alienated, or disappointed. Perhaps they felt they had wasted their time or even been betrayed. While our experience suggests this is a very unusual occurrence, it seems most likely to happen when the language and practices faculty use appear to betray that we are "using" rather than "working with" students, and when faculty promise to take students seriously but then are seen to dismiss or ignore their contributions. It can also happen when students are not sufficiently supported in developing constructive ways of and language for offering insights or feedback; when partners lose sight of the purpose of partnership (thinking the goal is facilitating profound and radical change when it might in fact be more about deepening understanding); or when there have not been sufficient opportunities for partners to gain perspective on their work—looking back over the partnership to identify lessons learned.

Rooting your partnership in respect, reciprocity, and shared responsibility—and regularly talking about both your commitments and your process—should minimize the chance of unfortunate outcomes from this work. But success is never guaranteed, for students or for you.

How do faculty who have worked in partnership with students return to more solitary or at least less collaborative relationships and situations?

Faculty who have participated in partnership indicate that it is difficult to return to previous ways of working. Sometimes they speak of partnership as a threshold that, once crossed, opens up new ways of understanding their work. More often, they describe trying to find ways to carry a more collaborative model into other contexts and relationships. In particular, they note both shifts in the vocabulary they use to talk about teaching and learning, and also a persistent commitment to dialogue across differences of position and power. Many look for ways to sustain the reflection they experience in partnerships.

Frequently faculty report that they consult with students who were previously in partnership with them about classes they are currently teaching or plan to teach. This can take the form of asking for advice or input about a syllabus or an assignment for the course, or it can take the form of actually coplanning a course with former students. In other words, faculty are thinking about teaching and learning as more of a shared project. So ask yourself: How can I collaborate with students enrolled in my courses? Can

I gather and act on student feedback more often? Can I co-design with them some of the course assignments or projects? Such activities will differ from student-faculty partnerships outside of the dynamics of a class in which a student is enrolled, but they can move away from the standard hierarchical model toward a more dialogic one.

Faculty who have worked in partnership with students not only find ways to invite greater engagement and participation from students in their classes, they invite more of their colleagues into discussions of teaching and learning. Having a positive language to talk about teaching and learning, and having experienced the gratification of talking in meaningful ways, inspires faculty to sustain and to extend such experiences.

How do students readjust to traditional courses with more hierarchical student-faculty relationships after having been invited into partnership?

Similar to their faculty partners, students who have worked in partnership develop the confidence and courage to respectfully approach other faculty members or employers to convey their perspectives in constructive ways—and to recognize when such efforts may not be wanted. Many have recalled stories of successful and gratifying interactions in which all parties learned from one another and were able to progress in their work as a result of the students initiating such communication. Others have recalled cases when, as one former student consultant explained, "you may just have to sit back and grit your teeth some because your feedback is not invited or may be clearly unwelcome" (Cook-Sather and Alter, 2011, p. 48).

Faculty can help students navigate this by encouraging them to apply the understandings and skills they develop through student-faculty partnerships—insights into learning processes, analytical capacities, ability to communicate across power differences, understanding of multiple perspectives, compassion—to other courses and other relationships with faculty. They should be reminded, as suggested that not all faculty will welcome such an approach, but that there are ways of infusing more traditional, hierarchical relationships with these qualities of engagement. And students benefit from a past partnership even when they cannot enact one in a future situation, like the student who read her paper assignment differently as a result of having collaborated with a faculty member. Students can transfer the qualities of attention and engagement they develop in partnership to other courses and relationships, regardless of whether there is an invitation to do so.

We outlined in Chapter 5 how many students experience a transformation in their metacognitive understanding of learning through being an active participant in student-faculty partnerships. It can be very difficult for students and faculty to return to more traditional lectures and transmission styles of teaching after this "awakening." We urge students and faculty to try to support one another in advocating for further partnership approaches within their colleges or universities rather than feeling the pressure to return to more hierarchical relationships between students and faculty that are pervasive in higher education. Partnership, after all, is one powerful way to help our students become the critical, independent thinkers and skillful global citizens that our universities aim to develop.

If I am a dean or provost, or a faculty member on a promotion and tenure committee, what can I do to encourage faculty to take up student-faculty partnerships?

Send a clear message to faculty, particularly junior faculty, that participation in such programs will be seen as a positive indication of attention to teaching. At the same time—and this is essential—ensure that criteria for promotion and tenure are structured and articulated in ways that value participation in partnership work.

Without both informal encouragement and formal structures in support of partnership, many faculty may not risk this kind of work. However, if it is supported, many faculty will participate. As we mentioned in Chapter 4, the provost at Bryn Mawr College has found that new faculty members reviewed for reappointment after having participated in the SaLT program have experienced fewer problems adapting to their new roles as professors and have received more positive reviews of their teaching than was the case for previous cohorts. As a result of the provost valuing faculty participation in the SaLT program—and no doubt for other reasons, too—virtually every new faculty member now chooses to participate in the program.

9

Assessing Processes and Outcomes of Student-Faculty Partnerships

In the previous eight chapters, we have shared research, stories, theories, and recommendations that we hope will be helpful to you as you consider taking up or expanding student-faculty partnerships. One last set of questions remains: how can we assess this work and how should we judge its effectiveness? Our main focus with assessment is not those familiar, institutionally mandated end-of-term student ratings. While we start with a discussion of that practice, our emphasis is on assessing student-faculty partnerships with the goal of documenting and improving them.

We recognize that the term "assessment" is used differently in different countries and even in different contexts within the same country. Here we use the term to refer to the process of stepping back from and analyzing progress in any educational endeavor—learning, teaching, research, pedagogical partnership—either in a formative way (during the process with the goal of using what is gathered to revise the approaches we are using) or in a summative way (with the goal of evaluating what has been learned, taught, or accomplished after the process is completed). In some contexts, what we discuss in this chapter might be called program or project evaluation.

We begin this chapter by contrasting the student course rating process with the sustained, collaborative model for assessment that we advocate. However, instead of only pointing out the differences, we also show how you can take those institutional processes as a starting point for expanding into a more collaborative, sustainable student-faculty partnership orientation toward assessment. We then discuss some ways you might conduct both formative and summative assessment of partnerships themselves. Finally, we offer some guiding principles for, and examples of, good practice in capturing and assessing the outcomes of those partnerships.

Students' Role in Assessing Teaching and Learning in Higher Education

Student ratings of courses have existed for decades (Kohlan, 1973; Marlin, 1987). On many campuses the student role in course ratings emerged as part of a larger movement that aimed to give students more voice in their educational experience. Over time, however, student ratings have often become a formalized process for students to express to decision-makers their perceptions of faculty performance in the classroom, rather than an opportunity for dialogue with faculty about how to enhance teaching and learning. At many colleges and universities, faculty are required to administer a standardized questionnaire at the end of all courses, and the results of those are included in materials used to make judgments about reappointment or promotion (Aleamoni, 1999; Caulfield, 2007; Goldstein and Benassi, 2006; Hativa, 2013; Melland, 1996).

We want to distinguish these forms of institutionally, and sometimes nationally, driven assessment from the gathering of student perspectives and suggestions on teaching and learning that are part of a collaborative and dialogic process either within a single course as it is unfolding or across courses as part of a larger research project. To move these processes toward a partnership orientation, faculty can think about how they use the feedback they receive from students. Could you invite students to help make sense of the feedback? Could these data be one part of the evidence used by partners to help redesign a course?

Assessing Teaching and Learning within Courses

In contrast to teaching, in which individual faculty often have considerable autonomy, institutionally driven forms of assessment tend to be regulated and managed—and students rarely have any input in the construction or use of the questionnaires. In addition, since these forms typically are administered at the end of the term, the feedback process is completed when the relationship between you and the students in your course is concluded. Thus, these course ratings do not afford students the chance to influence the course as it continues to unfold, nor does the process offer you as faculty the opportunity to respond to the students who gave you particular feedback (Caulfield, 2007; Clark and Redmond, 1982; Diamond, 2004; Lewis, 2001; Keutzer, 1993).

The requirement to gather end-of-term course ratings does, however, present you with an opportunity to develop more of a student-faculty partnership approach, if you conceptualize that culminating moment as one part of a multistep process of analyzing and revising the course. By adopting this stance, faculty not only gather useful feedback during the term, but they also find that they receive thoughtful and, quite often, positive end-of-term ratings. So one step toward partnership is to situate the institutionally required course rating process within a larger set of assessments of your course. The case study of Jody Cohen's practice that we presented in Chapter 3, including her invitation to students to provide feedback on teaching and learning during a course, illustrates one way to do this.

In a very different context, Cathy Bovill, while teaching at Queen Margaret University in Edinburgh, encouraged students to work with her to design a set of exercises that enabled students to determine what and how to assess the course as it progressed (Bovill et al., 2010). The students suggested focusing on elements of the course that it had not occurred to her to assess. This is particularly interesting as it highlights that there are often elements of teaching and learning that the students consider to be of high priority but that faculty may not believe to be of great importance.

If, like Cohen and Bovill, you gather student feedback at one or more points during the term and share it with the class, you can promote "two-way communication with learners" and facilitate "open discussions about course goals and the teaching-learning process" (Diamond, 2004, p. 226) in which students feel "empowered to help design their own educational process" (Keutzer, 1993, p. 239). In addition, research demonstrates that when faculty gather student feedback in appropriate and well-supported ways during the term, their end-of-course ratings improve (Cohen, 1980; Penny and Coe, 2004).

Another way of drawing students into more of a partnership model in the course assessment process is to ensure that they have an opportunity to reflect upon their own role within learning and teaching. Typically end-of-term student surveys, as well as many midcourse feedback processes, focus on faculty performance and how the faculty might improve the course. For instance, the "stop, start, and continue" technique originally devised by George and Cowan (1999) usually applies only to the faculty member's behavior—what students would like the teacher to stop doing, start doing, and continue doing in order to enhance learning. However, with a modest reorientation, students can also be asked to offer three statements of what they individually should stop, start, and continue doing in order to enhance their own learning and that of their peers (Bovill, 2011).

A partnership approach to gathering midsemester feedback combines the in-class collaborative approach with a student-faculty partnership based outside of the class. Through the SaLT program, for instance, faculty members work in partnership with student consultants who are not enrolled in the course under study to generate a list of questions to ask students in a course. These can be as simple as questions like the following: (1) In what ways is this class and the instructor supporting your learning? (2) In what ways could the class and instructor better support your learning? (3) What are you doing to ensure a successful learning experience for yourself in the course and what could you do differently? Or they could be more specific to the course. As with a modified "stop, start, and continue" technique, this approach asks students, as well as faculty, to analyze what they are doing and what they could be doing to support their own learning.

Once faculty members and student consultants have agreed on the questions to ask as part of gathering midsemester feedback through the SaLT program, the consultant types them up and creates forms to distribute to the students in the course. The collaborative process does not end there, however, and the student-led portion of the process distinguishes it from more common approaches to gathering midsemester feedback such as the Small Group Instructional Diagnosis (Clark and Bekey, 1979; Millis, 2004). On the day that the feedback session is to be conducted, the faculty member leaves the classroom for 15–20 minutes, and the consultant conducts the session. She first explains the importance of the opportunity, which is rare for many students and so warrants some framing. This both helps the students focus on the request as one genuinely worthy of considered responses and to make clear to students that what they write will be typed up and shared not only with the faculty member but also with the entire class. The consultant then asks students to respond to the questions in writing, and after the students have completed their written responses, she conducts a short discussion in which she invites the students to elaborate on their responses.

The final step in the process constitutes another opportunity for collaboration and partnership. The consultant takes all the student responses, aggregates them by question, types them up, and shares them with her faculty partner. The faculty member and the student consultant discuss together how the professor can frame what he or she has learned from the feedback in discussion with the students in the class. The faculty member then engages in dialogue with the students enrolled in his or her class, discussing what can change and why, what cannot change and why, and what emerged more generally from the feedback. (See Cook-Sather, 2009b, for examples of how faculty members have chosen to share the student feedback with their students.)

Faculty who have tried this approach indicate that although they can feel vulnerable, the process is also reassuring. One stated that having a student gather feedback on the class and share it with him "gave me confidence that [the feedback] was thorough and trustworthy, unlike end-of-the-semester course [ratings]." Another professor reflected:

> Previously I had decided against the midterm [assessment] because I was skeptical that students would provide honest, constructive feedback at a point in the semester when their final grades were not yet determined and in a situation in which it would be difficult to preserve their anonymity. My enthusiasm for the process at this moment came largely from the role that a . . . student consultant could play as an interlocutor with students, explaining the purpose of the exercise as well as helping to generate honest, useful feedback.
>
> [My consultant] and I agreed that she would collaborate in composing the questionnaire as well as introduce it to the students and facilitate a follow-up discussion. These arrangements were essential for creating an environment in which students' comments could be frankly expressed as well as effectively distilled into specific, constructive suggestions. (Walker, 2012)

In addition to their appreciation of the process, faculty also describe the shared responsibility they feel as a result of taking this approach. One faculty member said about his choice to gather and discuss midsemester student feedback: "'I want them to know that they are in control, too. Things don't have to spin out of control if they speak up about it.'" Another faculty member, after gathering and responding to midsemester feedback, said: "'I definitely feel like there's more of a sense that we all own the class a little more'" (Cook-Sather, 2009b, p. 237; see also Giles et al., 2004).

Assessing Teaching and Learning across Courses

Shifting from fostering a collaborative and dialogic process within a single course as it is unfolding to assessing teaching and learning across courses as part of a larger research project, we turn now to consider how you can work in partnership with students outside of the courses you are teaching. Collaborating with students to investigate educational practices across courses has a precedent in student voice activities in primary and secondary schools that focus on students as researchers. This work "promotes 'partnerships' in which students work alongside teachers to mobilize their knowledge of school and become change agents of its culture and norms" (Fielding and Bragg, 2003, p. 4).

The practice of student-faculty partnerships also has deep roots in the Scholarship of Teaching and Learning (SoTL). For example, in the first issue of the *International Journal for the Scholarship of Teaching and Learning*, several articles focused on students' perspectives as essential to assessment of courses. For instance, Askell-Williams et al. (2007) invited teacher education students to address the question, "What happens in my university classes that helps me to learn?" In addition, in a report from the Carnegie Foundation for the Advancement of Teaching called "Listening to Students about Learning," Bueschel (2008) argued that paying close attention to students talk about learning "can help them become more active partners in their own education, more engaged in the classroom, and better positioned to succeed" (p. 4).

Both the student voice work in schools and partnership projects in SoTL share a commitment to "inviting students into emerging communities of practice, seeing roles for them not as objects of study, but as co-inquirers, collaborators, and partners in formulating questions, generating and analyzing data, making sense of findings, and lobbying for change" (Hutchings et al., 2011, pp. 39–40; see also Werder et al., 2010, and Kavadlo et al., 2012). One of the most widely known assessment projects that invites students into this kind of active, collaborative role is the Wabash National Study of Liberal Education (Wabash College, 2013). In many aspects of the Wabash National Study, student-faculty and student-staff teams work collaboratively "to put together appropriate processes for capturing students' perspectives—including surveys, interviews, focus groups (run in some cases by students themselves), and Town Hall gatherings" (Hutchings et al., 2011, p. 79). This approach also encourages collaboration through which "faculty, staff, and students reflect on and consider responses to the evidence" they gather (Blaich and Wise, 2011, p. 13).

Other institutions have built on this approach. As we discussed in Chapter 5, for instance, at North Carolina A&T State University, undergraduate students, designated Wabash-Provost Scholars, have been "trained to conduct student focus groups and other types of institutional assessment, including training on institutional review board (IRB) protocols" (Baker, 2012). The focus of the students' research has varied, but it has included understanding more about student responses to the Wabash Study data collected, A&T's intellectual climate, and issues such as admissions and dress code policies. Baker (2012) explains that, in addition to conducting focus groups and collecting focus group data, the Wabash-Provost Scholars "asked students follow-up questions to help better understand that year's concentration . . . analyzed and summarized the data, developed written reports (with recommendations), and presented their results to faculty and administrators, including the provost and chancellor" (North Carolina A&T, 2011).

Including students in assessment efforts such as those described above enacts "a commitment to more shared responsibility for learning among students and teachers, a more democratic intellectual community, and more authentic co-inquiry" (Hutchings and Huber, 2010, p. xii). As we have discussed, such an approach requires new notions of power (Mihans et al., 2008) that in turn "mean greater ability to act and thus a greater sense of responsibility" (Manor, Bloch-Schulman, Flannery and Felten, 2010, p. 10; Bovill, Cook-Sather, and Felten, 2011). As you plan to research teaching and learning with student partners, you will want to think about the culture and practices in your institution and how best to pursue this more collaborative approach to assessment within and across courses in your particular context.

Assessing Outcomes: Principles of Good Practice

In this section we switch from a focus on students' roles in assessing teaching and learning in higher education to students' roles in assessing student-faculty partnerships in themselves. While most of the formal assessment of student-faculty partnerships is undertaken by faculty or faculty developers, we advocate students being involved in this process. In a sense, student partners are always engaged in assessing processes and outcomes throughout this work, not necessarily through a formal process of judgment but rather in the original, Latin root meaning "assessment"—of "sitting beside" in order to appraise. Indeed, the notion of faculty and students sitting side by side and inquiring, both to affirm and to revise pedagogical practice, is precisely what we mean to emphasize in student-faculty partnerships overall.

To assess student-faculty partnerships effectively, good practice suggests capturing both the outcomes of this work and the processes of partnership (which may, in fact, also contribute to other outcomes). Because these collaborations are so process-oriented, focusing only on outcomes is a mistake (Ivanic, 2000). In other words, student-faculty partnerships are not simply a means to an end. The complex and intricate processes of relationship-forming and learning that unfold within negotiations of pedagogical processes have the potential to enhance metacognition in learning and develop more democratic spaces within universities.

These changes benefit students, faculty, and institutions. In the same way that students can be partners to us as faculty in explorations of teaching and learning, they can be partners with us in assessing the processes and outcomes of student-faculty partnership work focused on those explorations.

Good practice also involves attention to both formative and summative assessment. You will want to create the combination of approaches that will be most helpful to you in your context and with your goals. Different forms of investigating student-faculty partnerships are appropriate, and different ways of documenting partnership processes and outcomes are useful to different audiences. For instance, the audience for your assessment might include those doing the work of student-faculty partnerships, or those supporting partnerships from within the institution, as well as external funding agencies and others (such as university trustees or politicians) who may provide resources from beyond the institutions. Finally, we recommend that you carefully consider the aims of any assessment and where the findings are likely to be used, for example, as part of faculty development, for quality assurance purposes, or for dissemination to wider audiences.

Below are some recommendations that attempt to address the varied demands of any assessment process. We suggest some criteria for good practice in capturing and assessing the outcomes of student-faculty partnerships in different contexts.

Formative Assessment

In previous chapters we have discussed the importance of communication before and during the creation of student-faculty partnerships. Formative assessment is one way for you to ensure that you are engaging in just such intentional communication. As programs and projects develop, we recommend that you strive to provide regular opportunities for participants and, where relevant, facilitators to step back from their work and analyze how it is unfolding. This form of dialogue gives everyone involved the chance to make midcourse corrections, to change directions when necessary, and to clarify and affirm what is working in the partnership. Examples include

- Faculty engaged in designing or redesigning a course with students might ask: Do you feel that our collaboration has given you meaningful opportunities to share your perspectives, and to understand my perspectives, on assignments and activities for this course? How could we structure our work differently to ensure even more interchange?

- Students in the role of consultant to a faculty member teaching a course might ask their faculty partners simple questions, such as: Do you want to continue to focus on this particular aspect of your teaching? Is the kind of feedback I am offering useful? Should we shift the focus of our work?

- Faculty developers might ask both faculty and students: Are our meetings structured and facilitated in a way that elicits both faculty and student perspectives on the issues we are exploring? If so, what is most effective in making that dialogue happen? If not, how could these sessions be structured or facilitated differently?

Cook (1992) has argued that we should ensure that we prepare and support students well enough for engaging in partnership work. As we invite students to become part of assessing the processes and outcomes of student-faculty partnerships, we benefit from bringing to the conversation a range of possible examples, approaches, methodologies, and suggestions in order to stimulate student-generated ideas for assessing shared work.

It is also important to plan for more formal moments of reflection and feedback that are intended to involve a broader audience, such as interested colleagues and funders, in the process of formative assessment. This situates the partnership work within a larger frame and allows for comparison of experiences with other student-faculty partnerships and documentation of the process of partnerships unfolding. This kind of assessment addresses basic questions, including: What is working and needs to be affirmed? What should be revised? Responses are useful to participants, but they also engage other stakeholders in conversations about the process of partnership. Here are some questions you might consider using:

- What were your expectations as you approached this partnership, and how have they been met or not met thus far?

- What do see as the most, and the least, effective practices within this partnership?

- What do you see as the emerging outcomes of this work?

- What appear to be some of the meaningful questions or issues that this partnership seems not to be addressing, and how might we engage with those?

- What insights about teaching and learning have you derived from your reflection on this partnership?

Summative Assessment

While formative assessment gives participants an opportunity to reflect on, revise, and learn from their work in progress, summative assessment of student-faculty partnerships provides the opportunity to take a step back to gain perspective on the arc of the work and to document its outcomes for both internal and external audiences.

Consider using an end-of-partnership questionnaire or discussion with questions such as

- Looking back over the way the partnership was organized, which aspects of the structure contributed most positively to your learning or research experience, and why? Which were less positive, and why?

- What were the most significant benefits and challenges you experienced in working with your student/faculty partners? In what way, if any, has what you learned in and through that partnership shaped how you think about yourself as a student or a teacher?

- What are the most important pedagogical insights you gained from this experience? How have they informed your teaching or your learning, and how do they position or prepare you to continue to develop as a learner/teacher/researcher?

- Beyond specific pedagogical insights, what overall benefits did you derive from this opportunity? Why are these important?

- What advice do you have for student participants in future student-faculty partnerships?

- What advice do you have for faculty participants in future student-faculty partnerships?

- What advice do you have for the director of the program (where relevant) or others who are coordinating such initiatives in the future?

You might also consider asking participants to create a portfolio to document development over the course of a partnership. These can be used for faculty members' own professional development or for their processes of review, and they can be helpful to students as they prepare to apply for employment or advanced degrees. Such integrative activities often yield significant new learning, but because they take considerable time they should not be a requirement of a partnership program.

To gather evidence about the long-term outcomes of partnership, and perhaps also to build community around partnerships on your campus, you might host periodic gatherings of past and present participants to reflect together on their experiences. Surveys of past partners can generate similar information without the benefit (or the costs) associated with community-building events. Reflection and survey prompts might include

- Please complete the following statements and speculate about or explain any connections you see to your work through the partnership experience:

    - I am more aware of . . .

    - I am more comfortable with . . .

    - I work and/or interact with students/faculty . . .

    - I am less comfortable and/or I am concerned by . . .

- Please describe 1–3 pedagogical or curricular approaches or practices you have developed or revised since participating in the partnership and any ways in which your work through the partnership informed those.

- What do you need over time to sustain partnerships? Ideally, what kind of follow-up support would you like to have?

- If you could make one statement to share with others (students, faculty, administrators, funders) about this work, what would it be?

As with any assessment, reflection activities or postpartnership surveys may yield mixed results—variations, contradictions, or simply comments that are not always clear. Experiences of partnerships will be diverse, shaped not only by the structure and goals of the particular project but also by factors including personalities and events in participants' lives outside of this work. To make sense of the reflections you gather, we recommend (after you remove personally identifiable information from the materials) working in partnership with a few students and faculty to help you interpret the feedback and understand the different perspectives captured in the data. To make this reflective activity valuable for program improvement, you and your assessment partners may want to list and then discuss what the feedback suggests about what to change and what to affirm in existing partnership practices.

As you go through this or any assessment process, it is helpful to explain and model for your partners the importance of honestly capturing and representing the benefits and disadvantages, as well as the contradictions and nuances, of different individual and shared experiences. Like other partnership processes, collaborating on assessment can provide powerful opportunities for all participants to learn about the particulars of doing this work well and also about larger issues related to navigating differing perspectives with integrity.

10

Next Steps . . . Toward a
Partnership Movement?

We hope that this book has inspired some of the same enthusiasm in you that we have for student-faculty partnerships.
We also hope that the guiding principles and concrete suggestions
we have offered will be useful as you embark upon new, or expand,
existing partnerships with students. Finally, we hope that if you
are not already engaged in student-faculty partnerships you might
consider stepping forward, however cautiously, to join in this work.
The future shape of higher education depends on it.

If that seems like a bold claim, we invite you to think about
what is most valuable to you about your practice as a teacher and
scholar. If you are like the faculty we work with, you care deeply
about learning, both your students' and your own—learning that
leads to the creation of new knowledge and the development of
new capacities; learning that contributes to the growth of not only
strong individuals but also resilient communities. In an increasingly interconnected world, when educational institutions sometimes seem to be more interested in income and endowments than
learning, we need to reimagine higher education in ways that are
more rooted in principles of respect, reciprocity, and responsibility.
Partnership is a powerful yet flexible approach to achieve our
aspirations for colleges and universities.

In this chapter, we briefly review what we think has been accomplished by our many colleagues, students and faculty alike, who

have engaged in partnership. We also point to some areas we see as ripe for developing or extending student-faculty partnerships. In both our conclusions and our suggestions for next steps, the emphasis is on how we can best help students and faculty to learn and develop.

The Fruits of Partnership

Our experiences coordinating partnership programs, our research across different contexts and kinds of institutions, and our reflections on this work in these pages and elsewhere have clarified and confirmed for us what is so powerful and effective about student-faculty collaboration. On the one hand, partnerships can build upon familiar practices, such as gathering feedback to make changes in our practice; on the other hand, they can shift the very ground that we are standing on by asking us to rethink our foundational understandings of teaching and learning. By premising student-faculty relationships on respect, reciprocity, and shared responsibility, we can take common practices to a much deeper level. Doing this entails working within and sometimes against norms in higher education. By developing and sustaining partnerships, we can build on small-scale examples of collaborative practice among faculty and students as well as pioneer larger scale initiatives and create new visions of ways of working more suited to our emerging global society.

As the individual and institutional examples we offer in this book illustrate, partnerships between faculty and students that are rooted in principles of respect, reciprocity, and shared responsibility have the potential to transform what happens in individual classrooms and, more broadly, institutions of higher education. The kinds of partnership we write about in these pages help tp create completely different educational spaces. We remain vigilant to the dangers of empty claims of partnership and are highly aware that context, regulations, power relationships, reward structures, traditions, and habits of mind may interfere with the potential of partnerships. But with sensitivity to culture and context, position and power, you too, whether an isolated faculty member in a less-than-ideal environment for partnership or a member of a team of colleagues focused on changing your departmental or institutional norms, can integrate the spirit and practice of student-faculty partnerships into your work.

What we call for here is a reclaiming of the transformative possibilities of higher education. In this, we speak with students: the United Kingdom's National Union of Students argues that "partnership should be something identifiable and meaningful to students from their first encounter with an institution through to graduation" (NUS, 2012, p. 7). Although we may have some way to go before this is a reality for all students, all of us can play a role in inviting students into different learning and teaching partnerships that are relevant and appropriate to our different roles and contexts.

When created with sensitivity to institutional situations, departmental norms, individual pedagogical goals, and particular student populations, the kinds of collaborative efforts we have featured in his book can significantly deepen both faculty and student engagement in the learning process. They can energize partners as they move from traditionally divided, if not adversarial, positions toward shared roles and responsibilities. They can shift institutional culture, in both subtle and more substantial ways, so that respect, reciprocity, and shared responsibility become principles upon which all our practice is founded and through which, as one student suggested, we can be "re-invigorated."

This is not just about those of us who labor in higher education feeling good about what we do. It is about improving and making our work more meaningful, with more significant processes and outcomes, for all of those involved. For many faculty and students, working in partnership offers a way of reclaiming some of the original purpose for entering universities in the first place—to learn and develop as individuals and within communities, and to make ourselves and our world at least a little bit more wise, humane, and just. These changes connect to the possible next steps we see for this work.

Next Steps

We see several interrelated areas in which student-faculty partnerships can help those of us in higher education to clarify our enduring commitments and also to imagine and create new ways of learning and teaching:

- Expanding student-faculty partnership work into new contexts
- Connecting with more diverse students
- Preparing a new generation of faculty for a new kind of higher education

Expanding Student-Faculty Partnership Work into New Contexts

The landscape of higher education is changing. Technology is enabling the creation of new pedagogies and disruptive educational formats. While some of these may be antithetical to the aims and practices of partnership, others might present powerful opportunities. The examples we provide from Derek Bruff's (2012) and Cathy Davidson's (2009, 2012) work, for instance, each demonstrate different kinds of what Henry Jenkins at MIT has called "participatory culture" (2006). Web-based communities, like some grassroots organizations, that enact participatory culture are characterized by

- Low barriers to entry
- Strong support for sharing one's contributions
- Informal mentorship, from experienced to novice

- A sense of connection to each other

- A sense of ownership in what is being created

- A strong collective sense that something is at stake (Bass, 2012, p. 27)

Except perhaps for the low bar for entrance, these characteristics also describe an excellent teaching and learning environment— and an effective student-faculty partnership.

Advocates and practitioners of partnership, therefore, should consider both what we can learn from online participatory cultures and how web-based tools might foster new partnership practices (see Williams et al., 2011). Faculty member Howard Glasser and student Maggie Powers at Bryn Mawr College, for instance, used Twitter to decenter power in a classroom, "140 characters at a time" (2011), which they did while maintaining a firm commitment to principles of respect, reciprocity, and responsibility.

Connecting with More Diverse Students

Another area we wish to highlight and that we have just begun to explore in our own work is how student-faculty partnerships can facilitate more and deeper connections with diverse students. As we have discussed in relation to working in partnership with students of color (Cook-Sather and Agu, 2012, 2013), international students (Cook-Sather and Li, 2013), and deaf students (Felten and Bauman, 2013), the experiences and perspectives of students who self-identify and/or are identified in ways that position them outside of the mainstream have a great deal to teach us about themselves, about ourselves, about teaching and learning, and about higher education. Each differently positioned student has unique insights to offer, and at the same time, collectively, differences can be conceptualized not only as resources but also as what we have in common, elements that can unite us (Solomon, 2012).

This work, while emphasizing the importance of including and accommodating "unheard voices" (Harper and Quaye, 2009), also argues for creating a new space in which diversity and difference are seen as the very conditions for engagement in the first place, rather than being viewed as an add-on or a separate issue (Felten et al., 2013). Attending to what these particular differences have to teach us will help us explore, across differences, what is possible if we reframe what are commonly understood to be deficits that hinder student engagement and achievement. Such attention raises larger questions about how our assumptions about particular students might mask opportunities for, and learning from, deeper engagement among all of our students.

Preparing a New Generation of Faculty for a New Kind of Higher Education

The kind of partnerships featured in this book prefigure or suggest a completely different kind of university classroom—a classroom that is different for all students, not just those who participate in projects and programs like those we have highlighted. Another area for further exploration, then, is the way in which these opportunities prepare the next generation of faculty to be teachers and opportunities for partnership programs to be integrated into preparing future faculty initiatives (Walker et al., 2008; Higher Education Academy, n.d.). Some students come to partnership with the goal of becoming a professor already in mind, but others come to that aspiration through experiencing partnerships focused on teaching and learning. Working closely with faculty to explore teaching and learning not only from the other side of the desk but also, as many students put it, "behind the scenes," gives students a more realistic idea of what it takes to teach at the university level. It also prepares them to lead the way in creating higher education cultures and institutions that embrace the potential of student-faculty partnerships.

A common and striking outcome of this partnership work is that students develop deeper understanding of what faculty do, empathy with the struggles of faculty, and new ideas about what faculty work could be. As we suggested in Chapter 5, students become, in one partner's words, "teacher advocates" and challenge themselves and their peers to think critically about what they as students could do differently to improve their own and others' learning. Others become passionate about the potential for partnership, carrying the values of respect, reciprocity, and shared responsibility into other classrooms and forums across higher education as well as into their future careers. The capacity these students develop to work across differences and engage confidently and openly in the complex processes of teaching and learning, and the desire to make colleges and universities places where such engagement is common, provide us with a promising outlook for the future of higher education.

Toward a Partnership Movement?

In a recent report Gärdebo and Wiggberg (2012) describe students as the university's "unspent resource" and argue that "if there is to be a single important structural change during the coming decades, it is the changing role of students who are given more room in defining and contributing to higher education" (p. 9). Or as an Elon University student partner once commented: "I think some faculty are so focused on getting stuff done that they don't pay attention to their students, who I think are the most valuable resources in a classroom." We agree.

Student-faculty partnerships often have transformative results for individual courses, students, and faculty. They also have the potential for institutional and cultural change. This kind of change emerges from a single group or program, at first causing only small but productive disruptions in the status quo of a campus. As partnership practices deepen and spread, those disruptions reinforce each other, beginning to change the very foundations of a university.

This is not the typical path toward reform in the academy. Most efforts at wide-scale change in higher education chart a more conventional path. Palmer (1992) refers to this as the "organizational approach" because it is "premised on the notion that bureaucracies—their rules, roles, and relationships—define the limits of social reality within which change must happen" (p. 10). Those seeking change through this approach focus on issues of formal power, striving to achieve their aims by reorganizing structures and negotiating with established authorities. In other words, change comes through curricular reform or administrative shake-ups or external disruptions. Because administrators dominate most university power structures, they are the source of power and the arbiters of change on campus. Students typically have little or no role in this organizational framework, although occasionally they might persuade those with real power to change direction. This dependency often frustrates reformers and constrains visions of change to what seems practical or doable within a given context.

Palmer contrasts the organizational approach to change with what he calls "the way of the movement." In social movements, like those for racial and gender equality in the United States, activists developed power sources outside of formal organizational structures. Only after building capacity and momentum among like-minded individuals did they attempt to reform social frameworks. "The genius of movements is paradoxical," Palmer concludes. "They abandon the logic of organizations in order to gather the power necessary to rewrite the logic of organizations" (p. 12).

In Palmer's analysis, movements typically progress through four stages. In the first, "isolated individuals decide to stop leading divided lives [i.e., they start acting in ways congruent with their own values, even though that is outside the norm]" (p. 12). This first step requires individuals to break from the kinds of habits we described in Chapter 1—those structures and practices that keep hierarchy as the standard way that higher education is structured and through which systems operate. The next step in Palmer's model has these individuals discovering each other and forming groups for mutual support. We see the work the three of us have done, and the work of colleagues we feature in this book, as a version of that discovery and formation of support networks within and across institutions.

The third step in Palmer's model moves from linked individuals to a more public presence and effort. In Palmer's words, "empowered by community, [individuals] learn to translate 'private problems' into public issues" (p. 12). Here the metaphor of movement suggests terms such a "momentum." As the movement gains momentum, it enters the forth stage: "Alternative rewards emerge to sustain the movement's vision, which may force the conventional reward system to change" (p. 12).

Movements rarely flow neatly through these four stages, however. More often, progress is halting or inconsistent. Sometimes change stalls and a local movement must begin again from the start. Other times, small steps build steadily at a pace that even the most optimistic participants could not have anticipated—a phenomenon historian Rebecca Solnit (2005) has called "hope in the dark."

We are not so bold as to equate student-faculty partnerships with the civil rights or women's movements. However, this work has a lineage dating from John Dewey more than a century ago and that has continued through student calls for democratic education fifty years ago (Bovill, 2013b). Despite the solid roots, the potential for institutional change sparked by the current wave of student partnerships is too new to prompt any claims of certainty. Still, we believe that Palmer's "way of the movement" aligns with the practice of student-faculty partnerships at individual universities and across higher education. Seeds of change are planted when one partnership takes root on a campus. From there, in our experience, the potential for individual and institutional change begins slowly to emerge. Perhaps this is a metaphor you can embrace—and a budding movement that you can join.

As we have stated many times throughout this book, start small; but remember Margaret Mead's assertion: We should "never doubt that a thoughtful group of committed citizens can change the world. Indeed, it is the only thing that ever has." We invite you to join us in establishing and nurturing student-faculty partnerships to enhance teaching and learning—and perhaps also to transform higher education.

Appendix I

The Ladder of Active Student
Participation in Curriculum Design

A conceptual model that is potentially helpful in considering the nature of student-faculty partnerships is the "Ladder of Active Student Participation in Curriculum Design" (Bovill & Bulley, 2011) (see Figure A.1).

This model outlines a range of levels of student participation that might be possible or desirable in different contexts. On this model, the rung that is labeled "partnership—a negotiated curriculum" is near the top of the ladder, recognizing that in many contexts student-faculty partnerships might be considered a high-level aspiration.

This ladder will be familiar to some of you as an adaptation of Arnstein's (1969) Ladder of Citizen Participation. Other authors have adapted and referred to Arnstein's model in attempts to conceptualize levels of participation in different settings and with different people (see for example, Hart, 1992, for a ladder of young people's participation). The Ladder of Active Student Participation in Curriculum Design was intended by the authors to be used as a tool to stimulate discussion among faculty and students about levels and types of student participation in different settings and about the different kinds of student-faculty relationships that are imagined and enacted at each rung of the ladder. Many colleagues have questioned whether students being in control is possible or desirable—the idea of completely removing the role of the

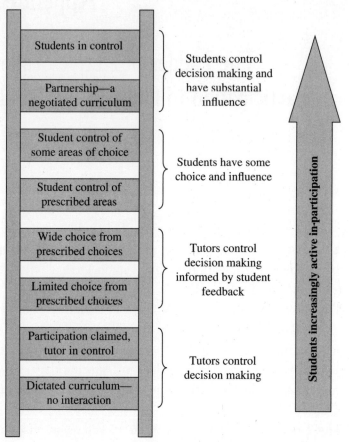

Figure A.1   Ladder of Student Participation in Curriculum Design

faculty seeming a step too far. This is consistent with Breen and Littlejohn's (2000) acknowledgment that teachers' subject expertise and their key role in facilitating learning is not removed in a negotiated classroom. Most colleagues with whom we have discussed the ladder model seem to agree that the partnership rung is a more appropriate goal for redefining faculty-student relationships.

There is a possible implication with any ladder model that the higher you go, the better—but the ladder need not be read that way. We acknowledge that, for example, faculty with a large group of undergraduate students in a course that is regulated by a professional body might aim for different levels of student participation than faculty with a small group of graduate students. Professional requirements usually relate to outcomes in terms of "fitness to practice" and less frequently dictate the ways in which the knowledge, skills, and values required of a professional graduate are to be achieved. This leaves flexibility in choosing pedagogical approaches most suitable to engender these graduate attributes.

What is possible will be heavily influenced by the goals, experiences, and creativity of the faculty and students involved and the context within which they are working. Therefore, higher up the ladder may not always be considered more desirable, depending upon the context. Indeed, Bovill and Bulley (2011) argue that "the second rung, 'participation claimed but tutor in control,' is particularly concerning. Students are led to believe falsely that they can participate in a process" (p. 181). What is worrying here is that "participation that is claimed but not genuine can be damaging to the participative process and can lead to mistrust" (p. 181). Some might argue that "the second rung could be placed lower than the first, because the 'dictated curriculum' does not deceive students with an empty claim of participation" (p. 181).

We have had some productive discussions about faculty-student partnerships with colleagues in different countries as a result of presenting the ladder model. Key issues raised by colleagues include: the different perspectives of where on the ladder a particular initiative is aiming or performing; how the curriculum is conceptualized (e.g., whether emphasis is placed on content, processes, structure, or underpinning principles); and whether the focus is on one class session, a single course, or a larger program.

The model is not intended to be a static view of the world, but rather as Carey (2013) has commented in relation to the ladder model, it is intended to be a useful heuristic to stimulate ideas among faculty and students about what might be possible and desirable in reconceptualizing the ways in which we relate to one another. Many colleagues and students have suggested new or alternative rungs or have wanted to swap around some of the rungs. Some have wanted to tip the ladder on its side, realizing that this might help reduce the feeling that some rungs are inherently better than others. For others the ladder seems too simple and there is a need for complementary ladders to represent different aspects of learning or the curriculum, or to represent different people's perspectives and visions. For example, in a particular classroom initiative, a few students may become involved intensively and their perspectives may be very different from other students less overtly involved or engaged in the class.

Tritter and McCallum (2006), within the context of user involvement in health systems, criticized Arnstein's original ladder for the overt emphasis on power while overlooking the importance of considering the different forms of knowledge and expertise that individuals bring to any relationship. They emphasized the need to place a greater value on the processes of participation, involvement, and partnership—so within this frame—student-faculty partnership experiences and processes become as important to learning as the more usually emphasized learning outcomes. They also argue that the diversity of knowledge and experience in any relationship must be valued and this implies that forming student-faculty partnerships is not just about a shift of power in who makes pedagogical decisions, but it is also about a fundamental change to accepted beliefs about who should take part in knowledge construction processes within higher education.

The discussions we have had about the ladder highlight what many people experience as a tension between the theoretical and the practical. We offer the ladder as an entry or jumping-off point for further exploration and experimentation.

Appendix II

Guidelines for the Students as Learners and Teachers (SaLT) Program at Bryn Mawr College (Modified for This Volume)

The SaLT program supports student-faculty partnerships undertaken while faculty members are teaching a course. Through this program, a student who is not enrolled in the faculty member's course visits the classroom once a week and takes detailed observation notes, meets weekly with the faculty member, and meets weekly with other students in similar partnerships and with the coordinator of the program. If you are planning to create a version of such partnerships or a program like this, the guidelines below might be directly applicable. If, however, you are thinking about pursuing a different form of student-faculty partnership, such as planning or revising a course before it is taught, you will need to modify these guidelines.

In the SaLT program, students who visit faculty members' classrooms are designated "consultants." Drawing on some of the root meanings of the word "consult"—to deliberate, to confer—the emphasis here is on the dialogic nature of these encounters between faculty members and student consultants: the idea that people benefit from seeking out one another's perspectives and discussing how those might inform teaching and learning. Ideally, the relationship is one of shared inquiry in which both faculty member and student consultant contribute to and learn from the partnership.

Note that this understanding of "consultation" differs funda-mentally from the slightly negative connotations of "consultation" implied on the lower rungs of the "ladder of active student partici-pation in curriculum design" in Appendix I, where consultation is used to confer the idea of an instrumental approach to checking stakeholders agree with something that is often already decided. This variation in terminology is important to consider, and you should give some thought to what language you want to use to name and describe your partnership work or program. The purpose of this particular name in this context was to confer legitimacy on students without naming them and their role in a way that might be threatening or scary.

The guidelines developed for faculty participants in the SaLT program aim to acknowledge the complexity of creating new roles and relationships within conversations about teaching and learning, as well as the equal but different risks that participants take in open-ing their classrooms to consultants and that consultants take in of-fering their perspectives on aspects of faculty members' teaching. They also strive to support the community building and learn-ing that all participants can experience when those involved are respectful, thoughtful, and communicative throughout the process.

1. Establishing Relationship/Rapport

The first step in building a partnership is to establish a relationship as people.

- During your initial meeting, introduce yourself and say something about why you are participating in this program. What interests, questions, and hopes do you bring?

- Learn from the Student Consultant about why she or he is participating and what questions and hopes she or he brings to the table.

- This first part of your initial discussion should be about you two as people, not yet about the work you will do together during the partnership, although it will lead into a discussion of the collaborative work you will undertake.

2. Establishing a Focus for Your Work

During your initial meeting, before the Student Consultant visits your class, talk with him or her to clarify what your teaching and learning goals are for the partnership overall. You may want to tell the Student Consultant

- What the course goals are

- Some specific pedagogical goals you have within the course

- What kinds of learning experiences you want students to have and why

Make sure the Student Consultant understands what you want him or her to focus on when he or she visits your class. Based on what you discuss with the Student Consultant, formulate a clear statement of what the focus of his or her observations should be, knowing that this focus will likely evolve and/or shift as the semester progresses.

3. Clarifying the Student Consultant's Role and Responsibilities

Discuss with the Student Consultant what his or her role will be.

- Will she or he be silent and simply take notes?

- Will she or he participate, and if so, how and when?

There are no set answers to these questions: it depends on the class, you, the Student Consultant, and so forth, but you and the Student Consultant should decide up front what she or he will do and then, as the partnership unfolds, reconsider these questions.

- Set a regular time to meet (right before your class is not generally a good time, although some people have made it work).

- Confer with your Student Consultant about whether he or she should email his or her observation notes prior to the post-visit discussion or bring the notes with him or her to the meeting.

4. Discussing How the Student Consultant Will Be Introduced to Your Class

The recommended approach is

- You explain to your class that you are choosing to take part in the SaLT program in order to engage in dialogue about teaching and learning in ways you would not otherwise have the opportunity to do and that the project is not about judgment in any remedial or punitive sense but rather about critical reflection on teaching and learning for the purpose of improving both, and then . . .

- The Student Consultant introduces himself or herself. He or she should reiterate that the purpose of the program is to foster dialogue about teaching and learning, and that he or she is there to hear from students as well as work with you regarding what might improve teaching and learning in the course. If you are both comfortable with it, the students in the class should be invited to approach or contact the Student Consultant to talk about their experiences in the course.

5. Classroom Observations and Note Taking

- When the Student Consultant visits your classroom, he or she should be on time, respectful, and stay focused on what you want him or her to focus on.

- The Student Consultant will take detailed notes for himself or herself with the goal of documenting and making sense of what he or she sees. These notes will not be shared with you (unless you both agree this is the better way to go); rather, the Student Consultant will draw on them to prepare a set of observations and thoughts to share with you at a subsequent meeting. The Student Consultant will use a specified structure for note-taking (see the example at the end of this Appendix) with a line down the center of the page with "Observations" on the left side and "Reflections" on the right side. The left side will describe in as much detail as possible, without analyzing, examples or instances of the issue you have asked the Student Consultant to focus on. He or she should note the time in this column so you know how much time is spent on what kinds of activities in the class. During and after his or her visit to the class, the Student Consultant will write in the right column thoughts, reflections, questions, ideas, and suggestions for you based on what she or he has observed and written in the left column.

- The Student Consultant will look over his or her notes and write or type up a version of his or her observations and reflections to share with you.

- As the semester progresses, you may want to revise this format and/or develop a different one. This is just a starting place to reflect back what an observer sees in your classroom.

6. Meetings with Your Student Consultant

When you meet with the Student Consultant, he or she will do the following:

- Start by asking you how you felt about the class and your treatment of the issue you had asked him or her to focus on.

- Share his or her notes and talk with you about what he or she saw and thought about.

Again, since partnerships are relationships, each develops something of its own way of shaping these conversations. You may start out one way and then shift as the semester progresses.

7. Conducting Midsemester Feedback

One of the most beneficial components of student-faculty partnerships through this program is the gathering of midsemester feedback. Faculty consistently cite this as a turning point for them with their classes. (See Cook-Sather, 2009b, for a discussion of faculty and student experiences of this process.)

A. Be sure you are willing to respond to the feedback the Student Consultant gathers—that is, that you are willing to make some sort of change in response to student feedback and thoughtfully explain why you can make those changes and cannot make other suggested changes. (This is critical: both educational research and students argue that it is worse to ask for feedback and ignore it or rationalize/defend all one's current practices than not to ask for feedback at all.)

B. It is important to think about the goals of your midsemester feedback. It could be for learning about the students' perspective on a specific question, about finding a new focus for the partnership, emphasizing expectations, and/or prompting students to think about their engagement in the class. Deciding what the goal of the process is can help you decide what types of questions to include.

C. Be clear about what you want feedback on. Given your goal(s), generate with your Student Consultant 3–5 questions to ask students in the class. Each set of questions should be tailored to the particular course within some more general parameters. Many faculty have found variations on the following basic questions very useful and informative:

   1. What is working well for you in this class? (perhaps specifying particular components of the class upon which you want feedback: readings, class discussions, assignments, class dynamic, etc.)

   2. What is not working or what are you struggling with?

   3. What is the professor doing to support your learning and what could the professor change to improve your learning experience in this class?

   4. What are you doing to further your own learning and what could you do differently to improve your learning experience in this class?

D. Communicate to students ahead of time that the Student Consultant will gather feedback and share it with you. It is important that students have a chance to prepare for the feedback session and that they know you will see what they write, not as it is written (in their own handwriting) but as it is transcribed, word for word, by the Student Consultant.

E. The Student Consultant will type up the questions on a sheet of paper with spaces for student responses and make enough copies for everyone in the class. (You can also do this electronically, but the response rate is lower, and students indicate that they appreciate the experience of all of them responding to the questions together, at once, in class.)

F. When the Student Consultant conducts the midcourse feedback session, he or she will first have the students in the class answer the feedback questions on paper in silence and, if there is time and if you wish him or her to, he or she can draw on what students have written to have a discussion in which he or she identifies broad categories of feedback, records these for you, and takes the written responses with him or her.

G. The Student Consultant will type up student responses in a form that can be shared with you and other students in the class. She or he will type up all student responses to each question and also provide an overview with the categories or themes she or he discerns.

H. Arrange to meet with the Student Consultant to discuss the feedback. This step has two parts: (a) processing the feedback with you and (b) helping you think about how to share the feedback with the class.

Talk with the Student Consultant about whether you would like to receive the typed-up feedback before you meet or when you meet. There are benefits and drawbacks to each: If you receive it ahead, you can work through it on your own first and then you can meet with your Student Consultant to discuss it; if the Student Consultant walks you through it, she or he can facilitate the process of sense making, but it might be harder for you to take it all in and formulate your responses to students. In either case, be sure there is a discussion in which you both interpret the feedback and consider how to share it with students.

Sharing the student feedback with the class is very important: students in the class, as well as you, need to see the range of responses and think about how to address the diversity of students' needs while still pursuing your goals for the course. The Student Consultant will assist you in identifying some meaningful changes to make and in formulating explanations—not defenses—for why other changes cannot be made.

8. Evolving Your Partnership

Some partners follow the above format for the entire semester; others start out following the above format and then, around week 8 or 10, shift to a different format and/or focus. Possibilities for such a shift of focus include

- Have the Student Consultant visit a different class you are teaching, if she or he is available to do so

- Shift your focus to planning for next semester's or subsequent courses; ask the Student Consultant to help you think through and plan for how to apply what you have explored this semester to other courses

- Ask your Student Consultant to research particular pedagogical approaches or "threshold concepts" within your discipline and discuss how they might inform your teaching

9. Concluding Your Partnership

- Discuss with the Student Consultant the possibility of her conducting the final feedback for the class, using the college's or a revised form, to afford the same benefits as her doing midcourse feedback and also to give her a chance to say thank you and good-bye to the class.

- Once you are finished with your partnership, you should have a final conversation with the Student Consultant with whom you have been working in which she or he will

  - Share with you what she or he got out of working with you.

  - Ask for some feedback about your work with him or her (i.e., What did he or she do that was particularly useful? What could he or she have done more of or better?). This latter is particularly important to make the exchange reciprocal—so the Student Consultant is also getting feedback on his or her facilitation of learning.

- Talk with you about how this work might inform future teaching/learning for you, him or her, and/or students in your class.

Observation Note Format and Excerpt from Sample Notes

Time	Observations	Reflections
11:35	Discussion with students about topical issues as well as life/temperature concerns before class begins	Obviously comfortable, easy, open dynamic; also great to see how you extend the teaching/learning time into these casual exchanges
11:41	Review from last week as well as preview of what will come today. You ask students to recollect and to define terms. You remind them of other, related terms.	Helps students create continuity across class meetings and to be clear on the meanings of key terms they will need for their analyses. You get students involved right away; it is clear that they need to remember the terms and know what they mean. You push for specificity, and they seem comfortable with that pressure.
11:45	You ask questions for which there are definite, specific answers.	Another way to check for understanding? Brief reflection time for students in which they define the key terms on index cards and pass them in to you?
11:50	You write terms on board	Good way to signal that these are essential and that students should write them too.
11:53	You state that you have a lot to cover today.	I wonder about the sense of rushing this creates.
11:55	Students ask one another questions and answer one another without looking at you.	This is a wonderful indication that students feel confident, active, engaged, and not as though they always have to defer or return to you. They can carry on the discussion without your intervention. So inspiring!

Appendix III

Practical Strategies for Developing Student-Led Research Projects

From the Students as Change Agents Program, University of Exeter, United Kingdom

The Students as Change Agents project invites students to engage in active research within their College looking into ways of improving the learning and teaching experience (see University of Exeter, undated). Applicants choose their own topic of research that addresses an area of learning and/or teaching that is of concern within their discipline or College, or even something that might affect all students.

This is a collaborative project involving both the University's Education Enhancement Department, coordinating staff in each College and the Students' Guild, with student representatives from Staff-Student Liaison Committees (SSLCs) taking responsibility for promoting evidence-based change.

Dunne & Zandstra (2011, p. 28) offer the following advice for developing student-led research projects:

1. Start with a small number of projects that are manageable; put time into making sure they are successful and that the results are worthwhile.
2. Maintain a constantly positive stance, looking for good practice rather than focusing on the less good, since this allows forward progress and the valuing and acknowledgment of faculty who are doing things well.

3. Ensure that students involved in any project have agreed who is going to be responsible for what, and be clear with students about expectations for working arrangements and their role.
4. Have high expectations of the students but always be available in the background, and make it clear they can contact you as they need.
5. Keep in contact with students throughout a project and gain ongoing feedback on progress. This keeps the momentum going but also ensures that help and support is given as required.
6. On occasion, students may need support in finding strategies to work in ways that are not seen as intrusive or threatening, and therefore alienating to faculty; talk through ideas for doing this.
7. Be sensitive to different perspectives (from senior management, academics, professional services, and support staff, as well as students) and get buy-in to ensure change is taken on board.
8. Make sure that positive outcomes are shared with appropriate parties and seek strategies for doing this—ongoing success may depend in part on visibility. Having a conference at the end of the year gives an absolute deadline that provides an incentive for completing projects.

References

Ahlfeldt, S., Mehta, S., and Sellinow, T. "Measurement and Analysis of Student Engagement Where Varying Levels of PBL Methods of Instruction Were in Use." *Higher Education Research and Development*, 2005, 24(1), 5–20.

Alcoff, L. M. "The Problem of Speaking for Others." In L. A. Bell and D. Blumfeld (eds.), *Overcoming Racism and Sexism* (pp. 229–254). Lanham, MD: Rowman & Littlefield, 1995.

Aleamoni, L. "Student Rating Myths versus Research Facts from 1924 to 1998." *Journal of Personnel Evaluation in Education*, 1999, 13(2), 153–166.

Altrichter, H., Posch, P., and Somekh, B. *Teachers Investigate Their Work: An Introduction to the Methods of Action Research*. London: Routledge, 1993.

Arnstein, S. R. A ladder of citizen participation, *Journal of the American Institute of Planners*, 1969, 35(4), 216–224.

Arum, R., and Roska, J. *Academically Adrift: Limited Learning on College Campuses*. Chicago: University of Chicago Press, 2010.

Askell-Williams, H., Lawson, M., and Murray-Harvey, R. "What Happens in My University Classes that Helps Me to Learn?: Teacher Education Students' Instructional Metacognitive Knowledge." *International Journal for the Scholarship of Teaching and Learning*, 2007, 1. Retrieved from http://hdl.handle.net/10518/2717

Astin, A. W. *What Matters in College? Four Critical Years Revisited*. San Francisco: Jossey-Bass, 1993.

Auster, C. J., and MacRone, M. "The Classroom as a Negotiated Social Setting: An Empirical Study of the Effects of Faculty Members' Behavior on Students' Participation." *Teaching Sociology*, 1994, 22(4), 289–300.

Azevedo, R. "Theoretical, Conceptual, Methodological, and Instructional Issues in Research on Metacognition and Self-Regulated Learning: A Discussion." *Metacognition Learning*, 2009, 4, 87–95.

Bain, K. *What the Best College Teachers Do*. Cambridge, MA: Harvard University Press, 2012.

Bain, K., and Zimmerman, J. "Understanding Great Teaching." *Peer Review*, 2009, 11(2), 9–12.

Baker, G. R. "North Carolina A&T State University: A Culture of Inquiry." (NILOA Examples of Good Assessment Practice). Urbana, IL: University of Illinois and Indiana University, National Institute for Learning Outcomes Assessment, 2012. Retrieved on March 17, 2013 from http://www.learningoutcomeassessment.org/CaseStudyNCAT.html

Baker, V. L., and Griffin, K. A. "Beyond Mentoring and Advising: Toward Understanding the Role of 'Faculty Developers' in Student Success." *About Campus*, 2010, January/February.

Barnes, E., Goldring, L., Bestwick, A., and Wood, J. "A Collaborative Evaluation of Student-Staff Partnership in Inquiry-Based Educational Development." In S. Little (ed.), *Staff-Student Partnerships in Higher Education*. (pp. 16–30). London: Continuum, 2011.

Barnett, R. *Higher Education: A Critical Business*. Maidenhead, UK: Society for Research into Higher Education and Open University Press, 1997.

Barr, R. B., and Tagg, J. "From Teaching to Learning: A New Paradigm for Undergraduate Education." *Change*, 1995, November/December, 13–25.

Bass, R. "The Scholarship of Teaching: What's the Problem?" *Inventio: Creative Thinking about Learning and Teaching*, 1999, 1(1).

Bass, R. "Disrupting Ourselves: The Problem of Learning in Higher Education." *EDUCAUSE Review*, 2012, 47(2).

Battat, J. "Facilitating Quantum Leaps: Reflections on How to Promote Active Student Learning in a Physics Classroom." *Teaching and Learning Together in Higher Education*, 2012, 6. Retrieved 5 January 2012 from http://teachingandlearningtogether.blogs.brynmawr.edu/archived-issues/sixth-issue-spring-2012/facilitating-quantum-leaps-reflections-on-how-to-promote-active-student-learning-in-a-physics-classroom

Baxter Magolda, M. B. *Making Their Own Way: Narratives for Transforming Higher Education to Promote Self-Development*. Sterling, VA: Stylus, 2001.

Baxter Magolda, M. B. "Learning Partnerships Model: A Framework for Promoting Self-Authorship." In M. B. Baxter Magolda and P. M. King (eds.), *Learning Partnerships: Theory and Models of Practice to Educate for Self-Authorship* (pp. 37–62). Sterling, VA: Stylus, 2004.

Baxter Magolda, M. B. "The Evolution of Self-Authorship." In MyintSwe Khine (ed.), *Knowing, Knowledge and Beliefs: Epistemological Studies across Diverse Cultures* (pp. 45–64). Dordrecht: Springer, 2008.

Baxter Magolda, M. B. *Authoring Your Life: Developing an Internal Voice to Navigate Life's Challenges*. Sterling, VA: Stylus, 2009.

Bird, C., and Koirala, B. *Partnership in Education: A Review of Modalities and Their Potential Application in Service Delivery within the Government Primary Education Sector*. Kathmandu: EC BPEP, 2002.

Blaich, C., and Wise, K. The Wabash National Study—The Impact of Teaching Practices and Institutional Conditions on Student Growth, 2011. Retrieved on 18 March 2013 from http://www.liberalarts.wabash.edu/storage/wabash-study-student-growth_blaich-wise_aera-2011.pdf

Bourner, T. "The Broadening of the Higher Education Curriculum, 1970–2002: An Ipsative Enquiry." *Higher Education Review*, 2004, 36(2), 39–52.

Bovill, C. "Sharing Responsibility for Learning through Formative Evaluation: Moving to Evaluation as Learning." *Practice and Evidence of the Scholarship of Teaching and Learning in Higher Education*, 2011, 6(2), 96–109. Retrieved from http://www.pestlhe.org.uk/index.php/pestlhe/article/view/112/222

Bovill, C. "An Investigation of Co-created Curricula within Higher Education in the UK, Ireland and the USA." *Innovations in Education and Teaching*

International, 2013a. Retrieved on 30 May 2013 from http://www.tandfonline
.com/doi/abs/10.1080/14703297.2013.770264

Bovill, C. "Students and Staff Co-creating Curricula: A New Trend or
an Old Idea We Never Got Around to Implementing?" In C. Rust (ed.),
Improving Student Learning through Research and Scholarship: 20 Years of ISL.
Oxford: The Oxford Centre for Staff and Educational Development (pp.
96–108), 2013b.

Bovill, C., Aitken, G., Hutchison, J., Morrison, F., Roseweir, K., Scott, A., and
Sotannde, S. "Experiences of Learning through Collaborative Evaluation from
a Postgraduate Certificate in Professional Education." *International Journal for
Academic Development,* 2010, 15(2), 143–154.

Bovill, C., and Bulley, C. J. "A Model of Active Student Participation in
Curriculum Design: Exploring Desirability and Possibility." In C. Rust (ed.),
*Improving Student Learning (18) Global Theories and Local Practices: Institutional,
Disciplinary and Cultural Variations* (pp. 176–188). Oxford: The Oxford Centre
for Staff and Educational Development, 2011.

Bovill, C., Cook-Sather, A., and Felten, P. "Students as Co-Creators of Teaching
Approaches, Course Design and Curricula: Implications for Academic Developers."
International Journal for Academic Development, 2011, 16(2), 133–145.

Bovill, C., Sheward, L. and Smyth, K. "Underground and Undervalued: A
Survey of Scottish Pedagogic Research in Higher Education. In C. Rust (ed.),
Improving Student Learning through Research and Scholarship: 20 Years of ISL (pp.
27–39). Oxford: The Oxford Centre for Staff and Educational Development,
2013.

Bovill, C., Sheward, L. and Smyth, K. *Higher Education Research in Scotland:
Report of a Survey Undertaken for Universities Scotland Educational Development
Sub-Committee.* Edinburgh: Universities Scotland, 2012.

Breen, M. P., and Littlejohn, A. "The Practicalities of Negotiation." In M. P.
Breen and A. Littlejohn (eds.), *Classroom Decision-Making: Negotiation and
Process Syllabuses in Practice.* Cambridge: Cambridge University Press, 2000.

Brew, A., and Barrie, S. "Academic Development Through a Negotiated Curriculum". *International Journal for Academic Development* 1999, 4(1), 34–42.

Brookfield, S. *Becoming a Critically Reflective Teacher*. San Francisco, CA: Jossey-Bass, 1995.

Bruff, D. Leveraging Student Interests through Social Bookmarking. CIRTL Network 2012. Retrieved on 25 July 2013 from http://www.cirtl.net/node/7769

Bryson, C., and Hand, L. "The Role of Engagement in Inspiring Teaching and Learning." *Innovations in Education and Teaching International*, 2007, 44(4), 349–362.

Bueschel, A. C. "Listening to Students about Learning: Strengthening Pre-Collegiate Education in Community Colleges (SPECC)." Stanford, CA: The Carnegie Foundation for the Advancement of Teaching, 2008.

Carey, P. "Student as Co-Producer in a Marketised Higher Education System: A Case Study of Students' Experience of Participation in Curriculum Design." *Innovations in Education and Teaching International*, 2013, 50(3), 250–260.

Carleton College Student Observer Program. Learning and Teaching Center. Retrieved July 1, 2013 from http://apps.carleton.edu/campus/ltc/services/observers

Caulfield, J. "What Motivates Students to Provide Feedback to Teachers about Teaching and Learning? An Expectancy Theory Perspective." *International Journal for the Scholarship of Teaching and Learning*, 2007, 1 (1 January). Retrieved 15 July 2007 from http://www.georgiasouthern.edu/ijsotl

Chickering, P., and Gamson, Z. "Seven Principles for Good Practice in Undergraduate Education." *The Wingspread Journal*, 1987, 9(2), 1–10. Retrieved from http:// www.uis.edu/liberalstudies/students/documents/sevenprinciples.pdf

Clark, D. J., and Bekey, J. "Use of Small Groups in Instructional Evaluation." *Journal of the Professional and Organizational Development Network in Higher Education*, 1979, 1, 87–95.

Clark, D. J., and Redmond, M. V. "A Practical Approach to Improving Teaching." *AAHE Bulletin*, 1982, February, 8–10.

Cleaver, F. "Institutions, Agency and the Limitations of Participatory Approaches to Development," in B. Cooke and U. Kothari (eds.), *Participation the New Tyranny?* (pp. 102–121). London: Zed, 2001.

Cohen, J., Cook-Sather, A., Lesnick, A., Alter, Z., Awkward, R., Decisu, F., Hummer, L., Guerrier, S., Larson, M., and Mengesha, L. "Students as Leaders and Learners: Towards Self-Authorship and Social Change on a College Campus." *Innovations in Education and Teaching International*, 2013, 50, 1, 3–13. Retrieved on January 6, 2012 from http://dx.doi.org/10.1080/1470 3297.2012.746511

Cohen, J., Donnay, V., and Hein, C. "Multiple Layers of Participation: Working with Student Leaders in Our 360." *Teaching and Learning Together in Higher Education*, 2012, 6. Retrieved January 5, 2012 from http://teachingandlearning-together.blogs.brynmawr.edu/archived-issues/sixth-issue-spring-2012/1084-2

Cohen, P. "Effectiveness of Student-Rating Feedback for Improving College Instruction: A Meta-Analysis of Findings." *Research in Higher Education*, 1980, 13(4), 321–341.

Collini, S. *What Are Universities For?* London: Penguin, 2012.

Conner, J. "Steps in Walking the Talk: How Working with a Student Consultant Helped Me Integrate Student Voice More Fully into My Pedagogical Planning and Practice." *Teaching and Learning Together in Higher Education*, 2012, 6. Retrieved 5 January 2012 from http://teachingandlearningtogether. blogs.brynmawr.edu/archived-issues/sixth-issue-spring-2012/steps-in-walking-the-talk-how-working-with-a-student-consultant-helped-me-integrate-student-voice-more-fully-into-my-pedagogical-planning-and-practice

Cook, B. J., and Córdova, D. I. "Minorities in Higher Education: Twenty-Second Annual Status Report: 2007 Supplement." American Council on Education, 2006.

Cook, C. "On Beginning to Negotiate." In G. Boomer, N. Lester, C. Onore and J. Cook (eds.), *Negotiating the Curriculum: Educating for the 21st Century*. London: Falmer Press, 1992.

Cook-Sather, A. "Re(in)forming the Conversations: Student Position, Power, and Voice in Teacher Education." *Radical Teacher*, 2002a, 64, 21–28.

Cook-Sather, A. "Authorizing Students' Perspectives: Toward Trust, Dialogue, and Change in Education." *Educational Researcher*, 2002b, 31(4), 3–14.

Cook-Sather, A. "Sound, Presence, and Power: Exploring 'Student Voice' in Educational Research and Reform." *Curriculum Inquiry*, 2006, 36(4), 359–390.

Cook-Sather, A. "'What You Get Is Looking in a Mirror, Only Better': Inviting Students to Reflect (on) College Teaching." *Reflective Practice*, 2008, 9(4), 473–483.

Cook-Sather, A. *Learning from the Student's Perspective: A Sourcebook for Effective Teaching.* Boulder: Paradigm Publishers, 2009a.

Cook-Sather, A. "From Traditional Accountability to Shared Responsibility: The Benefits and Challenges of Student Consultants Gathering Midcourse Feedback in College Classrooms." *Assessment & Evaluation in Higher Education*, 2009b, 34(2), 231–241.

Cook-Sather, A. "Students as Learners and Teachers: Taking Responsibility, Transforming Education, and Redefining Accountability." *Curriculum Inquiry*, 2010, 40(4), 555–575.

Cook-Sather, A. "Layered Learning: Student Consultants Deepening Classroom and Life Lessons." *Educational Action Research*, 2011a, 9(1), 41–57.

Cook-Sather, A. "Lessons in Higher Education: Five Pedagogical Practices That Promote Active Learning For Faculty and Students." *Journal of Faculty Development*, 2011b, 25(3), 33–39.

Cook-Sather, A. "Teaching and Learning Together: College Faculty and Undergraduates Co-Create a Professional Development Model." *To Improve the Academy*, 2011c, 29, 219–232.

Cook-Sather, A. "Amplifying Student Voices in Higher Education: Democratizing Teaching and Learning Through Changing the Acoustic on a College Campus." *Revista de Educación*. Ministerio de Educación. Madrid, Spain, 2012.

Cook-Sather, A. "Student-Faculty Partnership in Explorations of Pedagogical Practice: A Threshold Concept in Academic Development." *International Journal for Academic Development*, 2013a.

Cook-Sather, A. "Catalyzing Multiple Forms of Engagement Through Student-Faculty Partnerships Exploring Teaching and Learning." In E. Dunne & D. Owen (eds.), *The Student Engagement Handbook: Practice in Higher Education*. Emerald Publishing Group, 2013b.

Cook-Sather, A. "Dialogue Across Differences of Position, Perspective, and Identity: Reflective Practice In/On a Student-Faculty Pedagogical Partnership Program." *Teachers College Record*, forthcoming.

Cook-Sather, A., and Agu, P. "Students of Color and Faculty Colleagues Developing Voice in the 'Counter-Spaces' of a Professional Development Program." Paper presented at the 37th Annual POD Conference Seattle, WA, October 2012.

Cook-Sather, A., and Agu, P. "Students of Color and Faculty Members Working Together Toward Culturally Sustaining Pedagogy." *To Improve the Academy*, 2013, 32, 271–285.

Cook-Sather, A., and Alter, Z. "What Is and What Can Be: How a Liminal Position Can Change Learning and Teaching in Higher Education." *Anthropology & Education Quarterly*, 2011, 42(1), 37–53.

Cook-Sather, A., and Li, H. "Lessons from International Students on Campus Living and Classroom Learning." Conference of the Professional and Organizational Development Network in Higher Education. 9 November 2013. Pittsburg, PA.

Cooke, B. "The Social Psychological Limits of Participation?" in B. Cooke and U. Kothari (eds.), *Participation the New Tyranny?* London: Zed, 2001.

Cooke, B., and Kothari, U. "The Case for Participation as Tyranny." In B. Cooke and U. Kothari (eds.), *Participation the New Tyranny?* pp. 1–15 London: Zed, 2001.

Cousin, G. "Neither Teacher-Centred nor Student-Centred: Threshold Concepts and Research Partnerships." *Journal of Learning Development in Higher Education*, 2010, 2, February. Retrieved 9 October 2012 from http://www.aldinhe.ac.uk/ojs/index.php?journal=jldhe&page=article&op=view&path[ ]=64

Cowan, J., and Westwood, J. "Collaborative and Reflective Professional Development: A Pilot." *Active Learning in Higher Education: The Journal of the Institute for Learning and Teaching*, 2006, 7(1), 63–71.

Cox, M. D. "Student-Faculty Partnerships to Develop Teaching and Enhance Learning." In J. E. Miller, J. E. Groccia, and M. S. Miller (eds.), *Student-Assisted Teaching: A Guide to Faculty-Student Teamwork*, 168–171. Bolton, MA: Anker Publishing Company, Inc., 2001.

Cox, M. D. "Proven Faculty Development Tools that Foster the Scholarship of Teaching in Faculty Learning Communities." In C. M. Wehlburg and S. Chadwick-Blossey (eds.). *To Improve the Academy: Vol. 21. Resources for Faculty, Instructional, and Organizational Development* (pp. 109–142). Bolton, MA: Anker, 2003.

Cox, M. D., and Sorenson, D. L. "Student Collaboration in Faculty Development." In M. Kaplan (ed.), *To Improve the Academy: Vol. 18. Resources for Faculty, Instructional, and Organizational Development* (pp. 97–106). Bolton, MA: Anker, 2000.

Crawford, K. "Rethinking The Student-Teacher Nexus: Students as Consultants on Teaching in Higher Education." In M. Neary, H. Stevenson, and L. Bell (eds.), *Towards Teaching in Public: Reshaping the Modern University* (pp. 52–67). London: Continuum, 2012.

Creswell, J. W. *Qualitative Inquiry and Research Design: Choosing among Five Approaches*. 2nd edition. New York: Sage, 2006.

Darder, A., Baltodano, M., and Torres, R. D. "Critical Pedagogy: An Introduction." In A. Darder, M. Baltodano, and R. D. Torres (eds.), *The Critical Pedagogy Reader* (pp. 1–26). New York: RoutledgeFalmer, 2003.

Davidson, C. N. "How to Crowdsource Grading." HASTAC Blog. 2009. Retrieved from http://hastac.org/blogs/cathy-davidson/how-crowdsource-grading

Davidson, C. N. "Collaborative Learning for the Digital Age." *Chronicle of Higher Education*, 2011 (August 26).

Davidson, C. N. *Now You See It: How Technology and Brain Science Will Transform Schools and Business for the 21st century*. New York: Penguin Books, 2012.

Delpish, A., Holmes, A., Knight-McKenna, M., Mihans, R., Darby, A., King, K., and Felten, P. "Equalizing Voices: Student-Faculty Partnership in Course Design." In C. Werder and M. M. Otis (eds.), *Engaging Student Voices in the Study of Teaching and Learning* (pp. 96–114). Sterling, VA: Stylus, 2010.

Delpit, L. "The Silenced Dialogue: Power and Pedagogy in Educating Other People's Children." *Harvard Educational Review*, 1988, 58(3), 280–298.

Dewey, J. *Democracy and Education*. New York: Macmillan, 1916.

Dewey, J. *Experience and Education*. Touchstone Edition. New York: Simon & Shuster, 1997 (orig. 1938).

Diamond, R. M. "The Usefulness of Structured Mid-Term Feedback as a Catalyst for Change in Higher Education Classes." *Active Learning in Education*, 2004, 5(3), 217–231.

Dreier, O. "Learning in Personal Trajectories of Participation." In N. Stevenson, H. L. Radtke, R. Jorna, and S. Henderikus (eds.), *Theoretical Psychology: Critical Contributions* (pp. 20–29). Toronto: Captus Press, 2003.

Duah, F., and Croft, T. "Students as Partners in Mathematics Design." CETL-MSOR Conference, 2011. Retrieved from https://dspace.lboro.ac.uk/dspace-jspui/bitstream/2134/9904/3/Duah_Croft_2011final.pdf

Dunne, E., and Zandstra, R. "Students as Change Agents. New Ways of Engaging with Learning and Teaching in Higher Education." Bristol: ESCalate Higher Education Academy Subject Centre for Education / University of Exeter, 2011. Retrieved from http://escalate.ac.uk/8064

Edwards, N. M. "Student Self-Grading in Social Statistics." *College Teaching*, 2007, 55(2), 72–76.

Elbaz, F. "Teachers' Knowledge of Teaching: Strategies for Reflection." In J. Smyth (ed.), *Educating Teachers: Changing the Nature of Pedagogical Knowledge*. Philadelphia: Farmer Press, 1987.

Farley-Lucas, B., and Sargent, M. "Enhancing Out-of-Class Communication: Students' Top Ten Suggestions." *The Teaching Professor*, December 1, 2010.

Feiman-Nemser, S. *Teachers as Learners*. Cambridge, MA: Harvard Education Press, 2012.

Felten, P. "Monet Moments and the Necessity of Productive Disruption." *Teaching and Learning Together in Higher Education*, 2011, 2. Retrieved 7 January 2013

from http://teachingandlearningtogether.blogs.brynmawr.edu/archived-issues/
spring2011-issue/from-the-advisory-board

Felten, P. "Principles of Good Practice in the Scholarship of Teaching and
Learning." *Teaching and Learning Inquiry*, 2013, 1(1), 121–125.

Felten, P., and Bauman, H.-D. "Engaging Unheard Voices: Insights from Deaf-
Gain." In E. Dunne and D. Owen (eds.), *Student Engagement Handbook: Practice
in Higher Education*. Bingley, U.K.: Emerald, 2013.

Felten, P., Bagg, J., Bumbry, M., Hill, J., Hornsby, K., Pratt, M., and Weller, S.
"A Call for Expanding Inclusive Student Engagement in SoTL." *Teaching and
Learning Inquiry*, 2013, 1(2), 63–74. Retrieved from http://www.jstor.org/page/
journal/teachlearninqu/about.html

Feuerverger, G., and Richards, E. "Finding Their Way: ESL Immigrant and
Refugee Students in a Toronto High School." In Thiessen, D., and Cook-Sather,
A. (Eds.), *International Handbook of Student Experience in Elementary and Second-
ary School*, 555–575. Dordrecht: The Netherlands: Springer, 2007.

Fielding, M. "Radical Collegiality: Affirming Teaching as an Inclusive
Professional Practice." *Australian Educational Researcher*, 1999, 26(2), 1–34.

Fielding, M. "'New Wave' Student Voice and the Renewal of Civic Society."
London Review of Education, 2004, 2(3), 197–217.

Fielding, M. "Leadership, Radical Student Engagement and the Necessity of
Person-Centred Education." *International Journal of Leadership in Education*,
2006, 9(4), 299–314.

Fielding, M., and Bragg, S. *Students as Researchers: Making a Difference*.
Cambridge: Pearson Publishing, 2003.

Fine, M., Torre, M. E., Burns, A., and Payne, Y. "Youth Research/Participatory
Methods for Reform." In D. Thiessen and A. Cook-Sather (eds.), *International
Handbook of Student Experience in Elementary and Secondary School*
(pp. 805–828). Dordrecht, The Netherlands: Springer, 2007.

Fink, D. *Creating Significant Learning Experiences: An Integrated Approach to
Designing College Courses*. San Francisco: Jossey-Bass, 2003.

Flavell, J. H. "First Discussant's Comments: What Is Memory Development the Development Of?" *Human Development*, 1971, 14, 272–278.

Flavell, J. H. "Metacognition and Cognitive Monitoring: A New Area of Cognitive-Developmental Inquiry." *American Psychologist*, 1979, 34(10), 906–911.

Francl, M. "To Find Fruit: A Contemplative Assessment of a 360 Experience." *Teaching and Learning Together in Higher Education*, 2012, 6. Retrieved January 5, 2012 from http://teachingandlearningtogether.blogs.brynmawr.edu/seventh-issue-fall-2012/to-find-fruit-a-contemplative-assessment-of-a-360-experience

Freire, P. *Pedagogy of the Oppressed*. New York: Continuum, 1970.

Freire, P. "From Pedagogy of the Oppressed." In A. Darder, M. Baltodano, and R. D. Torres (eds.), *The Critical Pedagogy Reader*. New York, RoutledgeFalmer, 2003.

Fries-Britt, S. L., Rowan-Kenyon, H. T., Perna, L. W., Milem, J. F., and Howard, D. G. "Underrepresentation in the Academy and the Institutional Climate for Faculty Diversity." *The Journal of the Professoriate*, 2011, 5(1), 1–34.

Gärdebo, J., and Wiggberg, M. "Importance of Student Participation in Future Academia." In J. Gärdebo and M. Wiggberg (eds.) *Students, The University's Unspent Resource: Revolutionising Higher Education using Active Student Participation*. Pedagogical Development Report 12. Report series from the Division for Development of Teaching and Learning. Uppsala Universitet, 2012.

George, J., and Cowan, J. *A Handbook of Techniques for Formative Evaluation*. London: Kogan Page, 1999.

Gibson, L. "Self-Directed Learning: An Exercise in Student Engagement." *College Teaching*, 2011, 59(3), 95–101.

Giles, A., Martin, S. C., Bryce, D. and Hendry, G. D. "Students as Partners in Evaluation: Student and Teacher Perspectives." *Assessment & Evaluation in Higher Education*, 2004, 29(6), 681–685.

Gilligan, C. *In a Different Voice: Psychological Theory and Women's Development*. Cambridge, MA: Harvard University Press, 1993.

Giroux H. A. *Theory and Resistance in Education. A Pedagogy for the Opposition.* London: Heinemann, 1983.

Glaser, B. G., and Strauss, A. L. *The Discovery of Grounded Theory: Strategies for Qualitative Research.* New York: Aldine De Gruyter, 1967.

Glasser, H., and Powers, M. "Disrupting Traditional Student-Faculty Roles, 140 Characters at a Time." *Teaching and Learning Together in Higher Education,* 2011, 2. Retrieved from http://teachingandlearningtogether.blogs.brynmawr.edu/ archived-issues/spring2011-issue/disrupting-traditional-roles

Goldstein, G., and Benassi, V. "Students' and Instructors' Beliefs about Excellent Lecturers and Discussion Leaders." *Research in Higher Education,* 2006, 47(6), 685–707.

Habermas, J. *Theory and Practice.* London: Heinemann, 1974.

Hamer, J., Kell, C., and Spence, F. "Peer Assessment Using Aropa." In Proceedings 9th Australasian Computing Education Conference (ACE2007), Ballarat, Australia. Conferences in Research and Practice in Information Teachnology (SRPIT), Vol. 66, 43–54, 2007. Retrieved 26 July 2013 from http://www .cs.auckland.ac.nz/~j-hamer/peer-assessment-using-Aropa.pdf

Harrison, R., Mann, G., Murphy, M., Taylor, A., and Thompson, N. *Partnership Made Painless: A Joined-Up Guide to Working Together.* Lyme Regis: Russell House Publishing, 2003.

Harper, S. R., and Quaye, J. "Beyond Sameness, with Engagement and Outcomes for All". In S. R. Harper and S. J. Quaye (eds.), *Student Engagement in Higher Education: Theoretical Perspectives and Practical Approaches for Diverse Populations* (pp. 1–15). New York: Routledge, 2009.

Hart, R. *Children's Participation from Tokenism to Citizenship.* Florence: UNICEF, 1992.

Hativa, N. *Student Ratings of Instruction: Recognizing Effective Teaching.* CreateSpace, 2013.

Havnes, A. "Students as Partners in Educational Development: Practice, Policy, and Theory." Paper presented at the 4th International Consortium for Educational Development Conference, Austin, TX, Apr. 1998.

Healey, M. "Students as Producers and Change Agents." Plenary session presented at the Meeting of the International Society for the Study of Teaching and Learning. Ontario, Canada, Oct., 2012.

Healey, M., Bradford, M., Roberts, C., and Knight, Y. "Bringing about Change in Teaching and Learning at Departmental Level." Report of the GEES Subject Centre departmental change initiative, 2010. Retrieved 26 July 2013 from http://insight.glos.ac.uk/tli/resources/toolkit/eal/Documents/ChangeEventReport.pdf

Healey, M., and Jenkins, A. "Developing Undergraduate Research and Inquiry." York: Higher Education Academy, 2009.

Heron, J. "The Politics of Facilitation: Balancing Facilitator Authority and Learner Autonomy." In J. Mulligan and C. Griffin (eds.), *Empowerment through Experiential Learning: Explorations of Good Practice* (pp. 66–75). London: Kogan Page, 1992.

Higher Education Academy. "UK Professional Standards Framework (UKPSF)." No date. Retrieved 13 November 2013 from http://www.heacademy.ac.uk/UKPSF

Hildyard, N., Hegde, P., Wolvekamp, P., and Reddy, S. "Pluralism, Participation and Power: Joint Forest Management in India." In B. Cooke and U. Kothari (eds.), *Participation the New Tyranny?* (pp. 56–71). London: Zed, 2001.

hooks, b. *Teaching to Transgress: Education as the Practice of Freedom*. New York: Routledge, 1994.

Huber, M. T., and Hutchings, P. *The Advancement of Learning: Building the Teaching Commons*. San Francisco: Jossey-Bass, 2005.

Hudd, S. S. "Syllabus Under Construction: Involving Students in the Creation of Class Assignments." *Teaching Sociology*, 2003, 31(2), 195–202.

Hunt, C. "Diversity and Pedagogic Practice: Reflections on the Role of an Adult Educator in Higher Education." *Teaching in Higher Education*, 2007, 12(5–6), 765–779. DOI: 10.1080/13562510701596406

Huston, T., and Weaver, C. L. "Peer Coaching: Professional Development for Experienced Faculty." *Innovative Higher Education*, 2008, 33(1), 5–20.

Hutchings, P., Borin, P., Keesing-Styles, L., Martin, L., Michael, R., Scharff, L., Simkins, S., and Ismail, A. "The Scholarship of Teaching and Learning in an Age of Accountability: Building Bridges." *Teaching and Learning Inquiry*, 2013, 1(2), 35–47.

Hutchings, P., Huber, M. T., and Ciccone, A. *The Scholarship of Teaching and Learning Reconsidered: Institutional Integration and Impact*. Jossey-Bass/ Carnegie Foundation for the Advancement of Teaching. San Francisco: Jossey-Bass, 2011.

Imel, S. "Reflective Practice in Adult Education." ERIC Digest No. 122. Columbus, Ohio, ERIC Clearinghouse on Adult Career and Vocational Education, 1992.

Ivanic, R. "Negotiation, Process, Content and Participants' Experience in a Process Syllabus for ELT Professionals." In M. P. Breen and A. Littlejohn (eds.), *Classroom Decision-Making: Negotiation and Process Syllabuses in Practice* (pp. 233–247). Cambridge: Cambridge University Press, 2000.

Jenkins, A. "Discipline-Based Educational Development". *International Journal for Academic Development*, 1996, 1(1), 50–62.

Jenkins, H. *Confronting the Challenges of Participatory Culture: Media Education for the 21st Century*. Chicago, IL: MacArthur Foundation, 2006.

Jiang, Y., and Wang, Y. "An Equal Partnership: Preparing for Faculty-Student Team Teaching of 'Cultural history of Chinese Astronomy.'" *Teaching and Learning Together in Higher Education*, 2012, 6. Retrieved 5 January 2012 from http://teachingandlearningtogether.blogs.brynmawr.edu/archived-issues/sixth-issue-spring-2012/1084-2

Kadi-Hanifi, K., Dagman, O., Peters, J., Snell, E., Tutton, C. and Wright, T. "Engaging Students and Staff with Educational Development through Appreciative Inquiry." *Innovations in Education and Teaching International*, 2013. http://dx.doi.org/10.1080/14703297.2013.796719

Kaplan, M., Silver, N., LaVaque-Manty-, D, and Meizlish, D. *Using Reflection and Metacognition to Improve Student Learning: Across the Disciplines, Across the Academy*. Sterling, VA: Stylus, 2013.

Karkowski, A. M., and Fournier, J. S. "Undergraduate Research as a Catalyst for Institutional Change." *Council on Undergraduate Research Quarterly*, 2012, 32(5), 13–16.

Kavadlo, J., Nicoloff, A., Burgess, J., Coplen, A., and Olson, K. "Magic Words: Students Learning and Teaching Writing in First Year Seminar." *Teaching and Learning Together in Higher Education*, 2012, 5. Retrieved 19 October 2013 from http://teachingandlearningtogether.blogs.brynmawr.edu/archived-issues/fifth-issue-january-2012

Kearns, S. E., Miller, R. K., and Kerns, D. V. "Designing from a Blank Slate: The Development of the Initial Olin College Curriculum." In Committee on the Engineer of 2020, Phase II, Committee on Engineering Education, National Academy of Engineering. *Educating the Engineer of 2020: Adapting Engineering Education to the New Century* (98–113), 2004. Retrieved from https://download.nap.edu/catalog.php?record_id=11338

Kegan, R. *In Over Our Heads: The Mental Demands of Modern Life*. Cambridge, MA: Harvard University Press, 1994.

Keutzer, C. "Midterm Evaluation of Teaching Provides Helpful Feedback to Instructors." *Teaching of Psychology*, 1993, 20(4), 238–240.

King, K., and Felten, P. "Threshold Concepts in Educational Development: An Introduction." *Journal of Faculty Development*, 2012, 26(3), 5–7.

Klenowski, V., Askew, S., and Carnell, E. "Portfolios for Learning, Assessment and Professional Development in Higher Education." *Assessment & Evaluation in Higher Education*, 2006, 31(3), 267–286. doi: 10.1080/02602930500352816.

Kothari, U. "Power, Knowledge and Social Control." In B. Cooke and U. Kothari (eds.), *Participation the New Tyranny?* (pp. 139–152). London: Zed, 2001.

Kuh, G. D. *High-Impact Educational Practices: What They Are, Who Has Access to Them, and Why They Matter*. Washington, DC: Association of American Colleges and Universities, 2008.

Kuh, G., Kinzie, J., Schuh, J. H., and Whitt, E. J. *Student Success in College: Creating Conditions that Matter*. San Francisco: Jossey-Bass, 2010.

Larrivee, B. "Transforming Teaching Practice: Becoming the Critically Reflective Teacher." *Reflective Practice*, 2000, 1(3), 293–307. doi: 10.1080/713693162.

Lawler, P. "Teachers as Adult Learners: A New Perspective." *New Directions for Adult and Continuing Education*, 2003, 98, 15–22. doi: 10.1002/ace.95.

Lawrence-Lightfoot, S. "Respect: To Get It, You Must Give It." *Swarthmore College Bulletin*. March 2000.

Lesnick, A. "The Mirror in Motion: Redefining Reflective Practice in an Undergraduate Field Work Seminar." *Reflective Practice*, 2005, 6(1), 33–48. doi: 10.1080/1462394042000326798.

Lesnick, A. "360 Degrees of Pedagogy." *Teaching and Learning Together in Higher Education*, 2012, 6. Retrieved 5 January 2012 from http://teachingandlearningtogether.blogs.brynmawr.edu/seventh-issue-fall-2012/360-degrees-of-pedagogy

Lewis, K. G. "Using Midsemester Student Feedback and Responding To It." *New Directions For Teaching and Learning*, 2001, 87 (Fall), 33–44.

Light, R. J. *Making the Most of College: Students Speak Their Minds*. Cambridge, MA: Harvard University Press, 2004.

Little, D., and Green, D. A. "Betwixt and Between: Academic Developers in the Margins." *International Journal for Academic Development*, 2012, 17(3), 203–215.

Little, S., Sharp, H., Stanley, L., Hayward, M., Gannon-Leary, P., O'Neill, P., and Williams, J. "Collaborating for Staff-Student Partnerships: Experiences and Observations." In S. Little (ed.), *Staff-Student Partnerships in Higher Education*. (pp. 215–225). London: Continuum, 2011.

Lodge, C. "From Hearing Voices to Engaging in Dialogue: Problematising Student Participation in School Improvement." *Journal of Educational Change*, 2005, 6(2) (June), 125–146.

Lundy, L. "Voice Is Not Enough: Conceptualizing" Article 12 of the United Nations Convention on the Rights of the Child. *British Educational Research Journal*, 2007, 33(6), 927–942. doi: 10.1080/01411920701657033.

Maher, F. "John Dewey, Progressive Education, and Feminist Pedagogies: Issues in Gender and Authority." In K. Weiler (ed.), *Feminist Engagements: Reading, Resisting, and Revisioning Male Theorists in Education and Cultural Studies* (pp. 13–32). New York: Routledge, 2001.

Mann, S. J. "Alternative Perspectives on the Student Experience: Alienation and Engagement." *Studies in Higher Education*, 2001, 26(1), 7–19.

Mann, S. J. *Study, Power and the University*. Society for Research into Higher Education. Maidenhead: Open University Press, 2008.

Manor, C., Bloch-Schulman, S., Flannery, K., and Felten, P. "Foundations of Student–Faculty Partnerships in the Scholarship of Teaching and Learning." In C. Werder and M.M. Otis (eds.), *Engaging Student Voices in the Study of Teaching and Learning* (pp. 3–15). Sterling, VA: Stylus, 2010.

Marlin, J. J. "Student Perceptions of End-of-Course Evaluations." *The Journal of Higher Education*, 1987, 58(6), 704–716.

McHenry, N., Ziegenfuss, D., Martin, A., and Castaldo, A. "Learning Assistants Program: Faculty Development For Conceptual Change." *The International Journal of Teaching and Learning in Higher Education*, 2009, 22, 3, 258–268.

McIntyre, D., Pedder, D., and Rudduck, J. "Pupil Voice: Comfortable and Uncomfortable Learning for Teachers." *Research Papers in Education*, 2005, 20, 149–168.

Melland, H. I. "Great Researcher . . . Good Teacher?" *Journal of Professional Nursing*, 1996, 12(1), 31–38.

Merriam, S. B., Caffarella, R. S., and Baumgartner, L. M. *Learning in Adulthood: A Comprehensive Guide*. San Francisco, CA: Jossey Bass, 2006.

Meyer, J. H. F., and Land, R. "Threshold Concepts and Troublesome Knowledge (2): Epistemological Considerations and a Conceptual Framework for Teaching and Learning." *Higher Education*, 2005, 49, 373–388.

Mezirow, J. *Transformative Dimensions of Adult Learning*. San Francisco, CA: Jossey-Bass, 1991.

Mihans, R., Long, D., and Felten, P. "Student-Faculty Collaboration in Course Design and the Scholarship of Teaching and Learning." *International Journal for the Scholarship of Teaching and Learning*, 2008, 2(2). Retrieved 7 November 2009 from http://www.georgiasouthern.edu/ijsotl.

Millis, B. J. "A Versatile Interactive Focus Group Protocol for Qualitative Assessment." *To Improve the Academy*, 2004, 22, 125–141.

Moore, J. L., Altvater, L., Mattera, J., and Regan, E. "Been There, Done That, Still Doing It: Involving Students in Redesigning a Service Learning Course."

In C. Werder and M. M. Otis (eds.), *Engaging Student Voices in the Study of Teaching and Learning* (pp. 150–159). Sterling, VA: Stylus, 2010.

Moore, N., and Gilmartin, M. "Teaching for Better Learning: A Blended Learning Pilot Project with First Year Geography Undergraduates." *Journal of Geography in Higher Education*, 2010, 34(3), 327–344.

Nath, S. "Finding Voices in Reflection: How My Work Through the TLI Changed My Classroom Dynamics." *Teaching and Learning Together in Higher Education*, 2012, 6. Retrieved 5 January 2012 from http://teachingandlearning-together.blogs.brynmawr.edu/archived-issues/sixth-issue-spring-2012/finding-voices-in-reflection-how-my-work-through-the-tli-changed-my-classroom-dynamics

Neary, M. "Student as Producer: A Pedagogy for the Avant-Garde?" *Learning Exchange*, 2010, 1, 1.

North Carolina A&T Wabash Provost Scholars Program, 2011. Retrieved 24 October 2013 from http://www.ncat.edu/divisions/academic-affairs/atl/wabash-provost-scholars/

NUS, A Manifesto for Partnership, 2012. Retrieved 24 October 2013 from http://www.nusconnect.org.uk/news/article/highereducation/Rachel-Wenstone-launches-a-Manifesto-for-Partnership/

Nussbaum, M. *Cultivating Humanity: A Classical Defense of Reform in Liberal Education*. Cambridge, MA: Harvard University Press, 1997.

Nygaard, C., Brand, S., Bartholomew, P., and Millard, L. "Why Student Engagement Matters." *Student Engagement: Identity, Motivation, and Community*. Faringdon, England: Libri Publishing, 2013.

O'Neill, G. (ed.) *A Practitioner's Guide to Choice of Assessment Methods within a Module*, Dublin: UCD Teaching and Learning, 2011. Retrieved 24 October 2013 from http://www.ucd.ie/teaching/resources/assessment/howdoyouassessstu-dentlearning/

Orner, M. "Interrupting the Calls for Student Voice in 'Liberatory' Education: A Feminist Poststructuralist Perspective." In C. Luke and J. Gore (eds.), *Feminisms and Critical Pedagogy*. New York: Routledge, 1992.

Palmer, P. "Divided No More: A Movement Approach to Educational Reform." *Change Magazine*, 1992, 24(2), 10–17.

Palmer, P. "The Heart of a Teacher." *Change Magazine*, 1997, 29(6), 14–21.

Partridge, L., and Sandover, S. "Beyond 'Listening' to the Student Voice: The Undergraduate Researcher's Contribution to the Enhancement of Teaching and Learning." *Journal of University Learning and Teaching Practice*, 2010, 7(2) Article 4, 1–19. Retrieved from http://ro.uow.edu.au/jutlp/vol7/iss2/4/

Patitu, C. L., and Hinton, K. G. "The Experiences of African American Women Faculty and Administrators in Higher Education: Has Anything Changed?" *New Directions for Student Services*, 2003, 104, 79–93. doi: 10.1002/ss.109.

Peel, D. "Peer Observation As a Transformatory Tool?" *Teaching in Higher Education*, 2005, 10(4), 489–504.

Penny, A. R., and Coe, R. "Effectiveness of Consultation on Student Ratings Feedback: A Meta-Analysis." *Review of Educational Research*, 2004, 74(2), 215–253. doi: 10.3102/00346543074002215.

Pintrich, P. R. "The Role of Metacognitive Knowledge in Learning, Teaching, and Assessing." *Theory into Practice*, 2002, 41(4), 219–225.

Pope-Ruark, R. "'We Scrum Every Day': Using Scrum Project Management Framework for Group Projects." *College Teaching*, 2012, 60(4), 164–169.

Popovich, C., and Green, D. *Understanding Undergraduates: Challenging Our Preconceptions of Student Success.* Abingdon: Routledge, 2012.

Reiman, A. J., and Thies-Sprinthall, L. *Mentoring and Supervision for Teacher Development.* New York: Longman, 1998.

Richlin, L., and Cox, M. D. "Developing Scholarly Teaching and the Scholarship of Teaching and Learning Through Faculty Learning Communities." In M. Cox and L. Richlin (eds.), *New Directions for Teaching and Learning: Vol. 97. Building Faculty Learning Communities* (pp. 127–135). San Francisco: Jossey-Bass, 2004.

Robinson, C., and Taylor, C. "Theorising Student Voice: Values and Perspectives." *Improving Schools*, 2007, 10, 5–17.

Rodgers, C. "Redefining Reflection: Another Look at John Dewey and Reflective Thinking." *Teachers College Record*, 2002, 104(4), 842–866. doi: 10.1111/1467–9620.00181.

Rogers, C., and Freiberg, H. J. *Freedom to Learn*. 3rd ed. New York: Macmillan Publishing, 1969.

Roxå, T., and Mårtensson, K. "Significant Conversations and Significant Networks: Exploring the Backstage of the Teaching Arena." *Studies in Higher Education*, 2009, 34(5), 547–559.

Roxå, T., and Mårtensson, K. "Understanding Strong Academic Microcultures: An Exploratory Study." Report from a pilot-project, Lund University. Lund: Media Tryck, Lund University, 2013. Retrieved from http://www5.lu.se/upload/EQ11/ReportAcademicMicrocultures.pdf

Rudduck, J. "Student Voice, Student Engagement and School Reform." In D. Thiessen and A. Cook-Sather (eds.), *International Handbook of Student Experience in Elementary and Secondary School* (pp. 587–610). Dordrecht, The Netherlands: Springer, 2007.

Rudduck, J., and McIntyre, D. *Improving Learning through Consulting Pupils*. London: Routledge, 2007.

Sambell, K., and Graham, L. "Towards an Assessment Partnership Model? Students' Experiences of Being Engaged as Partners in Assessment for Learning (AfL) Enhancement Activity." In S. Little (ed.), *Staff-Student Partnerships in Higher Education* (pp. 31–47). London: Continuum, 2011.

Sambell, K., McDowell, L. and Montgomery, C. *Assessment for Learning in Higher Education*. Abingdon: Routledge, 2012.

Sanon, F., Baxter, M., Fortune, L., and Opotow, S. "Cutting Class: Perspectives of Urban High School Students." In J. Shultz and A. Cook-Sather (eds.), *In Our Own Words: Students' Perspectives on School* (pp. 73–92). Latham: Rowman & Littlefield Publishers, Inc., 2001.

Scandrett, E. "Popular Education in the University." In S. Amsler, J. E. Canaan, S. Cowden, S. Motta. and G. Singh (ed.), *Why Critical Pedagogy and Popular Education Matter Today*. Birmingham; C-SAP, 2010. Retrieved 23 October 2013 from http://eprints.aston.ac.uk/9145/1/Critical_Pedagogy_Popular_Education.pdf

Scandrett, E., O'Leary, T., and Martinez, T. "Learning Environmental Justice through Dialogue." PASCAL Conference Proceedings: Making Knowledge Work. Leicester: NIACE, 2005.

Schlechty, P. *Engaging Students: The Next Level of Working on the Work*. San Francisco: Jossey-Bass, 2011.

Schön, D. A. *Educating the Reflective Practitioner*. San Francisco: Jossey-Bass, 1987.

Seale, J. "Doing Student Voice Work in Higher Education: An Exploration of the Value of Participatory Methods." *British Educational Research Journal*, 2010, 36(6), 995–1015.

Selover, G., and Miller-Lane, J. "Fostering a Pedagogy of Mutual Engagement through a Shared Practice of Aikido." *Teaching and Learning Together in Higher Education*, 2011, 4. Retrieved 6 January 2013 from http://teachingandlearning-together.blogs.brynmawr.edu/archived-issues/current-issue/fostering-a-pedagogy-of-mutual-engagement-through-a-shared-practice-of-aikido

Shadiow, L. *What Our Stories Teach Us: A Guide to Critical Reflection for College Faculty*. San Francisco: Jossey-Bass, 2013.

Shor, I. *Empowering Education: Critical Teaching for Social Change*. Chicago: University of Chicago Press, 1992.

Shor, I. *When Students Have Power: Negotiating Authority in a Critical Pedagogy*. London: University of Chicago Press, 1996.

Shore, E. "'Changing Education': Helping to Conceptualize the First 360." *Teaching and Learning Together in Higher Education*, 2012, 6. Retrieved 5 January 2012 from http://teachingandlearningtogether.blogs.brynmawr.edu/seventh-issue-fall-2012/changing-education

Shulman, L. "Teaching as Community Property: Putting an End to Pedagogical Solitude." *Teaching as Community Property: Essays on Higher Education* (pp. 140–144). San Francisco: Jossey-Bass, 2004a.

Shulman, L. "Visions of the Possible: Models for Campus Support of the Scholarship of Teaching and Learning," 1999. Reprinted in P. Hutchings (ed.),

Teaching as Community Property: Essay on Higher Education. San Francisco: Jossey-Bass, 2004b.

Singham, M. "Moving Away from the Authoritarian Classroom." *Change*, 2005 (May/June), 50–57.

Singham, M. "Death to the Syllabus!" *Liberal Education*, 2007, 93(4), 52–56.

Smith, M. B., Nowacek, R. S., and Bernstein, J. L. *Citizenship across the Curriculum*. Bloomington, IN, Indiana University Press, 2010.

Snell, E., Peters, J., and Tutton, C. "*The Student Voice in Staff Development Through Student-led Appreciative Inquiry for Inclusion*." Paper presentation at Staff and Educational Development Association (SEDA) Conference, 2012, May 17–18, 2012. Retrieved 23 October 2013 from http://www.seda.ac.uk/index.php?p=14_2&e=425&x=1

Solnit, R. *Hope in the Dark: Untold Histories, Wild Possibilities*. New York: Nation Books, 2005.

Solomon, A. *Far from the Tree: Parents, Children, and the Search for Identity*. New York: Scribner, 2012.

Solórzano, D., Ceja, M., and Yosso, T. "Critical Race Theory, Racial Microaggressions, and Campus Racial Climate: The Experiences of African American College Students." *The Journal of Negro Education*, 2000, 69(1/2), 60–73. Retrieved from http://www.jstor.org/stable/2696265

Solórzano, D., Villalpando, O., and Oseguera, L. "Educational Inequities and Latina/o Undergraduate Students in the United States: A Critical Race Analysis of Their Educational Progress." *Journal of Hispanic Higher Education*, 2005, 4, 272–294. doi: 10.1177/1538192705276550.

Somekh, B., and Zeichner, K. "Action Research for Educational Reform: Remodelling Action Research Theories and Practices in Local Contexts." *Educational Action Research*, 2009, 17(1), 5–21.

Sorenson, D. L. "College Teachers and Student Consultants: Collaborating about Teaching and Learning." In J. E. Miller, J. E. Groccia, and M. S. Miller (eds.), *Student-Assisted Teaching: A Guide to Faculty-Student Teamwork*, 179–183. Bolton, MA: Anker, 2001.

SPARQS. "Staff Workshop." PowerPoint Presentation, Undated. Retrieved 26 July 2013 from http://www.sparqs.ac.uk/institute.php?page=92

Stefani, L.A.J. "Assessment in Partnership with Learners." *Assessment and Evaluation in Higher Education*, 1998, 23(4) 339–350.

Strauss, A., and Corbin, J. *Basics of Qualitative Research: Grounded Theory Procedures and Techniques*. Newbury Park, CA: Sage Publications, 1990.

Sunderland, M. E. "Using Student Engagement to Relocate Ethics to the Core of the Engineering Curriculum." *Science and Engineering Ethics*, 2013. doi 10.1007/s1194.

Swennnen, A., Lunenberg, M., and Korthagen, F. "Practice What You Teach! Teacher Educators and Congruent Teaching". *Teachers and Teaching: Theory and Practice*, 2008, 14, 531–542.

Tabak, K. G. "From a Teaching Focus to a Student Centered Classroom: Building Collaboration in the Classroom." *Teaching and Learning Together in Higher Education*, 2011, 5. Retrieved 6 January 2013 from http:// teachingandlearningtogether.blogs.brynmawr.edu/archived-issues/fifth-issue-january-2012/from-a-teaching-focus-to-a-student-centered-classroom-building-collaboration-in-the-classroom

Taylor, H. "Insights into Participation from Critical Management and Labour Process Perspectives." In B. Cooke and U. Kothari (eds.), *Participation the New Tyranny?* (pp. 122–138). London: Zed, 2001.

Thiessen, D. "Knowing about, Acting on Behalf of, and Working with Primary Pupils' Perspectives: Three Levels of Engagement with Research." In A. Pollard, D. Thiessen, and A. Filer (eds.), *Children and Their Curriculum* (pp. 184–196). London: Falmer Press, 1997.

Thiessen, D. "Teaching and Learning Together: Towards a Pedagogy of Mutual Engagement." *Teaching and Learning Together in Higher Education*, 2010, 1. Retrieved January 6, 2013, from http://teachingandlearningtogether.blogs.brynmawr.edu/archived-issues/fall2010-issue/from-the-advisory-board

Tierney, A. "How Undergraduate Students Tackle Staff Development Roles." HEA Centre for Bioscience Representatives Forum, Newcastle University, 11–12th September 2008. Retrieved from http://www.bioscience.heacademy.ac.uk/ftp/events/repforum08/tierney.pdf

Tompkins, J. *A Life in School: What the Teacher Learned.* Perseus Books, 1996.

Tritter, J. Q., and McCallum, A. "The Snakes and Ladders of User Involvement: Moving Beyond Arnstein." *Health Policy* 2006, 76, 156–168.

Umbach, P. D. "The Contribution of Faculty of Color to Undergraduate Education." *Research in Higher Education*, 2006, 47(3), 317–345.

Underwood, T. "On Knowing What You Know: Metacognition and the Act of Reading." *The ClearingHouse*, 1997, 71(2) (November/ December), 77–80.

University of Ballarat Succeed@UB, 2013. Retrieved from http://www.ballarat.edu.au/staff/learning-and-teaching@ub/clipp/succeed@ub

University of Essex, *About Students As Change Agents*, undated. Retrieved 24 October 2013 from http://as.exeter.ac.uk/support/educationqualityandenhance-mentprojects/current_projects/change/about/

Wabash College. Wabash National Study 2006–2009, 2013. Retrieved from http://www.liberalarts.wabash.edu/study-overview/

Walker, A. " The Mid-Semester Challenge: Filtering the Flow of Student Feedback." *Teaching and Learning Together in Higher Education*, 2012, 6. Retrieved 5 January 2012 from http://teachingandlearningtogether.blogs.brynmawr.edu/archived-issues/sixth-issue-spring-2012/the-mid-semester-challenge-filtering-the-flow-of-student-feedback

Walker, G. E., Golde, C. M., Jones, L., Bueschel, A. C., and Hutchings, P. *The Formation of Scholars: Rethinking Doctoral Education for the Twenty-First Century.* San Francisco: Jossey-Bass, 2008.

Webber, T. "Orientations to Learning in Midcareer Management Students." *Studies in Higher Education*, 2004, 29(2), 259–277.

Werder, C. "Democratizing Teaching and Learning through Real Dialogue across Differences." *Diversity & Democracy*, 2013, 16, 1. Retrieved 17 March 2013 from http://www.aacu.org/diversitydemocracy/vol16no1/werder.cfm

Werder, C., and Otis, M. M. (eds.) *Engaging Student Voices in the Study of Teaching and Learning*. Sterling, VA: Stylus, 2010.

Werder, C., Thibou, S., and Kaufer, B. "Students as Co-Inquirers: A Requisite Threshold Concept in Educational Development?" *Journal of Faculty Development*, 2012, 26(3), 34–38.

Wiggins, G., and McTighe, J. *Understanding by Design*, Expanded 2nd ed. Alexandra, VA: Pearson, 2005.

Wilkinson, M., and Scandrett, E. "A Popular Education Approach to Tackling Environmental Injustice and Widening Participation." *Concept*, 2003, 13(1/2), 11–16.

Williams, J., Alder, D., Cook, J., Whinney, M., O'Connell, R., Duffin, W., and King, P. "Students and Staff as Educational Partners in the Development of Quality-Assured Online Resources for Medical Education." In S. Little (ed.), *Staff-Student Partnerships in Higher Education* (pp. 76–91). London: Continuum, 2011.

Wolf-Wendel, L., Ward, K., and Kinzie, J. "A Tangled Web of Terms: The Overlap and Unique Contribution of Involvement, Engagement, and Integration to Understanding College Student Success." *Journal of College Student Development*, 2009, 50(4), 407–428.

Wood, M. "Investigating Undergraduate Student Engagement in Group Learning from the Students' Perspectives." Paper presented at Research Symposium: Student Engagement in Higher Education. York St John University, 2 July 2012.

Wortham, S. "The Interdependence of Social Identification and Learning." *American Educational Research Journal*, 2004, 41(3), 715–750.

Zeichner, K. M., and Liston, D. P. "Teaching Student Teachers to Reflect." *Harvard Educational Review*, 1987, 57(1), 23–48.

Index

O